Inexcusable Omissions

History of Schools and Schooling

Alan R. Sadovnik and Susan F. Semel
General Editors

Vol. 10

PETER LANG
New York • Washington, D.C./Baltimore • Bern
Frankfurt am Main • Berlin • Brussels • Vienna • Oxford

Inexcusable Omissions

Clarence Karier and the Critical Tradition in History of Education Scholarship

EDITED BY
Karen Graves, Timothy Glander,
& Christine Shea

PETER LANG
New York • Washington, D.C./Baltimore • Bern
Frankfurt am Main • Berlin • Brussels • Vienna • Oxford

Library of Congress Cataloging-in-Publication Data

Inexcusable omissions: Clarence Karier and the critical tradition in history of education scholarship / edited by Karen Graves, Timothy Glander, and Christine Shea.
p. cm. — (History of schools and schooling; vol. 10)
Includes bibliographical references.
1. Karier, Clarence J. 2. Education—United States—Philosophy. 3. Education—United States—History. I. Graves, Karen. II. Glander, Timothy Richard. III. Shea, Christine Mary. IV. History of schools and schooling; v. 10.
LB885.K32 I54   370'.973—dc21   00-030460
ISBN 0-8204-4879-6
ISSN 1089-0678

Die Deutsche Bibliothek-CIP-Einheitsaufnahme

Inexcusable omissions: Clarence Karier and the critical tradition in history of education scholarship / ed. by: Karen Graves....
_New York; Washington, D.C./Baltimore; Bern; Frankfurt am Main; Berlin; Brussels; Vienna; Oxford: Lang.
(History of schools and schooling; Vol. 10)
ISBN 0-8204-4879-6

Cover design by Nancy Karier

The paper in this book meets the guidelines for permanence and durability of the Committee on Production Guidelines for Book Longevity of the Council of Library Resources.

© 2001 Peter Lang Publishing, Inc., New York

All rights reserved.
Reprint or reproduction, even partially, in all forms such as microfilm, xerography, microfiche, microcard, and offset strictly prohibited.

Printed in the United States of America

To teachers,
who go about their work with intellectual integrity.

To the democratic ideal.

To Clarence,
who has sharpened our perceptions regarding both.

In memory
of

Paul Constantine Violas

(1937–1999)

Contents

Preface   xiii

Part One: Personal Reflections on Karier and His Work

Honoring a Lost and Forgotten Tradition: The Teacher
    as Mentor
    Christine M. Shea   1

Searching for Truth: Meeting Clarence Karier in the 1960s
    Richard Ognibene   19

Liberalism and Education
    Joel Spring   27

Marching to the Beat of His Own Drum: An
    Epigrammatic Analysis of Understanding and
    Applying Philosophy and Ethics in the Writing
    of History
    Peter A. Sola   41

Part Two: Karier's Impact and Legacy

To the Nonalienated: Navigating a Course
    Between False Security and Despair
    Karen L. Graves   51

An Audacious Analysis of Power and Control:
    The Significance of *Roots of Crisis* and *Shaping the
    American Educational State* for Current Critiques of
    American Bureaucratic Educational Systems
    Stuart McAninch   67

Freud, Karier, and the Therapeutic State
    Joseph L. DeVitis   79

Clarence Karier on War, Race, and Other Dynamics
    at the Intersection of Economics and Education
    Ronald Rochon and Paul Theobald   89

Clarence Karier's Influence on Two Careers in
    Native American Policy Studies
    Mark W. Sorensen and Guy Senese   101

The Preparation of School Practitioners: Social
    Foundations of Education, Critical History
    of Education, and Educational Change
    Steve Tozer   119

Democratic Agitations: Transformation of a
    Critical Historian
    James D. Anderson   139

Part Three: Implications for Future Scholarship

Resistance to Standardized Testing: From Issues
    of Validity to "Testing for Order and Control"
    Timothy Glander   157

Contradictions of Domestic Containment: Forestalling
    Human Development During the Cold War
    Stephen Preskill   181

"What Really Happened": Implications for the Study
    of African American Educational History
    Katrina M. Sanders and Joy Ann Williamson   195

The Ideology of Progressive Education and Its
   Implications for American Imperialism
   Gilsang Lee   211

Arthur Bestor and Anti-Intellectualism in American
   Education
   Marlene Wentworth   231

The Emancipatory Power of Language: Critical
   Language Awareness and the Legacy of
   Clarence J. Karier
   Timothy Reagan   245

Appendix   263

Notes   269

Contributors   309

Preface

The title for this book is drawn from Clarence Karier's review of Lawrence A. Cremin's 1977 text *Traditions of American Education*. Cremin's history had made the case for the emergence of an American *Paideia* in the nineteenth century that reflected the expansion of liberty and republican virtue and opportunity throughout the land. Cremin's was the naïvely hopeful view of American schooling that tended to downplay conflict and exploitation and accentuate a generally positive view of the past and future. In his review Karier focused on Cremin's use of the expression "inexcusable omissions" to reference those whose lives, Cremin acknowledged in passing, were excluded from this historical progress. Karier spoke of those with dreams deferred, the "Irish who died building the railroads and canals in the East, the children who died in the coal mines of Pennsylvania, the women who died chained to their machines in factories, the Polish laborers burned to death in the steel mills of Gary, the Indians wasted by the Gatling gun in the West, [and] the slave who felt the white man's lash . . ." and wondered at what point do "these 'inexcusable omissions' cease to be 'omissions' and when do they become an organic part of American history?"[1] At what point does the oppression, violence, and injustice found throughout the American historical record cease to be regarded as occasional aberrations and are understood instead to be consistent and systemic features of the American experience? In Cremin's view these omissions were "inexcusable" precisely because they failed to fit with his idyllic image of American education and society. From Karier's view these omissions defined the very nature of Cremin's historical interpretation, which itself provided a convenient excuse for present inequities and injustices. For Karier, what was really "inexcusable" was the manner in which mainstream scholarship in the history of American education, of which Cremin was the dominant figure, defined reality to meet the needs and interests of those who continued to profit from contemporary social and economic arrangements.

Today the term "inexcusable omissions" might be understood to take on additional connotations. In basic ways the term might refer to the gaping holes that remain in our historical understanding of the experiences of marginalized and subjugated people. So much remains fundamentally and inexcusably omitted from the historical record that it is impossible to lay claim to an adequate view of our educational past. The term might also refer to the collective and selective amnesia that surrounds many of the circumstances and events of the American century, particularly those implicated in the development of the national security state during the Cold War. Here the record remains sparse and largely classified, again inexcusably omitting and obscuring fundamental realities that would doubtlessly cast the present in starkly different ways. Finally, the expression "inexcusable omissions" might be understood to refer to the increasing and inexcusable omission of much critical scholarship from the discourse on social and educational policy. As tolerance for dissent of any sort has waned, critical history of education scholarship has been pushed further to the margins and key questions and lines of inquiry that might well inform policies have been further displaced by the apologetics provided by the neo-conservatives who now dominate the field. What becomes "inexcusable" now is the increasing omission of the kind of thorough critical analysis that several decades ago sought to make a difference in the lives of people by providing a more accurate historical account than those written in the interests of the wealthy and privileged.

This book aims to be a small corrective to this situation by examining the work and legacy of arguably the leading critical historian of education in the second half of the twentieth century, Clarence J. Karier. Karier authored five books and scores of articles, served as head of the Department of Educational Policy Studies at the University of Illinois for over twenty years, and supervised the study of countless doctoral and master's degree students. By revisiting Karier's work, contributors hope to reintroduce a set of historical matters that remain highly important for both historians of education and educational practitioners. By adopting a decisively personal cast, the authors of these essays hope to recover the essential link between Karier's intellectual craftsmanship and the way he approached his teaching and worked with students.

Born in 1928, Clarence Karier's work in education spans nearly fifty years. Following service in the U.S. Army during the Korean

War, Karier began his career in 1953 as a social studies teacher at Marinette High School, in Marinette, Wisconsin, where he also served as President of the Marinette Teachers Association. He received a full scholarship to attend the University of Wisconsin and completed the requirements for the doctorate in the history of education in 1960, writing his dissertation on the neo-humanist protest in American education. The University of Wisconsin during the 1950s was well known for its critical scholarship, and his education there prepared him well for the significant and unique contribution he would make to the debates about our educational past. As a professor at the University of Rochester from 1960 to 1969, and as a professor at the University of Illinois from 1969 and continuing after his retirement in 1995, Karier has been a leading critical voice in the discussion over such key issues as the origins of standardized testing, the educational and social implications of John Dewey's pragmatic philosophy, the role of the arts and humanities in the public school curriculum, and the values implicit in the educational and psychological traditions that still continue to shape our work as educators.

As a scholar and person of profound integrity, Karier has had enormous influence on the people with whom he has worked. This volume is divided into three major sections and provides essays by Karier's former students and colleagues, people who have worked closely with him at various stages of their careers. Part One examines Karier as a teacher and mentor; Part Two assesses his impact on scholarship in the history of education and social foundations of education; and Part Three explores some of the implications of Karier's work for further scholarship in the field. Clarence is a person of considerable modesty and humility. We offer an apology for holding his life and work up for this kind of inspection and celebration. We know that he is not pleased with such attention.

The editors wish to thank Nancy Karier for her excellent work on the cover. Tim Glander and Christine Shea would like to give special acknowledgment to Karen Graves, who engaged in the lion's share of work pertaining to formatting and organizing the work, and for keeping us on task during particularly hectic times. Finally, the editors would like to thank the individual contributors to this volume. In each essay, we have tried to retain their original voice and style.

Part One

Personal Reflections on Karier and His Work

1

Honoring a Lost and Forgotten Tradition: The Teacher as Mentor

Christine M. Shea

> "Things men have made with wakened hands, and put soft
> life into are awake through years with transferred touch,
> and go on glowing for long years.
> And for this reason, some old things are lovely
> warm still with the life of forgotten men who made them." [1]
>
> —D. H. Lawrence

It is believed that the word "mentor" dates back to ancient Greece when Odysseus first entrusted his friend Mentor with the education of his son, Telemachus, as he embarked on a lengthy voyage. As a surrogate parent, Mentor gave support, love, guidance, and protection to the young child until the return of his father. Thus, we have come to know mentors as those who gently guide and nurture the growth of others during various stages of their development.[2] For historians and philosophers of education, however, the nature of these mentored relationships, so essential for any education of depth and substance, has remained a constant topic of academic controversy and conversation. Are we to believe that the philosopher-king in Plato's *The Republic* provides the ideal framework for the education of the tutor/expert? Or is it Rousseau's *Emile*, often thought to be the standard Western text of the mentored relationship, that we should embrace? Our more contemporary Western understanding of the term "mentor" we derive pragmatically from our notions of craft production. The craftsperson does not begin life as a master; there must be a certain knowledge gained in apprenticeship, upon which the craft itself is grounded. The goal, of course, is to transmit from one generation to the next a narrowly defined and prescribed set of skills, usually understood as those most able to help one "earn a living" or "be successful."[3] As such, this mentored skilled learning was thought to be unrelated to, and often in conflict with, the education of the whole person.

It is to the alternative voices in the American landscape and the ancient Eastern intellectual traditions that we must look to recapture our own more sacred and holistic notions of the ideal mentored relationship. Certainly any discussion of mentoring must examine Eastern notions of the teaching relationship; it is the Eastern intellectual traditions that have continued their thousands-of-years-old traditions and rituals to honor and revere those they call "teacher." In the Tao tradition, Jing Hwa—the Golden Flower—symbolizes the quintessence of Tao. The petals of the Hwa (the flower) represent the blossoming and awakening of one's real self and the realization of wholeness in each human being. Jing (gold) represents the alchemy, the art of finding the way to actualize the potential for transformation and transcendence in each individual. In the great spiritual tradition of Taoism, every relationship is invited to enter this "heartmind" mentoring journey toward wholeness. Both mentor and student benefit from this dynamic interaction as advice, support, and the joys of learning are shared in the Tao dance, Tai Ji, the dance of joining hands in joyful cooperation and synergy in human relationships.[4] What then is this process of "mentored learning"? of "apprenticeship"? of collaborative stewardship? I have discovered many of my own answers to these questions by reexamining my own relationship to my doctoral advisor, Dr. Clarence J. Karier.

Creating a Free and Friendly Space

"The German word for hospitality is 'Gastfreundschaft' which means, friendship for the guest. The Dutch use the word 'gastorijheid' which means, the freedom of the guest. . . . Hospitality, therefore, means primarily the creation of a free space where the stranger can enter and become a friend instead of an enemy. Hospitality is not to change people, but to offer them space where change can take place. . . . It is not to lead our neighbor into a corner

where there are no alternatives left, but to open a wide spectrum of options for choice and commitment." [5]
—Henri Nouwen, *Reaching Out: The Three Movements of the Spiritual Life*

As a new graduate student, I had arrived at the University of Illinois directly from my Peace Corps service in Tunisia, North Africa. Even twenty-eight years later, I can still vividly remember those first few years in the department. As one of a small group of female graduate students in the department, I was distinctly aware that the others were worlds ahead of me in terms of their academic preparation and career goals. I had completed a wonderful Peace Corps experience and had even been fortunate enough to work on an early childhood curriculum development manual for the preschools of Tunisia. I "discovered" the University of Illinois when one of the well-known "Peace Corps Green Sheets" had contained an advertisement announcing a new doctoral training program there focusing on the professional preparation of international relief workers with children in developing countries. I arrived at Illinois less than a month after returning from my Peace Corps tour abroad.

When I arrived at Illinois, I was dumbfounded to learn that most of the philosophy doctoral students had come to Illinois to study exclusively under the tutelage of specific faculty members—Burnett, Feinberg, Petrie, Ennis, or Smith, etc. The "philosophy group" was composed of an extraordinarily competent group of young scholars, including Ralph Page, Bruce and Felicity Haynes, Philip Stedman, Bob Halsted, Guitty Nassehy, Mary Leach, Steven Tozer, Ernie Kahane, Joe Hamilton, Jon Fennell, Graham Oliver, Michael Oliker, Steven Norris, Jeffrey Tank, Tom Tomko, among others. The group of male analytic philosophy of education students from Australia, England, and New Zealand was particularly awesome. I remember day after day leaving the graduate student office with a headache after attempting to make sense of the seemingly endless forays into "conceptual analysis." Week after week, I attempted to pick up one of John Dewey's books and make sense of it. I remember thinking to myself, "I wonder if I can get a doctorate here and not have to 'do' John Dewey?" Oftentimes, at noon, the male graduate students would go running with some of the male faculty, and usually, came back to the department after having had an obviously enjoyable "bonding experience." As a woman, I sometimes felt socially excluded, academically incompetent, and completely overwhelmed.

Following Your Bliss

> *"If you follow your bliss, you put yourself on a kind of track which has been there all the while, waiting for you, and the life that you ought to be living is the one you are living. . . . I feel that if one follows what I call one's 'bliss'—the thing that really gets you deep in the gut and that you feel is your life—doors will open up. They do! They have in my life, and they have in many lives that I know of."*[6]
>
> —Joseph Campbell, *An Open Life*

During my second semester at the university, by chance, I took Clarence Karier's History of American Education course, and it changed my life. I couldn't believe that any academic subject could be so interesting, so compelling, so unsettling. It opened me in a dramatically new and unfamiliar way to the academic life. Suddenly, it seemed, I went from someone who was merely "taking courses" with no particular passion for my work to someone who was a person who had opinions that mattered, whose research efforts had a clear focus, and who had a mentor who cared enough to leave little yellow pasted notes on top of my desk: "Could you give me your comments on this article draft?" "Have you seen this article?" "I have an extra copy of this book; this copy is yours." "Stop by my office . . . what did you think about our class today?" Pasted notes hurriedly scribbled in Clarence's nearly illegible handwriting, notes that a grateful graduate student has kept over these twenty-eight years! It was this personal touch, this one-on-one mentoring, that made Clarence such a revered and honored teacher amongst his students.

In a July 14, 1973, letter to my Mom, I announced the good news:

> Well, it's official. At last I've now changed into the Ph.D. program in History of Education. I asked Clarence (Karier) last Tuesday if he would accept me into the program and be my advisor. He said he "would be delighted." He operates on a tutorial system—that is, individual seminars for a couple hours a week. There are three of us interested in

early childhood education who are going to begin to look into the whole history of child-centered education. I have a feeling this is going to be a very exciting few years. It seems that I'm getting into something I really like!⁷

Cultivating the Ferment

"The stage of romance is the stage of first apprehension. The subject-matter has the vividness of novelty. . . .. Romantic emotion is essentially the excitement consequent on the transition from the bare facts to the first realizations of the import of their unexplored relationships. For example, Crusoe was a mere man, the sand was mere sand, the footprint was a mere footprint, and the island a mere island, and Europe was the busy world of men. But the sudden perception of the half-disclosed and half-hidden possibilities relating Crusoe and the sand and the footprint and the lonely island secluded from Europe constitutes romance. . . . In our conception of education. . . we are concerned alike with the ferment, with the acquirement of precision, and with the subsequent fruition."⁸
—Alfred North Whitehead, *The Aims of Education and Other Essays*

Clarence's history of education group was a very diverse one—actually, quite an odd assortment of seekers. Our small group gathered each week in the living room in Clarence's modest home, and there, week after week, we devoured vast amounts of coffee and sweet rolls, and books—from Hall, Emerson, Thorndike, and Thoreau to Fichte, Freud, Jung, Skinner, Hesse, Hegel, and Mosse. While the topics, treatments, and time periods were infinitely diverse, we had a deep sense of commitment to our collaborative Socratic gadfly quest—to understand, to question, and to critique the great master narratives of the American past. As students, I remember how much we enjoyed the process of following each other's research investigations and what a pleasure it was to do research in one of the nation's most outstanding university libraries. There was Joe Hamilton working on John Dewey; Marian Metzow digging into the early childhood education books; David Hogan working on the Progressive-era history of Chicago's public schools; Spiro Rasis studying the American humanist tradition; Gail Parks analyzing concepts of adolescence in Progressive era popular magazines; Tim O'Hanlon writing on Progressive-era school athletics movement; Brisbane Rouzane studying the history of African American education; Bob Barger working on the history of Catholic parochial school education; Tim Reagan researching the history of bilingual and multicultural education; Steven Yulish researching the history of Progressive-era character education movements; Mark Sorensen writing the history of Native American educational traditions; Lauren Weisberg puzzling over Karl Jung and the German youth movement; Erik Kristensen studying D. H. Lawrence's educational ideas; Micky Becker studying something with Clarence he revealed to us in whispered tones as "decadence"; and I was investigating the history of the Progressive-era American mental hygiene movement. Russell Marks, Peter Sola, Joe DeVitis, and Jim Anderson were in the final stages of their dissertation work with Dr. Karier and Professor Paul Violas.

Seeking Solitude and Taking Time

"While visiting the University of Notre Dame, where I had been a teacher for a few years, I met an older experienced professor who had spent most of his life there. And while we strolled over the beautiful campus, he said with a certain melancholy in his voice, 'You know . . . my whole life I have been complaining that my work was constantly interrupted, until I discovered that my interruptions were my work.'"[9]
—Henri Nouwen, *Reaching Out: The Three Movements of the Spiritual Life*

In mentoring each of us, somehow Clarence managed amidst his busy life as professor, department chair, father, husband, and mentor to help each of us discover those topics and themes about which we were most passionate and troubled. In retrospect, I wonder to myself: How DID he do it all? How DID he mentor SO MANY doctoral students? How DID he have time to provide individual tutorials for all these doctoral students? How DID he have time to publish year-after-year two major articles a year, a major text every few years, a continual stream of book reviews and scholarly responses to colleagues in the field? He did so by showing up at the office (almost) every day of the year; even Saturday mornings were devoted to more tutorials. Ah! but Sundays were for Clarence himself, and we tried not to disturb him. Typically, Clarence wrote his essays at the end of the semester when the rest of the faculty and students had left for their winter or summer break holidays.

"Going into the Woods"

> "I went to the woods because I wished to live deliberately, to front only the essential facts of life, and see if I could not learn what it had to teach, and not, when I came to die, discover that I had not lived. I did not wish to live what was not life, living is so dear; nor did I wish to practise resignation, unless it was quite necessary. I wanted to live deep and suck out all the marrow of life, to live so sturdily and Spartan-like as to put to rout all that was not life, to cut a broad swath and shave close, to drive life into a corner, and reduce it to its lowest terms, and, if it proved to be mean, why then to get the whole and genuine meanness of it, and publish its meanness to the world; or if it were sublime, to show it by experience and be able to give a true account of it in my next excursion "[10]
>
> —Henry D. Thoreau, *Walden*

One of the early doctoral level seminars that I took with Clarence was devoted to reading books on the topic of "Child-Centered Traditions in Western Education." During the semester, we read from a wide assortment of primary source reading, including Rousseau, Jung, Wickes, Dewey, Neill, Hall, Mead, and others. I was fascinated with G. Stanley Hall and chose his work as the topic of my seminar paper. Having completed over 60 term papers as an undergraduate major in History and Literature, I thought I had the term paper process mastered. My Hall paper, I thought, provided the reader with a well-polished summary of Hall's educational thought within the context of larger American intellectual traditions.

As a struggling doctoral student, I had bought my train ticket home to upstate New York and was eagerly looking forward to going home for the Christmas holidays. However, shortly after submitting my paper just after Thanksgiving, I got a call from Clarence. He wanted to talk with me about my paper. During our meeting, Clarence gently suggested to me that he didn't think I had totally immersed myself in the primary sources yet nor had I gotten in touch with "the real G. Stanley Hall." I remember walking down the hall away from Clarence's office with tears in my eyes. I felt angry, embarrassed, and bewildered all at the same time. I cancelled my train reservation, said goodbye to my friends leaving for their vacations, and settled down in my empty apartment complex to confront "the real G. Stanley Hall." For the next few weeks, I was completely consumed by my G. Stanley Hall paper. I am sure I am one of the few people alive who has actually read his two-volume book on *Adolescence* in its entirety (i.e., in addition to most of his other major works).[11] I do remember many times during these weeks of having no sensation of time, of being completely and entirely absorbed in my work. The redrafted paper I wrote and submitted as I finally took leave for my Christmas holiday is one of which I am still, to this day, justifiably proud. It captured, I think, a theoretical reading of Hall that I have not yet seen in print. This rather insignificant experience changed me as an individual and a scholar. I was joyful at the discovery that I could have the same complete absorption in my doctoral studies that I used to have painting in the garage loft at my home. This experience, Mihaly Csikszentmihalyi would refer to, I think, as "flow" learning; athletes would call it "being in the Zone."[12] When I returned from my Christmas holiday, and reread the paper I had submitted, I was in disbelief that I could have written such a profound essay. Wise teachers know when their students need to "go into the woods."

Being There

"A wise teacher learns to be a good listener. Empathy can come only from truly hearing and understanding what the student thinks. Listening does not imply agreement nor does it require a response. Very often the students who have shared their concerns with you, who have seen your attentive gaze and nodding, sympathetic head go on to say they can do the work or solve the problem themselves. Spend time with the students who need you to listen."[13]
—Nagel, The Tao of Teaching

I arrived at 4 p.m. for my weekly tutorial with Clarence. Those who have studied at Illinois know that the desk in Clarence's small, crowded office space is pushed directly against the floor-to-ceiling glass windows on the third floor of the education building. From his perch, Clarence was able to observe the expansive midwestern landscape and ever-changing weather patterns. Students usually sat in the chair directly beside Clarence's office desk with their back to the glass windows. The book I was to discuss this particular day was Herbert Marcuse's *Eros and Civilization*; I struggled to make sense of Marcuse's complex treatment of Freud. As usual, our conversation covered a vast terrain and Clarence was always there, providing all kinds of interesting information on both Freud and Marcuse. I remember feeling so carefully nurtured in these sessions, and knowing how lucky I was; what a rare privilege it was to have this kind of one-on-one mentoring. The time always went by so quickly for me, and today was no exception. Suddenly, I seemed to come out of our conversation and I heard Clarence saying, "Look behind you. Look at the beautiful sunset!" I turned around to view one of those glorious midwestern views; the clouds covered the winter sky in brilliant shades of pink, orange, purple, and gold. The sun was a huge blinding golden color. As I looked at the view, I became aware that in the approaching dusk I could see Clarence's reflection clearly in the glass. He was tugging at his sweater sleeve so he could quickly see what time it was on his watch. As he looked up, we caught each other's gaze in the reflective glass. We both laughed. Clarence was too much of a gentleman, too aware of his mentoring role to tell me that I had overstayed my appointed hour. It was after 5:30 in the evening! Clarence laughed apologetically and said, "I've got to leave. We're celebrating a birthday today and I've got to get home for supper!"

That moment has remained etched in my consciousness to this day. There have been numerous days when my students have lingered in conversation, and I have felt the urge to cut short our meeting so I could return to my own work and research. Each time, I remember the sunset, and I remember the hundreds of hours that my mentor spent helping me master my discipline. And I remember to listen and to create time and space for my student guest.

Live Simply that Others May Simply Live

To be a philosopher
is not merely
to have subtle thoughts
nor even to found a school
but so to love wisdom
as to live according to its dictates
a life of simplicity, independence,
magnanimity, and trust.
It is to solve
some of the problems of life,

> *not only theoretically,*
> *but practically.*[14]
> —Henry David Thoreau, *Walden*

Clarence often taught his most memorable lessons through silent example. Each spring, the midwestern fields surrounding the University of Illinois came alive with the work of putting in the new crops. Each year, Clarence would begin a list on his office door of all the pesticides, herbicides, and chemicals being advertised on local television stations for use on the incredibly rich, black, and fertile Illinois soil. Each year, the list seemed to grow longer and longer. The contrast between the thousands of Illinois farm families who were losing their precious family farms and the rapid expansion of the new corporate-run agribusiness conglomerates was not lost in this exercise. This annual cataloging of the environmental and social disaster that was occurring in our very midst served to connect us in a very concrete and specific way to the crises in the farming communities that surrounded our more sheltered ivy-tower lives.

Discovering "Who We Are"

> *"Education understood to involve formation and the whole person implies an effort to foster an increased openness, attentiveness, and truthful responsiveness to a deeper reality and a deeper experience and understanding of the whole self. The educator becomes one who initiates and shepherds, or collaborates in, a process of awakening and of acquiring perspective, and, in some sense, of experiencing oneself whole. . . . In order to build toward an understanding of an educative process which originates in and involves the whole person, we need to develop an awareness of person and personhood, of this 'who we are.'"*[15]
> —Thomas Del Prete, *Thomas Merton and the Education of the Whole Person*

One day Clarence came rushing into the graduate student offices. "I've finally figured it out!" he exclaimed to me. He continued, "All this time, I've been trying to figure out what your position is on issues. You seem to keep changing from meeting to meeting, and I haven't been able to figure it out! But then, I just realized that you always argue and support the person in the group in the worst-off position; you always come to the assistance of the person in the group that needs the most support with their arguments." My mind was racing; I hadn't even been aware that this had been a concern for Clarence. Clarence's quiet observations, such as this, over the years helped me acquire some deep understandings about myself. Even to this day, that particular observation has been replayed for me in many different contexts in my life. Each time I am reminded of the person who understood that the educative process always involves a search for the whole person and speaks to the "who we are."

The Teacher as Critical Gadfly

> *"You must renounce and sacrifice the approval that is only a bribe enlisting your support of a collective illusion. You must not allow yourself to be represented as someone in whom a few of the favorite daydreams of the public have come true. You must be willing, if necessary, to become a disturbing and therefore an undesired person, one who is not wanted because he upsets the general dream."*[16]
> —Thomas Merton, *Conjectures of a Guilty Bystander*

This same attentive listening that Clarence devoted to his students, he taught us to apply in equal measure to the subjects of our own historical research studies. It was this same quest for the essence of an individual, of what made each educator he studied "tick," that quickly crystallized Clarence's biographical sketches into classic portraits in the educational literature. Invariably, his articles generated wide discussion and controversy within the field. Clarence often remarked during these years that if he had to stop his current research to respond to all the misinterpretations of himself and his work that appeared in print that he would never get any new research completed. He produced a rich body of historical scholarship during this period. His coedited text with Paul Violas and Joel Spring, *Roots of Crisis: American Education in the Twentieth Century*, was published in 1973, followed in 1975 by *Shaping the American Educational State: 1900 to the Present*. During the late 1970s, Clarence researched some of his most penetrating critiques of American progressive liberal thought and also collaborated with David Hogan on some landmark critical essays on John Dewey's work. Beginning in the late 1970s, Clarence began research on an intellectual history of modern psychology, publishing *Scientists of the Mind: Intellectual Founders of Modern Psychology* in 1986. A major redraft of his classic history of education text, *The Individual, Society, and Education: A History of American Educational Ideas*, was also published in 1986.[17]

As Clarence's historical research progressed during the decade of the 1970s, he was deeply troubled and morally assaulted by what his research was revealing about the highly competitive, materialistic, and racist values underlying the policies of the American educational state. Clarence himself expressed most succinctly the direction of his work:

> The author writes from a perspective of the present which holds that American society is not structured to enhance the dignity of many but unfortunately, is structured to foster a dehumanizing quest for status, power, and wealth. We live, I believe, in a fundamentally racist, materialistic society which, through a process of rewards and punishments, cultivates the quest for status, power, and wealth in such a way so as to use people and institutions effectively to protect vested interests.[18]

In addition, Clarence's research during this decade began to focus on an examination of both the "child-centered" and the "efficiency-society-oriented" traditions in American education. He argued that the tendency in many mainstream liberal educational histories had been to picture the efficiency-society-oriented educators to be conservative, while those writing in the child-centered tradition were assumed to be radical.[19] His research began to reveal, clearly, that the thrust of both traditions has been in the direction of social control as well as social stability, with similar results.[20] As Clarence noted of the American child-centered tradition,

> If one goes further and examines the rhetoric and practice of many child-centered educators in both the nineteenth and twentieth centuries, the social control function of the "new" education is obvious.[21]

Much of my own historical research over the years has been devoted to a further understanding of this one, seemingly paradoxical insight that Clarence provided during my graduate years.

The culmination of Clarence's research into twentieth-century American education concluded with his yet-to-be-published work on the emergence of the American security state during the Cold

War years. The book, meticulously researched and supported by recently released Freedom of Information documents, relates the sordid and shameful history of the covert political policies and programs operated by America's intelligence agencies, thought necessary to secure the "defense of American liberties" at home and abroad.[22]

"Walking the Walk"

> "It isn't enough to complain about politicians and the 'system.' The power to achieve change is already in our hands. The next movement for a deeper and more meaningful democracy requires us to go beyond the limits of our current political imagination. We are, today, part of a long tradition of Americans who have endeavored over several centuries to achieve a more democratic and socially just society—from the abolitionists, women's suffragists, Populists, and early labor union activists of the nineteenth century, to the activists of nearly a generation ago who opposed Jim Crow segregation and the Vietnam War in the 1960s. . . . We, too, are America, and we shall not retreat until genuine equality and social justice are shared by all. And toward that end, we dedicate ourselves to the empowerment of all humanity and to the continued enrichment of the human spirit." [23]
> —Manning Marable, *Speaking Truth to Power: Essays on Race, Resistance, and Radicalism*

Each of the doctoral students had his or her own particular "issue" that they liked to discuss with Clarence. For some, it involved interpreting the motivations and actions of a particular historical figure in education—Jung, Rousseau, Dewey, etc. For others, the question of "fascism," particularly whether an American variety of "fascism" had developed, was always a hot issue of debate. My "issue" with Clarence centered on social activism. I was aware in my historical writing that I often wanted to end my historical research with a search for "a solution." Clarence was always insistent that one did not have to have a solution in order to write a good critique. To this day, the question of the nexus between "social critique" and "social transformation" theorizing has interested me. I've always been at a loss for words when students come up to me at the end of a "History of American Education" course and inquire, "Okay, so if things have been so bad, what do we do? What's the solution for all these questions?" One answer I remember Clarence offering one day was, "The solution is: You begin to live the alternative!" In retrospect, I can see that Clarence's own social activism has been dramatically expressed in the over twenty-four years that he spent as Chair of the Department of Educational Policy Studies at the University of Illinois.

When Clarence Karier arrived at the University of Illinois in the fall of 1969 to assume the position as Chair of the Department of History, Philosophy, and Comparative Education, the department had experienced the recent retirement of a number of distinguished faculty, including Bunny Smith, Bill Stanley, and Harry Broudy. Clarence's momumental task was to ensure that the department maintain its national leadership in the field and create an academic and social environment compatible with its democratic humanist traditions. The department had gathered a renown group of foundations faculty, including Clarence himself, and Paul Violas, James Anderson, Joe Burnett, Hugh Petrie, Robert Ennis, Walter Feinberg, Ralph Smith, Foster McMurray, Alan Peshkin, Mobin Shorish, Fred Coombs, among others. As the department chair, one of Clarence's first initiatives was to suggest that the department name be changed to the "Department of Educational Policy Studies." In a letter to Dean Myron Atkins, Clarence explained his position. "The uniqueness of this Department as compared to other departments across the nation will be that here at the University of Illinois will be a Department which brings together not only social science experts to work creatively on educational issues and problems, but also exceptionally strong expertise in philosophy and history."[24] He continued,

> In the recent past many of the programs, research, and studies which have emerged from educational policies departments have suffered on the one hand by too heavy emphasis on using social science models and techniques generated in the various disciplines, and on the other hand, by a far too superficial acceptance of practically-oriented research. For example, it is now fairly clear that both the Coleman and the Jencks studies could have been measurably improved if philosophers and historians of education had been part of the dialogue which produced these studies. In many ways the critical assumptions concerning the social and ethical consequences of our educational decision-making have gone unexamined.[25]

And, in concluding, Dr. Karier asserted:

> We believe that the kind of department we wish to create over the next few years, which will include a social science division, will be best able to ask the kinds of critical, penetrating questions so necessary for more reflective decision-making at all levels of education.[26]

During his final years in the department, Clarence transformed what had been an almost exclusively all-white male faculty into a wonderfully diverse group of talented scholars. While many other major university departments were complaining about their inability to find and attract "qualified" African-American, Latino, women, and other minority scholars for university appointments, Clarence was able to secure some of the nation's finest minority scholars as faculty in the department. Upon Clarence's retirement, Dr. James D. Anderson took over the leadership of the department and has maintained the ranking and reputation of the department as one of the premier educational policy departments in the country; a majority of women, African American, Asian American, international, and other scholars now continue to build and expand the proud Illinois tradition in educational policy studies. As the department chair, Clarence's activism on these issues will have dramatic consequences as generations of future scholars and mentees seek their doctoral education at the University of Illinois.

Mentoring With Transferred Touch

> *"It seemed to Goldmund that his life had been given a meaning. For a moment, it was as though he were looking down on it from above, clearly seeing its three big steps: his dependence on Narcissus and his awakening; then the period of freedom and wandering; and now the return, the reflection, the beginning of maturity and harvest. The vision faded again. But he had found a fitting relationship to Narcissus. It was no longer a relationship of dependence, but one of equality and reciprocity. He could be the guest of this superior mind without humiliation, since the other man had given recognition to the creative power in him."*[27]
>
> —Hermann Hesse, *Narcissus and Goldmund*

Last fall I had occasion to prepare my professional portfolio for tenure review at a new university where I have just begun teaching. The process allowed me the time to reflect on the contours of my own teaching career, and remind myself how much the mentoring process had defined the highlights of my own career. After leaving my own beloved mentor, the first three years of my teaching career were spent at Hampshire College, Massachusetts, one of the few remaining undergraduate institutions that continues to center its entire academic structure on the sacredness of the mentored relationship. As I compiled my portfolio for review, I was reminded that during my three-year sojourn at Hampshire, I had served on over 95 different mentored student project committees. In retrospect, I could see how effortlessly this mentoring role had been for me because I myself had been so well mentored. At the same time, I also requested some letters of recommendation from my recent doctoral student advisees in the curriculum studies program at Georgia Southern University, where I had recently taught. Their letters are ones that I will treasure for many years; their words are almost the same ones that I would have lovingly bestowed on my own doctoral mentor. I was struck and deeply satisfied knowing that perhaps the mentoring process had come full circle.

Conclusion

"Only when we dare to let go of control will we win the hearts of others and enable true learning and growth to occur. Let others find their own way by using very little intervention; refrain from manipulating, imposing morality, or coercing. . . . Confucius, in his discourse on education states that the 'superior teacher/mentor guides students but does not pull them along; urges them to go forward by opening the way yet refrains from taking them to the place.' . . . The Buddha says that the best way to raise your cow is to not control it. Offer instead a large, spacious meadow."[28]
—Huang and Lynch, *Mentoring: The Tao of Giving and Receiving Wisdom*

The concept of "the teacher as mentor" has become a lost and forgotten tradition in American education. At its core, the philosophy of mentoring encourages humble visions of healthy, harmonious lives treated as ends in themselves rather than as instruments in the global race for power, wealth, and status. While the creation of such a world grounded in caring, love, and social justice is probably beyond our reach, it is reasonable to expect that we can, at least, achieve much more harmonious and morally just educational institutions than those that presently exist. The texts of Clarence's academic career remain as rich sources of inspiration in helping us learn from our oftentimes corrupt, morally bankrupt, and vicious educational past. The text of his life is one that continues to beat in the hearts of each one of his grateful students.

2

Searching for Truth: Meeting Clarence Karier in the 1960s

Richard Ognibene

By the mid-1960s, I was tenured as a social studies teacher in an urban school system and held a master's degree in history from a university department that traditionally fared well in academic reputational rankings. Regrettably, as a student of history I had not encountered teachers with anything more than pedestrian pedagogical skills, or anyone who demanded much more than mastery of information found in texts. In part, because I possessed a great ability to memorize, I was successful both as student and as teacher. Critical thinking was not demanded by either my professors or my students, and there was every possibility that in the long career ahead of me this important trait would be inexcusably absent from my professional work. Then in 1966, I met Clarence Karier, a circumstance that so altered my intellectual outlook that it would not be an exaggeration to say that I was reborn. The college students to whom I have taught educational foundations since 1969 do not know that these courses have been cotaught with me in the foreground and Clarence in the background. Sadly, Clarence does not know it either because we have had virtually no contact during the past thirty years. This essay is to note some early developments in Clarence's career, and to reflect on some of the ways he influenced my life and work.

Clarence Karier came to the University of Rochester in 1960 after completing his Ph.D. work at the University of Wisconsin. Within a short time, he developed an array of courses and connections to other departments in the College of Education and the College of Arts and Science to create a doctoral program in the history of education. In 1965, Clarence obtained federal funds to support National Defense Education Act (NDEA) Fellowships in the history of education. From 1965 to 1968, approximately four NDEA students a year were admitted. Perhaps the best known graduates of this program were Paul Violas and Edward Stevens. Paul entered in 1965, completed his dissertation in 1969, and spent his career at the University of Illinois. Ed began the program in 1966, finished his dissertation in 1970, and taught at Ohio University. I also joined the program in 1966, and it was in that context that I met Clarence.

Establishing the history of education doctoral program was a significant achievement. The University of Rochester, founded in 1850, awarded only a handful of Ph.D.s starting in the 1920s, and it did not seriously get into graduate work until the 1950s. From the first doctorate awarded in 1925 until 1962, the University awarded a total of 1,108 Ph.D. degrees, primarily in the areas of science and music.[1] Professional education was a minor undertaking at the University and relegated to service offerings for local teachers and administrators scheduled on Saturdays and summers by the University's extension division. The College of Education was not established until 1958. In 1959, it was authorized to develop doctoral programs.[2]

Although I was too inexperienced to realize it at the time, what Clarence did was to construct a multidisciplinary doctoral program based on the courses he developed, course offerings from the history and political science departments, and selected courses from other departments in the College of Education. Taking history of education survey and "classics" courses with Clarence, intellectual history with Loren Baritz, political theory with William Bluhm, organization theory with Glenn Immegart, and school law with Henry Butler, among others, created a credible and exciting program of study given the limitations existing within the department in which the program was housed. As was typical then, the foundations faculty in the College of Education was divided into psychological and social foundations areas. Clarence's two social foundations colleagues, one in sociology and the other in philosophy, were not destined to have the kind of career that Clarence did. Although early on Clarence had become a "star professor" in the department (and in the College), there was no tension evident among the foundations group that affected students. In fact, the opposite was true; they were collegial, and when Clarence left for Illinois in 1969, both of his social foundations colleagues unhesitantly helped several of Clarence's students through the final stages of their dissertations. There was a generosity there based on the respectful, supportive, and good-natured relationships that evolved among that small faculty, with Clarence at the center.

The doctoral programs could not have been started or sustained if the various history of education courses Clarence developed did not enroll students. This was not an issue because Clarence's reputation as a teacher and scholar had grown enormously in a very short time. Although he began his career in Rochester in 1960 as an assistant professor, he was a full professor by 1968 with a joint appointment in the history department. Clarence's scholarship was top tier right from the beginning. From 1963 to 1967, he published articles in *Teachers College Record, Educational Theory, Studies in Philosophy,* and the *Journal of Contemporary History.* This was an especially productive period that culminated with the publication of his first book, *Man, Society and Education.* While these publications were important for their contributions to the revitalization that was beginning to occur in the history of education discipline in the 1960s, I want to focus instead on how the vitality displayed in Clarence's research was also present in his practice as a teacher and mentor.

Recently, and somewhat by accident, I happened upon Parker Palmer's book *The Courage To Teach.* In this text, Palmer makes several observations that are germane to my memory of Clarence Karier when I was his student from 1966 to 1969. Palmer writes, "Good teachers possess a capacity for connectedness. They are able to weave a complex web of connections among themselves, their subjects, and their students so that students can learn to weave a world for themselves."[3] Such connections, Palmer argues, help create a community of truth, with truth defined as *"an eternal conversation about things that matter, conducted with passion and discipline."*[4] The conception of truth as an "eternal conversation" is quite similar to the view Clarence expressed in the introduction to *Man, Society, and Education*: "Man the creator is a restless being who always dies a little when he fails to create and nothing inhibits his creating more than *the* truth. In this context one can agree with Lessing that 'the search for truth is more precious than its possession.'"[5] Searching for truth in an eternal conversation is how I remember Clarence's classes, and hallway and office interactions with him as well.

The first course in the history of education sequence was Clarence's "History of American Educational Thought." The course enrolled forty to fifty students, the vast majority of whom were not majoring in the subject but were enrolled in other graduate programs in the College of Education. It was the place where I met Clarence as teacher for the first time. The course text was the massive and difficult to use *A History of Education in American Culture* by Butts and Cremin, along with a few paperbacks.[6] Reading the text was necessary to respond to questions Clarence provided at the beginning of the semester that served as the basis of the final exam. The text, however, was never the basis of what took place in the class.

Before class, students often conversed with Clarence, and one could observe from the smiles and laughter that this was friendly talk, not course-related business. The class typically began with a lecture that might take a third to half of the three-hour period. It was fascinating to watch Clarence lecture. He would present information and ideas from a seemingly endless array of sources, compare what typically had been thought about the topic with his perspective and/or that of a new crowd of historians (Katz, Spring, Tyack, etc.) whose emerging work he knew well even in 1966. As he did so, his level of intensity rose to such a degree that everyone present could, to use Parker Palmer's terms, feel Clarence's passion for those ideas that mattered most to him. As teacher, Clarence's intellectual passion produced more questions than assertions, and debating these questions is what always happened next.

Clarence managed group discussion well. His enthusiasm provoked a similar response from students, enabling discussion to emerge naturally. More than that, he was masterful at building connections between what he said, other information he would provide during discussion, student questions and commentary, and the relationship of the historical issues to contemporary concerns. Recently, when I asked Adelia Peters, also a mid-sixties NDEA student, to characterize Clarence's teaching style thirty-five years ago, without hesitation she called him "an orchestra conductor of ideas."[7] This brilliant metaphor is quite apt.

The excitement that Clarence's first course created had numerous consequences. It helped to build enrollment in the next level of educational "classics" seminars he conducted, thus broadening the range of peers with whom history of education students would interact. Students read a book a week for these seminars, which Clarence conducted in a Socratic style, raising questions primarily, and occasionally providing supplemental information when appropriate. Since questions were the primary mode of dialogue, one did not dare to come unprepared. The books read for these seminars were an eclectic array of history, philosophy, and psychology texts that represented Clarence's diverse interests. When completing a program with Clarence, one owned a small library, and to this day book collecting remains one of my chief pleasures. When my children joke that our floors will collapse from the bookshelves, or my students roll their eyes at reading lists that are too long, I have a ready response: blame Clarence Karier. I was twenty-five years old when I met Clarence, and although I was a teacher, I did not have a wide range of intellectual interests. Clarence was the main influence in my life to help correct that deficiency.

Another consequence of the excitement generated by Clarence's teaching was that students wanted to spend time with him outside of class. His office was a perpetual open house. Clarence was there an amazing amount of time and seemed never to be alone. Conversations went on at length, included students from other programs, and reflected the same kind of intellectual enthusiasm as his classes, but at a lower key. There I saw a scholar working privately, with the same good effect as watching his public work in class or reading his published work. I do not believe that Clarence was aware of the then emerging faculty development literature that proclaimed that faculty who have the greatest impact on students are those who interact with them on a regular basis outside of class, but this was the professorial lifestyle he lived intuitively.[8]

I should not create the impression that Clarence and his students lived at some elevated academic plane all of the time. In fact, some of Clarence's best qualities were not rooted in academic life at all. One such quality was the ordinary care he displayed for others. Most of the students were older, and like Clarence, many were raising families. Family talk was a regular part of our outside of class conversation, a circumstance made easier by the fact that Clarence and Norma regularly invited students to their home for social gatherings. Another quality was Clarence's sense of humor. He laughed easily and saw the humor in the lunatic circumstances often found in academic settings. He shared his professional hopes and frustrations with those with whom he was in contact, including his graduate students. In short, although Clarence quickly earned a distinctively high reputation in the College of Education, he was anything but aloof. He was a person who showed his humanness fully. Shortly after I left the University in 1969, I read Carl Rogers' inspirational education book, *Freedom To Learn*. Rogers argued that genuineness and empathy were key qualities in a teacher that helped promote significant learning.[9] I understood and accepted Rogers' argument; I had, after all, just spent several years working with Clarence Karier.

Another thought-provoking book I discovered in 1969 was Neil Postman and Charles Weingartner's *Teaching as a Subversive Activity*. Postman and Weingartner argued that the acceptance of the status quo and surface level explanations offered by schools and teachers posed a threat to the continuation of our democratic society. Schools, they wrote, play a "game called 'Let's Pretend,' and if its name were chiseled into the front of every school building in America, we would at least have an honest announcement of what takes place there."[10] What our society needed, Postman and Weingartner suggested, were schools that helped students become good at "crap detecting," a metaphor they borrowed from Hemingway and which they used as a title of their first chapter. Crap detecting was the ability to see through the traditional interpretative frameworks imposed by the community in which one grew up, and to be able to critique institutions and societal changes and the kind of impacts they produced at deeper and more significant levels. The way to foster that ability, according to Postman and Weingartner, was through an inquiry-based instructional approach and a questions-centered curriculum.[11] From 1966 when I met Clarence Karier, until 1969 when we parted, training in crap detecting is what I experienced. It was not the kind of teaching I encountered in my prior undergraduate or graduate work, nor was it typical of the work of most college teachers of the era.[12]

Like Parker Palmer, "I was a child of the 1950s, with its many social fictions," and needed a teacher to fit me with "new lenses" so I could weave a more accurate, multidimensional worldview.[13] The body of Clarence's work after he left Rochester in 1969 demonstrates his commitment to and success at crap detecting, and the work of several authors in this volume attests to the vision he helped them acquire. My purpose in this essay is simply to note that those of us who knew Clarence in Rochester were also influenced by his perceptive criticism, as I hope the following example suggests.

When I completed my dissertation, I was teaching in a small, Catholic college in upstate New York. Several of my young contemporaries at the college thought the place too stodgy and formed a group to attempt to transform its curriculum and pedagogy. We gained recognition and modest financial support from the college president, but there was fierce opposition to our presumptuous assessment from veteran faculty. In order to involve that faculty, one of our first activities was a panel discussion on Gilbert Highet's *The Art of Teaching*, a book that was then more than twenty years old and much revered. The panel consisted of three senior faculty and me, and I was the last speaker.

The other panelists generally commented favorably on some aspect of Highet's commonsense recommendations about lecturing. My position, which shocked many, and became the focal point of discussion, was to reject Highet on the basis of his social views that rendered much of his pedagogy suspect. I selected examples from the text that revealed Highet's elitism, intolerance, sexism, and willingness to stereotype that made him an unacceptable model for college teachers in an era (early 1970s) when civil rights and multicultural education were in the forefront of many people's concerns about equitable educational outcomes and processes. The examples from the text were so numerous and so harsh that many audience members (and panelists) shook their heads in disbelief. This positive response to my work motivated me to develop the analysis further and submit it for publication. It turned out to be my first postdissertation publication.[14] I did not tell the audience that Clarence Karier taught me to do that kind of analysis, but I did cite him in a footnote in the article.

Parker Palmer writes that the power of mentors is "their capacity to awaken a truth within us," that we can "discover a teacher's heart in ourselves by meeting a great teacher. . . ."[15] Meeting Clarence Karier in the 1960s was a life-changing experience for me. He awakened me from my indifference to questions about the nature of knowledge, the person, and the good society. In doing so, this great teacher transformed me from one who taught primarily with facts that could be used to tell a good story, to one who understands the need to search for truth whenever I teach or write.[16]

It really is about time to say "thank you, Clarence."

3

Liberalism and Education

Joel Spring

I

The police shattered the glass doors with their batons and streamed into the lobby of the University of Wisconsin's Commerce Building ready to pounce on the demonstrators trying to block recruiting by Dow Chemical, the infamous manufacturer of Agent Orange. This was my initiation into the antiwar demonstrations of the late 1960s.

Obviously lacking any clear directions about the location of the demonstrators, the police charged the right-wing Young Americans for Freedom who stood near the door chanting, "Get those Commies! Get those Commies!" Bravely swinging their nightsticks, the police pushed the conservatives over the railing of a stairwell located near the entrance. Still lost, the police then charged a group of students who were changing classes. Trapped against the wall facing the entrance, these students, including myself, were suddenly plummeted by wild-eyed and frightened-looking police officers. A blue arm reached out and snatched a young woman standing next to me, her arms loaded with books. I watched as she was dragged across the hallway and out the doors while being beaten across her back.

I could see Clarence Karier outside the Commerce Building carrying bodies that had fallen during the police riot. I began swinging my briefcase full of weighty books about the failures and successes of American education. Down the hallway, demonstrators continued their chants against Dow's magical chemical that guaranteed to reduce jungle greenery to brown refuse and help speed up the cancer rate. I guess the police or their leaders finally realized that they were attacking the wrong groups, much to the relief of the conservative counter-demonstrators who were now huddled in a corner cursing their attackers. The police then turned their attention to students seated at the end of a long hallway in front of the recruiting offices screaming "Hell No! We Won't Go!"

The police blamed the students for breaking the glass doors and causing a riot by hurling rocks at them. I clearly remember police batons breaking the glass, and I don't remember any rocks on the building's floors. University officials announced their commitment to protect academic freedom by promising to expel any students participating in demonstrations or riots that infringed on the rights of other students. Always nervous about their supposedly left-leaning university, state legislators from rural and small-town Wisconsin threatened to reduce funds to higher education if University officials didn't take strong action against campus commies and hippies. The faculty was neatly divided between liberal arts professors railing against government interference in the university and Johnson's dirty war, and engineers and scientists, fearing that their government-sponsored projects were in danger, demanding more police action to control students.

Immersed in this heady stew of academic politics, we sat in Clarence Karier's seminar discussing the nature of American education. I was very naive. My interest in studying education was personal. I wanted to understand the influence of schools on my character development. But now I couldn't separate the influence of schools from the influence of politics. The relationship of the two had literally been beaten into the heads of college and high school students around the country. How could you avoid making the leap from the knowledge of the classroom to the blood of the battlefield?

So there we sat in Karier's seminar trying to sort out the meaning of an educational system that was being turned upside down. Could the school be a source of evil as well as good? I had always thought of the school as good—as helpful. I'd spent many years in school. Now I was attending school to avoid being drafted into a military machine that was fighting a war lacking any meaningful goals. Oddly, I had never given much thought to the fact that the government forced me to make a choice between going to school or into the military. I'd never made the obvious connection between the U.S. government's foreign policies and my decision to remain in school. I'd never thought politically.

Now the war and Karier were forcing me to think politically, which meant examining the exercise of power. How were knowledge and power linked? One academic we discussed in and out of class was Lawrence Cremin, who at the time was the major "star" in the field of educational history. A self-professed liberal, who asserted that the public schools were the backbone of democracy, Cremin taught at a private bastion of elite ivy-league power, Columbia University. Later, he would serve as president of Columbia University's Teachers College and help found the inner club of backslapping liberal and conservative educators, the National Academy of Education.

It was interesting that people ignored, because they were afraid or didn't see, the contradiction between teaching at an elite private university while professing faith in public schools. As far as I know, no one pointed out the same contradiction with Cremin's successor in the "star" system, David Tyack, who asserted the value of public education while teaching at the elite private university on the West Coast, Stanford. Tyack retired into a part-time faculty position at Harvard.

I will be crass and do the unspeakable by mentioning academic financial rewards. I know that academics sometimes claim that they only work because of love of knowledge and not because of status and money. However, private schools, like Columbia and Stanford, use both to buy their academic talent. Check any annual rating of the American Association of University Professors and you will find the elite private schools offering the largest financial rewards. Then look closely at the faculty of these schools and you will be hard pressed to find any so-called "radicals." Serving the elite, the elite schools teach and research ideologies supportive of the rich and powerful.

What does money buy in the case of educational history? In Lawrence Cremin it bought a defender of the liberal promise that American schools would save and protect something called "democracy." Cremin's greatest achievement was to twist the meaning of progressivism so that connections between educational thought and radical politics disappeared from the pages of history.

As the Wisconsin National Guard moved onto campus and took up sandbagged positions with machine guns pointing out from the entrance of the Education Building, we discussed the educational liberalism of scholars like Cremin. In the seminar, I felt close to Karier. We were both brought up in the school of hard knocks. From a small farm community in Wisconsin and a brief career as lumberjack, Karier had entered the middle-class world of the university. I always wondered if he felt as out of place as I did. Several years after the Wisconsin seminar, I convinced Clarence to go salmon fishing with me while we were both teaching summer school at the University of Washington. I quickly showed off my Alaskan fishing skills by getting us lost in the fog of Puget Sound. As we drifted inside a soft white cloud, Clarence recalled why he disliked camping and similar outdoor activities—too many years living in tents in the battlefields of Korea fulfilling the government's dream of stopping Communism.

So what was wrong with the connection between liberalism and education? Weren't the liberals always working for the poor? Didn't they support welfare and social security? Didn't liberals want schools to provide equality of opportunity for all people?

After reading and discussing Cremin, seminar members began to wonder if there was much difference between liberals and conservatives. What was the meaning of these political labels that we so readily tossed around? Reflecting the 1950s and the Cold War concern with consensus politics, as opposed to the Marxist view of antagonistic social classes fighting for control and resources, Cremin had lumped all progressive educators together. He put stern-faced psychologists and advocates of intelligence testing, such as Edward Thorndike and Lewis Terman, in the same bed with radical advocates of teacher unionism and child freedom, such as Margaret Haley and Margaret Naumberg, respectively. Cremin dismissed child-centered school advocates as romantic progressives. However, Cremin's writings proclaimed there were no real basic differences. They all wanted to help American children.

It was Clarence Karier who clearly pointed out that one group of so-called progressives, the psychologists, test advocates, and school administrators, had a very clear political agenda that was quite different from those of others. From Karier's standpoint, this particular set of progressives represented the true meaning of twentieth-century liberalism. They wanted to use the schools to engineer the good society. And, of course, they could drape themselves in the banners of benevolence by proclaiming a desire to help the poor and needy. This band of liberals wanted to use tests, tracking, and character development to create a society in which the distribution of jobs and income was determined by the schools. Future incomes should be determined by merit, these liberals proclaimed, and the schools should measure and determine merit.

When it was pointed out that the poor, minority cultures—Native Americans, African Americans, and the new wave of immigrants—didn't seem to do well on the new standardized tests and tracking systems, the liberals took the results as validation of their efforts. After all, weren't these groups inferior in intelligence?

On the other hand, many industrialists and other business people liked the idea. Liberal educators promised that schools would create an efficient society where workers were trained for their jobs and were happy. Liberals promised to reduce labor unrest and job dissatisfaction. Indeed, wages could be kept down because the schools through proper vocational guidance would ensure that there were no labor shortages in the various segments of the American labor market.

Liberal educators also promised to increase equality of opportunity while improving industrial efficiency. They claimed that the schools, using scientific instruments of measurement, could improve the efficiency of workers by placing students in the most appropriate school subjects and later in jobs according to their scientifically evaluated innate abilities. Wealth and family background would not be important, liberals proclaimed, only the merit of the student. Of course, liberals were still a little bit bothered by the close relationship between their scientific measurements and the student's family background. But, as Clarence Karier pointed out in the seminar, psychologists like Edward Thorndike used the close relationship to argue for eugenics.

Liberals were in favor of the planned breeding of humans? Between the Dow demonstration and the seminar, my ideas about politics were being stood on their head. Certainly, I could see the parallel between the rhetoric of liberalism and eugenics—everyone was going to benefit. No more poor and helpless. Eugenics would ensure that only the fit, hardy, and intelligent would be educated in the schools of democracy to work in the factories of capitalism.

But how were liberals different from conservatives? I thought the conservatives were the enemies. I thought they were the ones supporting government policies that favored the pocketbooks of the rich. Were the liberals doing the same thing as the conservatives?

In the seminar, we returned to Cremin's ability to gloss over important political differences. We discussed the 1950s, an era in which Cremin formulated his interpretation of the educational history of the twentieth century. The conservatives of this period were the fire-breathing stalkers of Communists in public school corridors. They railed against professional educators as having ruined the schools with doctrines of social promotion, abandonment of phonics instruction, and child-centered instruction. Conservatives called for bringing back the old-time discipline of nineteenth-century schools and the moral tales of McGuffey readers. They favored cutting back on school spending and reducing economic restraints on capitalism. The free market, they argued, would make everyone rich.

The liberals of the 1950s responded in horror at conservative criticism of schools. Cut back on educational spending! No, said the liberals, it's the public schools that promise equality of opportunity and the reduction of tensions between social classes. Capitalism would be destroyed, liberals argued, without the school as the great equalizer ensuring social harmony. We just need to get rid of those leftovers from the romantic progressives, they argued, such as education based on the interest of the child, and grease the wheels of social engineering with better tests and closer ties between schools and the labor markets. We'll use the schools to save capitalism from communism, liberals insisted.

Was the only difference between conservatives and liberals the use of different tactics to save capitalism? What a thought!

My political education in Clarence Karier's seminar was also being enhanced by campus events. The Dow demonstration had unleashed a flood of faculty rhetoric that seemed to mask an underlying fear about academic offices being raided by outraged flower children. "Reasoned discourse is the heart of academic life," proclaimed trustees, administrators, and the faculty. But this was the era when universities were adopting the model of higher education advocated by Clark Kerr, the President of the University of California. He called on higher education to function as service stations for U.S. corporations.

I couldn't get it straight in my head. There seemed to be some flaw in my reasoning or the reasoning of others. The university existed to help America. Dow made chemicals that helped America to conduct a war in a former French colony. Therefore, Dow should be allowed to recruit workers on campus and seek the help of university research. On the other hand, the U.S. was supposed to be an anti-imperialist power that avoided involvement in anticolonialist rebellions. But in this case, some members of the anticolonial movement were friends of the U.S. government, while others sided with China and the Soviet Union. Therefore, the U.S. should side with its friends against the virulent growth of communism. But Agent Orange killed plants, trees, and animals. It devastated the countryside, leaving friend and foe without croplands. In addition, Agent Orange promised to be evenhanded in causing cancer by including American troops within its grasp.

Then those crazy flower children were running around saying that they weren't causing violence but that the U.S. government was the major source of violence. "Reasoned discourse" was the weighty response of very knowledgeable professors. "Violence has no place on a college campus." I wondered how you could compare a few police officers who were slightly injured by unarmed students to the tens of thousands killed and maimed in Vietnam.

Campus life helped me understand Karier's discussion of liberalism and education. If schools were service stations pumping workers and ideas into the American economy, then the important thing would be controlling those stations. Who controlled U.S. schools? I noted in campus discussions that no member of the University's board of trustees was a flaming radical. In fact, I would classify them all as protectors of big business, with mindsets ranging from liberal to conservative.

Obviously, the social engineers of liberalism in U.S. schools, such as Thorndike, Terman, and later James Conant, were merely instruments for the real people with power. Or, to use the colorful language on campus, they were the running dog lackeys of the power elite. Clarence Karier helped me to understand that the key to the politics of knowledge was understanding how certain ideologies and personalities were selected from society's mix of conflict theories and ideas. Intellectuals did not rise to power because their ideas were more brilliant than others. They rose to power because their ideas appeared to be useful in maintaining the power of the social elite. Quite simply stated, standardized testing, tracking, and socialization became standard features of the American schools *not* because they were the best ideas or because they worked. These ideas became part of American schools because they promised big business a well-trained and compliant workforce.

Lawrence Cremin's interpretation of educational liberalism and progressivism won the accolades of the elite because it avoided any discussion about the relationship between educational policies, and political and economic power. Cremin's writings did not highlight differences in political goals between school reformers. He presented educators as good-hearted people trying to help children. This whitewash of educational history avoided any discussion of real alternatives regarding the political direction of U.S. schools. It ensured that the service station image would not be jarred by a critical interpretation of history.

So Karier's insights penetrated to the heart of the educational structure. It opened the door to a multifaceted understanding of the politics of knowledge. Certain ideas came to dominate institutions because they served the interests of those with power. Cremin, Thorndike, Terman, et al., gained honor and prestige because their ideas reflected and/or supported the thinking and interests of those with power. Of course, this did not make them hypocrites or dishonorable people. Their interests and ideas simply paralleled those of the power elite. As these academics gained influence, their ideas dominated the direction of U.S. schools.

But I was still confused. Karier had opened many doors; however, I was still puzzled how psychologists who were openly racist in their views—eugenics being the most extreme racist idea—could have so much influence on a school system that claimed to be democratic. Why didn't African Americans, Native Americans, Mexican Americans, and immigrants from southern and eastern Europe rise up against these academic pronouncements that they were from a genetically inferior stock and that they were inherently less intelligent than northern Europeans? How could a school system be built on these openly undemocratic and racist views?

Well, the answer turned out to be simple. These groups did revolt! And this turned out to be another example of the politics of knowledge. In fact, besides the antiwar movement, campus groups were struggling for civil rights. However, it was almost impossible at the time to find in the pages of standard educational histories any discussion of the struggles of these groups against an openly racist U.S. public school system.

The brilliance of Karier's insights involved the interconnection between racism, liberalism, U.S. schools, and the politics of knowledge. The very organizers of the U.S. test-driven school system were racist and biased against members of lower social classes. Segregation and school tracking that reflected racial differences were not errors of the educational system but were the result of its very purpose of grading and supplying workers to the labor market. Many Native Americans understood this in the 1960s when they demanded tribal control of their schools. Many African Americans and Mexican Americans understood that the system was rigged against them when they attacked the cultural bias of the school curriculum and standardized tests. The politics of knowledge and the politics of racism were the same!

II

There was a dusty taste when I licked my lips. The road wound up a hill past cacti and low-growing shrubs to the Center for Intercultural Documentation (CIDOC) located in Cuernavaca, Mexico. Little air funnels filled with grit and dried grasses spun across the road as I ascended to Ivan Illich's hopeful citadel dedicated to deschooling and liberatory education. Clarence Karier had met a man in a local hotel where he was staying who belonged to a group dedicated to finding the most difficult paths from place to place. I never understood if the purpose was physical exercise or some form of religious self-abuse. This man walked up the back of the hill over rocks, iguanas, and the occasional snake. Despite our differing paths, we are all going to the same place—the promised land of better education.

It was 1971 and we planned this meeting at CIDOC to organize a book of essays that would eventually be published under the descriptive title, *Roots of Crisis: American Education in the Twentieth Century*.[1] Illich had planned CIDOC as a model for deschooling where education would not be used to determine a person's status or income. Consequently, no records of course completion or graduation papers were issued. People did not study for the purpose of gaining something called "credit" that could be transferred to another institution. There was no distinction between students and teachers. If a person wanted to teach a course he/she put up a sign in the eating area announcing an introductory lecture or discussion. People attended the first class meeting and decided whether or not they wanted to participate in the remainder of the course. If people did decide to join the class, they paid a small fee to the institution to cover costs of the building and library. Anyone could teach and everyone could learn. There were no tests, entrance examinations, or mandated curricula. It was the hope of the future.

The goal of the CIDOC model was to make it difficult for those with power and money to use the educational system to advance their economic and political interests. From Clarence's perspective, the domination of schooling by economic and social elites was the root of the present educational crisis. In the opening sentences of *Roots of Crisis*'s first essay, Clarence argued, "The school, as a formal vehicle of education, exists as an instrument of social and economic power for the most influential elite groups as much as for the political and social organizations through which the society is managed. Thus, in the twentieth century, schools became the instruments of power under capitalism and fascism, as well as under communism."[2]

Similar to Illich, Clarence had expanded his critique of schooling and liberalism to include the very concept of school as it existed within any political structure. Inevitably, whatever group or person controlled the political structure, tried to use the schools to maintain ideological control. Under fascism, communism, or liberalism, schooling was the same—indoctrination of students to support the existing power structure. With regard to the roots of crisis and politics of knowledge in U.S. society, Clarence wrote, "American education in general has provided an effective service function to the business community in the training of both producers and consumers. . . . It is my contention that the schools throughout the history of American education have been used as instruments to teach the norms necessary to adjust the young to the changing patterns of the economic system as well as to the society's more permanent values."[3]

Clarence's argument was crystal clear. It followed the old capitalist line that everyone pursues their own self-interests. Those with power will use the schools to promulgate values and ideas that support their own economic, political, and social interests. How could anyone, particularly economic conservatives who proclaimed the value of self-interest, deny this analysis of the role of schooling in the twentieth century?

There were others at CIDOC worrying about the damage of schooling to the human spirit. With the front of his shirt lined with paper clips that he constantly plucked to keep his finger tips tough for playing the cello, John Holt urged home schooling as a means for saving the child from the damaging influences of government schools. His personal campaign and books launched a home schooling movement which by the 1990s enlisted participants from across the religious and political spectrum. Also, Jonathan Kozol was there warning about the racism of teachers and schools, and how schools contributed to "death at an early age." Purge the schools of racism and classism was Kozol's message. I had invited Michael Katz to join us but he was off on a honeymoon. He had also concluded from his study of a small Massachusetts town that schools were instruments of social control and domination.

During my daily walk to CIDOC, I often saw non-Spanish speaking Native Americans carrying silver lamps as they marched in single file on a pilgrimage to a mountain shrine. At the time, I hadn't given much thought to the fact that Mexico had one of the largest indigenous populations in the Americas. The issue of cultural domination was a missing ingredient in our discussions. We considered racism, but not the issue of cultural rights. Of course, this was implied in Clarence's argument that schools passed on a culture that reflected the interests of a power elite.

Leaving Cuernavaca with a group of students I had brought down from Case Western Reserve University, I carelessly tossed copies of revolutionary songs from around South America onto the dashboard of my van. The music had been distributed as part of a songfest honoring Paulo Freire. With my poor knowledge of Spanish, I wasn't even clear about the meaning of the songs. On the other hand, U.S. border guards knew their Spanish and, after reading the songs, removed everything from the van. They combed the ashtrays and the truck's interior and asked the students to unroll packed jeans so that they could examine the cuffs and pockets. Luckily, no seeds or grass were found. Welcome to the U.S.A.!

III

Roots of Crisis set the engines of the politics of knowledge in motion. Conservative and liberal scholars beat their chests in disbelief that anyone could suggest that schools could be used as instruments of domination. After all, weren't schools the backbone of democracy? Among conservatives, Diane Ravitch led the charge sending out the message that these new historians were simply conspiracy theorists who deliberately overlooked the importance of the school in providing equality of opportunity. She completely neglected the issue of ideological domination of the school curriculum. This neglect foreshadowed her advocacy in the 1980s and 1990s of national standards and tests. She became enamored with the idea of national standards for history. Of course, these national standards would define the curriculum and content of instruction which, according to her perspective, should indoctrinate students into a conservative interpretation of history. This was exactly what Clarence had been talking about as the major danger of schooling.

Liberals rallied around the rising star of David Tyack, who as I mentioned before, was a winner in the academic game by gaining a sinecure at Stanford. Distancing himself from Karier's ideas, Tyack claimed the problem with American schools was the growth of educational bureaucracy. This was safe territory. Conservatives since the 1950s had claimed that educational bureaucrats were responsible for all the ills of schooling. In fact, conservatives attacked all forms of government bureaucracy. Forgetting that bureaucracy was originally intended to protect government institutions from the power of outside interests, liberals joined the assault by claiming bureaucrats were responsible for racism and classism in schools.

Then liberal scholars tried to distort Karier's critique by claiming that it was simplistic. They argued that other groups put pressure on schools. Of course, Clarence never denied the political importance of other groups; he only argued that the most powerful were the most influential.

So the powerful machinery of academic politics and the politics of knowledge slowly pushed Clarence's ideas into the background, while during the 1980s and 1990s, business, now led by transnational corporations, called on American schools to prepare workers who would help U.S. businesses win the economic competition with Japan and Germany (later the European Union) for world markets. Time proved Clarence Karier right! He was right about the politics of knowledge in which he became a victim. He was right about the "roots of crisis." At the end of the twentieth century, ideological domination through schooling reached a high point as state after state tightened control over the curriculum by requiring more and more testing. "Teach to the test" was the new cry, which in simple terms meant teach the ideology of controlling economic and political interests.

4

Marching to the Beat of His Own Drum: An Epigrammatic Analysis of Understanding and Applying Philosophy and Ethics in the Writing of History

Peter A. Sola

> If a man does not keep pace with his companions, perhaps it is because he hears a different drummer. Let him step to the music he hears, however measured or far away.
>
> —H. D. Thoreau

Over the past forty or fifty years there have been a small number of books that have had a seminal effect on the writings of historians of education and their insight on the role of education in America.[1] *The Individual, Society, and Education* is in the topmost tier of these classics. This book was the first of several written or edited by Professor Clarence J. Karier. My thirty-year association with Professor Karier, first as student, continuing as friend and colleague, and my formal education in history and philosophy of education, have given me an uncommon perspective on this book. The book's influence on my thinking began in 1970, in my first seminar with Professor Karier. The impact of the text, on both my students and me, continues to the present.

Professor Karier's mentors, including the late Merle Borrowman, unveiled to him the philosophical hypothesis that has shaped and developed his critical analysis of educational institutions in this country. Karier's experience, the understanding of the importance of philosophy in the writing of history, was significant in the development of this text's conceptual framework. Professor Karier's historical assumptions have evolved over the past forty-odd years, and we are able to see clearly the development of his analysis of historical events. A close reading of the preface to the current edition of *The Individual, Society, and Education* discloses the ongoing evolution of his thought. For example, Karier acknowledges his lack of speaking to the role of women and minorities, as well as not addressing the racism of Jefferson, in the original edition.[2] Truth, for the historian, is always mutable. Yet, while some individuals may be able to adjust to the idea of truth being relative, not many persons, including some historians, have a solid foundation in philosophy that enables them to comprehend their own miseducation, and acknowledge it in a later edition.

The first assumption of any writer of history (herstory?) ought to be that the truth is relative. Here, I am using "truth" to mean that which one believes; "reality" changes with the acquisition of additional knowledge, the gaining of wisdom, reinterpreting the facts, and a myriad of variables that affect the writer's reporting of the past. Professor Karier always reminds us that Dewey's perspective on the past, present, and future is that "truth" is a moving target.[3]

Embracing this meaning of "truth" as relative could lead one to believe that historians might be liars. Few of us would make such a bold statement for fear of pointing the finger at the person in the mirror. Historians, however, do view the past through their own eyes, even as they work with historically proven data, scientifically verifiable facts, eyewitness accounts, written records, and other credible sources. An observer may understand history in a way distinct from commonly accepted notions of the present. When historians' interpretations of the facts are at variance with common beliefs, they may bring down the wrath of the public, other historians, and the ever-popular establishment on their heads. This was, and is, the issue of the so-called revisionist writers of history.

In writing history from their perspective, revisionist historians observe the past within the framework of their assumptions and interpretation of the facts. Many of these writers are accused of being anti-intellectual, biased, writing history backwards. This representation has been alluded to regarding the writings of Clarence Karier, as well as many individuals who have studied with him. It is deplorable that some—when their views of reality are threatened—react by personally attacking those who see the past from a different perspective, instead of trying to understand new paradigms. Historians, when arriving at this turning point, might look to philosophy to help find the way out of Plato's cave and discover the light of reality.[4] It is at this very moment that Professor Karier compels the reader to begin to acknowledge the predominance of personal perspective as a formidable limiting or liberating mechanism in the writing of history.

If the historian has used facts that are universally accepted, that are proven scientifically, why does the writing of history result in several versions of the truth, or, reality? If one accepts that the writing of history is a science, then it simplifies the reader's understanding of history as a process of simply reading the facts reported by the observer. Of course, interpretation is a necessary part of this process. It is not the facts that lead the writer into trouble but one's personal view of the facts. On the other hand, if one accepts that the writing of history is an art, and art is all about individual perspective, then understanding history becomes more complicated, and much more enjoyable to read. When historians write about the Age of Enlightenment, and view this period through their own perspectives, which may be antithetical to the generally accepted view, ought that interpretation to be rejected? On what bases do historians' perspectives become accepted or rejected? Is the rejection based on rational reasoning, a dispute of the facts? Is it philosophical or political in nature? Taking a different tack, the historian who sees the past as the foundation of the present will try and replicate, in his or her writing, the truth of the present by reinforcing those past events that support the present.

For example, fifty years ago many historians accepted the view that there was little to report, historically, regarding the role of African-Americans in the development of this country, in any context. The same was noted about women. When persons of color and women were afforded more opportunities to publish their work, a vastly different understanding of the roles of these groups emerged. We now read in our history books of African-Americans who were U.S. soldiers and cowboys, as well as women who shouldered an equal burden in many historical developments. My point is that the historian's perspective, one's view of reality, has an enormous effect on his or her writings.

If historians do not have a clear understanding of their historical-philosophical perspective, they will be in Plato's cave, seeing only faint reflections of the truth. Perceiving the past in a particular way, however, and proving that this past is true, are two very different notions. What forces other historians to at least take note of the writer's vision is the accumulation of facts, the consequences of these facts as viewed from the present, and a firm belief, garnered through a solid understanding of philosophy, that the writer is credible in reporting the truth as she or he sees it. The most difficult aspect of the historical-philosophical issue, that is "interpreting the facts," is the concept of intended and unintended consequences.

It is the historian's set of assumptions that place him or her in a specific frame of mind that shapes one's interpretation of history. The writings will clearly reflect these assumptions. For example, how do you, the reader, see the development of the common school system in the United States? Do you view it as the creation of a glorious institution that is a world-class model, or do you see it as an edifice to White Anglo-Saxon Protestant culture, or somewhere in between these positions? The historian's writings must take account of the writer's examination of her or his particular or peculiar belief system. The historian's personal belief system—what is moral, immoral; one's view of class, race, gender; the purpose of public institutions; etc.—is the baggage and freight that one carries when examining the past.

If this baggage carried by the historian is not understood, or is ignored, then the historian becomes a captive of his or her unexamined beliefs. More troubling are the historians that believe that they are truly objective in their narrative of the past. These individuals are unconscious of their beliefs, proclaiming the truth but blind to the notion that they may be merely reflecting their own assumptions. These individuals are parading their biases under the guise of objective truth. These individuals are, in fact, in Plato's cave, seeing reflections and glimmerings of reality and all the while believing they behold reality and the truth.

All history is written from the writer's perspective. Some writings may be more subjective than others, but the idea that historians see reality, or the truth, better than the average citizen is nothing but poppycock. What they see is their version of the truth.

Then, does it follow that historical writings from all perspectives are accurate? Not necessarily. History must reflect the facts as proven by the scientific method. Feelings, opinions, and beliefs are insufficient to give credence to a view of history. However, when an historian writes from a set of assumptions that contest the status quo, that goes to the core of believed fundamental assumptions about society, in general, or education, in particular, the readers' political and personal beliefs may be challenged. Was Jefferson a racist? Why did Lincoln free the enslaved? Did Horace Mann establish the common school to eliminate class hostility, to uplift the working class, to maintain public control of the populace, or all of the above? How one responds to these questions may reveal personal and public beliefs about figures writ large in U.S. history.

Finally, are we guilty of using current values to judge the past instead of applying the values of the past? In subsequent writings, Professor Karier states that he views society as essentially racist, structured to protect vested interests and institutions that serve to maintain those in power. These assumptions would certainly frame histories that reflect the truth as perceived by the author, and, by the way, make him persona non grata in particular historical circles. Those historians that represent the status quo, the Establishment so to speak, would lose creditability and the power bestowed upon them by the establishment, if, in fact, Professor Karier is correct in his assumptions. Many of the establishment historians simply launched an ad hominem attack on Professor Karier, instead of trying to refute his writings. In truth, they accused him of what they themselves were guilty of, not accepting the reality that another perspective may be more truth-telling than their own.

Any historian who has spent a lifetime defending a paradigm, only to be told that this life work is based on a set of hypotheses that are incorrect, would fight to protect his or her perspective of the past; that is only human. What is wrong, in my judgment, is that these historians have lost sight of the role they have accepted. They are to see reality and report it, not to protect their position, status, or role as the "defenders of the faith." They have forgotten to examine their own beliefs, as to why they see the world in a distinctive, unique pattern, and then to examine their views based on this new standpoint. Historians have to be honest to themselves in the first instance and then, and most importantly, to their readers.

Honesty to the reader is, at the minimum, what history ought to be about. The writer needs to ensure that what is presented is as accurate as possible and is the truth, the reality as he or she sees it. This, of course, assumes that the publisher will allow the writer control of the text. It is, perhaps, not well known why more than twenty years passed between editions of *The Individual, Society, and Education*. The text was well received and went into additional printings. After a few years, the publisher asked Professor Karier to update the contents. He refused to work with the publisher because of what occurred during the editing of the original galley proofs. Professor Karier wrote, I believe in chapter ten, a critical section about the John Birch Society, a conservative organization that was attracting national attention in the mid-sixties. The publisher pulled this section from the text. Professor Karier thought it was a printing error and told the book editor that a section was missing and needed to be included in the text. The editor stated that the omission was not an error; it was intentional because the section was too controversial to be included. Professor Karier then asked for his transcript to be returned, only to learn that according to his contract, the book rights belonged to the publisher and the book would be printed according to their needs. He never updated the text for that publisher. Twenty-one years later, the text plates were purchased by the University of Illinois Press, updated by Professor Karier, and republished.

Maybe I am judging the publisher too harshly. Perhaps my interpretation of the past is tinged with bias, and my personal feelings and beliefs have turned the publisher's actions into something that would have been acceptable from another viewpoint. I accept these possibilities. However, my perspective on the past includes the understanding that integrity to one's belief system far outweighs the quest for fame and fortune. Holding to truth as one sees it is the true mark of a person. If this society measured success by one's integrity, Clarence Karier indeed would be a very wealthy man. Fortunately, some of us march to the beat of a different drummer.

Part Two

Karier's Impact and Legacy

5

To the Nonalienated: Navigating a Course Between False Security and Despair

Karen L. Graves

> The truly alienated person who has come to believe that he cannot change the system under which he lives is not interested in seeing things as they are and asking why, or for that matter, even dreaming things that never were and asking, why not. . . . From a nonalienated perspective, one might ask not only why, but, indeed, how we got where we think we are.[1]
>
> —Clarence J. Karier

> To refuse to participate in the shaping of our future is to give it up. Do not be misled into passivity either by false security (they don't mean me) or by despair (there's nothing we can do). Each of us must find our work and do it.[2]
>
> —Audre Lorde

I

Some thirty-odd years after the initial publication of *The Individual, Society, and Education*, scholars gather to reflect upon Clarence Karier's contributions to the critical tradition in history of education scholarship.[3] His work has influenced the field significantly. Karier's efforts, with colleagues Paul Violas and Joel Spring, to identify the *Roots of Crisis* in U.S. education resulted in a watershed moment in the historiography of American education. In a 1974 review of their text, B. Edward McClellan determined that the "conclusions these essays reach, the point of view they express, and the issues they raise are certain to have an important impact on subsequent study of twentieth-century political, social, and educational thought."[4] As Michael Katz observed, Karier's research has been instrumental in displacing naïve, optimistic faith in the liberal tradition. Katz writes that with the publication of *Roots of Crisis* "the burden of proof no longer lies with those who argue that education is and has been unequal. It lies, rather, with those who would defend the system."[5]

"New Liberalism," as articulated by Karier, Violas, and Spring, is a central concept in this essay. The reference is to the dominant ideology that developed in the United States during the last decades of the nineteenth century. Drawing upon the rhetoric and reform policies of middle-class "progressives," educators, scholars, government officials, social workers, and industrialists, these historians diagramed the major tenets of this ideology, offering a new understanding of American liberalism. After Darwin, belief in the permanence of truth waned, and many considered human progress dependent upon the effective use of scientific method. In 1927 editors of *The New Republic* defined liberalism as an activity, "the effort to emancipate human life by means of the discovery and the realization of truth."[6] The vindication of truth, these new liberals continued, required the subordination of principles to method.[7] The message from the ivory tower, the halls of government, and the corporate boardroom was constant and clear: the rational capacity required to discern truth and to manage twentieth-century society was the propensity of an elite few. Decisions of moment were to be handed to the scientific expert. Seeking social change without conflict, new liberals embraced the notion of a well-ordered society in the form of government regulation of the economy and bureaucratic political reform. There was no place for the "rugged individual" in this society. Rather, new liberals looked upon the individual as a "cell" whose meaning is found only within the "social body," albeit a "cell" with particular functions to perform.

As one should expect, changes in schooling reflected the impact of the emerging dominant ideology. All states adopted compulsory schooling legislation by 1918, just one indicator of the "positive freedom" championed by new liberals. The adoption of the differentiated curriculum underscored the unprecedented importance of the school's role to sort and train students for specific societal roles. At the same time, extracurricular activities gained support for their value in cultivating a sense of collective unity during a time of decreasing political and economic power for the individual. The assault on the academic curriculum distanced many students from traditionally valued skills for critical analysis.[8] As an ideology, then, New Liberalism refers to the system of ideas from which twentieth-century Americans have created their understanding of social, political, and economic reality. As the dominant ideology in the United States, stretching back to the last decades of the nineteenth century, New Liberalism has permeated the thinking of persons aligned with different political parties, "conservatives" as well as "liberals." Booker T. Washington articulated New Liberal philosophy, as did Jane Addams, as did John Dewey. New Liberalism, with its emphasis on orderly change in a chaotic society, was the Zeitgeist of modern America.

By the late 1960s, however, political economic conditions in the United States forced many to reevaluate central New Liberal tenets, such as faith in progress, and the expectation that it could be achieved through meritocracy and the intelligent use of science and technology. Liberal theorists were hard pressed to explain how decades of melioristic social policies could result in the racist, sexist, class-biased structures under attack by the civil rights movement, the women's movement, and the many other organized forms of protest against oppression. Karier and his colleagues argued that it was time to question the perceptual framework of liberal historians that appeared out of sync with contemporary social conditions. The radical historians reasoned that the *Roots of Crisis* in American society were embedded in another history.[9]

Karier believes that late-twentieth-century Americans' failure to deal effectively with present social conditions is connected to a reluctance to analyze the centers of power and influence in U.S. society. In the early 1970s he cautioned that New Liberal doctrine is not an adequate substitute for a philosophy of humanity. The quality of life in the United States at century's end reaffirms Karier's concern regarding individual freedom, human dignity, and well-being.[10] As Cornel West documents, ours is a "twilight civilization" in which impressive scientific and technological innovations parallel a deteriorating public life marked by class polarization, racial balkanization, and a predatory market culture.[11]

Our contemporary condition is bleak, to be sure, but the struggle for justice continues. In warning that alienation is most significant when one turns away from critical examination, Karier points the way to our best hope for the future. He addresses his work to the nonalienated, to those who can still ask "why" and "why not." In sustaining that part of ourselves that, paraphrasing Audre Lorde, refuses to be led into passivity, either by false security or despair, knowing how we got to where we are is essential.[12] In this essay I revisit Karier's work on early twentieth-century liberalism, signaling ways in which the philosophy establishes a sense of false security. For those engaged in critical teaching and learning in the twenty-first century, a new course is needed. In the latter part of this essay I analyze Karier's approach to doing history, which, I believe, is a sound model for navigating between false security and despair.

Hayden V. White determined that the "contemporary historian has to establish the value of the study of the past, not as 'an end in itself' but as a way of providing perspective on the present that contributes to the solution of problems peculiar to our own times."[13] No one has accepted this responsibility with more thoughtfulness than Clarence Karier. His research has had a profound impact on the critical tradition in history of education scholarship. Karier's work is of primary importance for those for whom refusing to participate in the shaping of our future is no option. His steadfast commitment to unearth the *Roots of Crisis* in U.S. education is a model for each one seeking to find our work and do it.[14]

II

Clarence Karier knew he was cutting close to the bone, articulating his analysis of New Liberal ideology in history of education society circles during the 1970s. Fundamental assumptions held by such esteemed scholars as Cremin, Curti, and Hofstader dominated the field so that Karier's critical reflection on liberalism became, for many, self-reflection. To question the validity of shared notions of progress, rationality, science, and technology was to step beyond the pale.[15]

In "Liberal Ideology and the Quest for Orderly Change," Karier argues that modern liberals' acquiescence in the face of political, economic, and military power is indicative of a major weakness, if not a fatal flaw, in new liberal philosophy.[16] Together with his colleagues, he presents a convincing case that New Liberal ideology promotes a compulsory state in which the individual is to be shaped and controlled in order to fulfill the nation's destiny. The efficiency and effectiveness of the social structure is to be maintained through orderly social change, under the direction of social science experts.[17] Pragmatism is the epicenter of Karier's critique: the central weakness of New Liberal thought is that, in times of crisis, survival emerges as the fundamental value. Expediency governs, leaving the new liberal with only a philosophy of accommodation to the most powerful.[18]

The security that the new liberal seeks through accommodation is, upon close examination, a false security. It is helpful to begin this argument by revisiting a key point in Karier's analysis: in times of severe crisis, most new liberals will move to the right of the political spectrum. He cites, for example, the about-face regarding U.S. involvement in World War I, participation in the 1939 Committee for Cultural Freedom, and the embrace of "law and order" against student protests during the 1960s and 1970s.[19] Karier finds the move to the right telling of new liberal philosophy. Liberals themselves, he explains, justify choices which may be interpreted as a capitulation to the right (trampling on civil rights in the name of "law and order," for example) as an effort to preserve democracy. The premise for this line of thought is that attacks on the liberal center from the left and the right will weaken and destroy democratic institutions. If the institutions are to survive, the thinking goes, there must be some relief from assault. Apparently, the only choice new liberals discern is curtailing critiques from the left or experiencing a fascist nightmare.[20] Trying to establish a safe haven from totalitarianism, to secure democracy, the new liberal is willing to sacrifice the very freedoms that define a democratic state. Karier gives a classic example.

In the days prior to U.S. involvement in World War I, John Dewey wrote on "getting things done"—politics—in a democracy. The eminent pragmatic philosopher recognized the difficulty of "getting things done," which seemed to run counter to the interests of the masses, and argued in favor of certain devices of manipulation. Dewey preferred a "businesslike psychology" for this end, to achieve social objectives in an efficient and effective manner as possible.[21] Retreating to the right, characterized by the jettison of free thought, expression, and independent decision making, did not, however, secure democracy. Manipulation of public opinion ran counter to democratic principles. In moving to the right in times of crisis to "protect" democracy, new liberals compromised on fundamental democratic tenets, and democracy was weakened in any case. New liberals, then, often found themselves redefining democracy. In the new system of ideas, democracy was a malleable concept.

New liberals such as Jane Addams, Herbert Croly, John Dewey, and Walter Rauschenbusch sought to serve individual interests through the larger corporate society. Classical liberal faith in rugged individualism gave way to pursuit of a harmonious, organic community, with the social science expert at the helm. Charles Eliot enunciated the New Liberal perception of the role of the expert in a "democracy" quite clearly in 1897:

> Confidence in experts, and willingness to employ them and abide by their decisions, are among the best signs of intelligence in an educated individual or an educated community. . . .. Democracies will not be safe until the population has learned that governmental affairs must be conducted on the same principles on which successful private and corporate business is conducted; and therefore it should be one of the principal objects of democratic education so to train the minds of the children that when they become adult they shall have within their own experience the grounds of respect for the attainments of experts in every

branch of governmental, industrial, and social activity, and of confidence in their advice.[22]

Seeking a nonviolent, coercive means of social control in the tumultuous years at the turn of the last century, new liberals embraced the "intelligent" use of education and technology with an intensified boldness. The objective, political and economic stability, was nothing new; emphasis on expert application of scientific method as the vehicle for achieving social stability, however, was a significant development. Dewey advised, "Take science . . . for what it is, and we shall begin to envision it as a potential creator of new values and ends."[23] Here again, new liberalism lent itself to a false security by placing the well-being of individuals in the hands of social engineers. For, as Karier stated, it was not at all clear that New Liberal policy served the interests of the individual, except when those interests coincided with the needs of corporate society.[24] New liberals assumed an inherent connection between democracy on the one hand, and the surrender of independent decision making for many citizens on the other. Educational psychologist E. L. Thorndike argued that 95 to 99 percent of the population should trust its fortunes—in government, industry, law, religion, and education—to an educated elite.

> [I]n the long run, it has paid the "masses" to be ruled by intelligence. . . . The argument for democracy is not that it gives power to all men without distinction, but that it gives greater freedom for ability and character to attain power.[25]

Thorndike's comment notwithstanding, the nexus between democracy and social control as described by new liberals is problematic. The American liberals' "flirtation with fascism" is a case in point. Karier's argument, that prominent Americans' early response to Italian fascism was a logical outcome of certain characteristics of New Liberal thought, is compelling and of great consequence. Reading Charles Beard's "Making the Fascist State," or Herbert Croly's "An Apology for Fascism," one is not hard pressed to draw connections between the New Liberal philosophy of social unity, efficiency, and social engineering, and *New*

Republic reports on Mussolini's Italy.[26] Karier does not tag Beard and Croly as fascists, nor does he confuse liberalism with fascism. His point is that the deep-seated desire for orderly change that is fundamental to New Liberal thought can, and indeed has, led to nondemocratic action in the name of democracy. In retrospect, it is easy to see Charles Beard's account, that the events in fascist Italy may turn to a "new democratic direction," as false security in a twentieth-century experiment to reconcile individualism and socialism, politics and technology.[27] Karier would have us examine the system of thought that served as a foundation for Beard's analysis.

In "Making the World Safe for Democracy: An Historical Critique of John Dewey's Pragmatic Liberal Philosophy in the Warfare State," Karier examined the Deweyan position that using up one's influence on lost causes is not consistent with pragmatic philosophy.[28] An analysis of this ethical weakness in new liberal philosophy brought to light, yet again, the false sense of security embedded in New Liberalism. Dewey criticized those who held on to principles, absolutely, and argued that one could avoid coercion by compromise. Croly's *New Republic* printed:

> Principles do not exist for a liberal in the form of rules which are formulated by reason and which human life is under some obligation to obey. They are vistas and clues which in the circumstances may or may not work. . . . They are not by way of being vindicated until they are wrought into the continuing experience of an individual or a community.[29]

This pragmatic ethic which allows one to rationalize abandonment of principles paved the way for intellectuals who became servants of power in the twentieth-century liberal state. Karier perceptively drew upon Randolph Bourne's work to explain that New Liberal philosophy as articulated by Dewey sanctioned technique over values. New liberals sought security in technical prowess, at the cost of a privation in values. Bourne rightly characterized this end as merely the illusion of security.[30]

Karier's critique of New Liberal ideology is consistent with the historical evidence dating from the Progressive Era; it resonates with events of the 1960s and 1970s (the period in which it was written), and it remains applicable to New Liberalism at the close of the twentieth century. The fundamental tendency that Karier discerned within new liberal philosophy—the crucial move to the right—has become commonplace. Consider former California governor Jerry Brown's defense of Operation Urban Warrior, the two-year exercise conducted by the U.S. Marines in Chicago; New York; Jacksonville, Florida; Charleston, South Carolina; and Oakland, California.

The Marines invaded Oakland in March 1999 for a week of military exercises designed to test tactics and technologies designed for urban warfare in the twenty-first century. Newly elected Mayor Brown welcomed the Marines to Oakland after San Francisco rejected the Marines' request to use the Presidio for the war exercise, noting that the Marines would spend $4.5 million in Oakland. The Coalition Against Urban Warrior, however, maintained a steady stream of protest during the Marines' occupation of Oakland. Antiwar veteran groups, church groups, and chapters of the American Federation of Teachers joined others constituting the coalition. During the second day of the military exercise, a group of students and youth took over Mayor Brown's office. After a one-hour standoff they were forcibly removed; twenty-two were arrested.[31]

In the context of this essay, the salient point is Brown's defense of his political decision to bring the Marines to Oakland. Taking a page from Dewey, Brown argues that supporting Urban Warrior is the only realistic policy. Brown refers to the protestors' perspective as "narrow," and turns, in classic pragmatic form, to compromise. "If you are against even military training, you are not going to be listened to on the really critical issues."[32]

To the extent that new liberals urged compromise at the expense of integrity and embraced "democratic" processes that favor the expert over the common citizen, they established a false sense of security. More than twenty-five years ago Karier mapped out the twentieth-century liberal position with a painstaking degree of accuracy. He explained that new liberals consented to demands from the right out of fear of elimination. Jerry Brown used this very rationale a few months ago when he condemned opposition to the U.S. military. Brown warned, "If the 'left' persists in living in lies, it will disappear—and rightfully so!"[33]

Perhaps, at the end of a century of ideological domination, the new liberal position *is* disappearing, but as a result of its own maneuvers. How far, and how often, after all, can new liberals slide to the right, and still represent a philosophy distinct from their worst nightmare? How far to the right can new liberals slide without dismantling democracy altogether?

III

Karier understands that all history is written from a particular standpoint. History, from his perspective, is an art in that the value of historical analysis rests upon interpretation in the present. To understand that we all sift our accounts of the past through a conceptual screen constructed from our present, however, is not to make the past solely dependent on the present.[34] In his writing and in his teaching, Karier underscores the importance of staying open to new possibilities; historical inquiry ought to precede the formulation of social theory, rather than the other way around. Good history requires a playful curiosity on the part of the historian. The creative process of writing history, however, is one that must be validated by reason, logic, and empirical analysis. Context, internal consistency, cross-references, and authenticity of documentation are the tools with which the historian works.[35]

Karier's perception of history requires that one let loose of historical certainty, a proposition that one would expect a range of scholars, from Dewey's students to postmoderns, to appreciate. If we are reluctant to prescribe a definitive present, Karier suggests, how is it possible to recapture a definitive past? To argue that history reflects the cultural standpoint of the historian, however, is not to lapse into pallid relativism. Karier's point is that there are many pictures of the past, some more or less true than others, some more or less useful in the present.[36] Proficient in his scholarship, and willing to render history that illumines a critical view of our present, Karier's work is marked by a strong sense of integrity.

The conviction that the search for truth cannot be partial is a fundamental element in Karier's scholarship. But, his is not a positivistic truth: "Hard, rigorous criticism is the corrective process through which a field of inquiry comes to know the 'truths' it tentatively holds."[37] Karier's study of new liberalism leads to a conclusion that the twentieth-century standard of the academician as a servant of power falls into sharp relief with the ancient calling of the intellectual—to strive to be a servant of truth.[38] Little wonder, then, at the fury which followed his 1978 Presidential Address for the History of Education Society. In the published essay containing the text of the 1978 address, "The Quest for Orderly Change: Some Reflections," Karier addresses charges hurled at the critical historians of education and, in so doing, outlines central elements of the critical history paradigm.

In acknowledging that history is written from a particular perspective of the present, critical historians drew the charge of "presentism" from fellow scholars. The critical history tradition, it should be noted, was not built on making the past perform what Paul Violas called whatever tricks necessary to support a given contemporary perspective. In his presidential address, Karier quoted Violas, who warned that history slips into propaganda when it fails to account for the evidential data, or otherwise warps, omits, rewrites, or pretends. Violas stated, one "cannot with impunity simply drag the 'naked' facts into his present in order to buttress his vision of appropriate social action."[39] Distorting history for the sake of the present, Karier continued, is simply bad history.[40]

"The Quest for Orderly Change" is a beautifully articulated, well-argued exposition of Karier's approach to the study of history. His theory centers on Marx's notion of ruthless criticism. That is, in order to determine to the best of one's abilities "what really happened," the historian must engage in criticism that does not shrink from its own conclusions, or from conflict with the power elite.[41] Karier refers to this approach as "critical realistic history." It shares common ground with W.E.B. DuBois' classic statement on criticism and democracy: "Honest and earnest criticism from those whose interests are most nearly touched—criticism of writers by readers, of government by those governed, of leaders by those led—this is the soul of democracy and the safeguard of modern society."[42] Criticism—the soul of democracy, the safeguard of modern society—is for Karier the crucial element in writing history.

When the authors of *Roots of Crisis* assessed traditional educational history, they found it short on meaningful criticism, long on apology. A more critical treatment promised to reveal the sources of weakness in the dominant philosophy, develop a more realistic assessment of its strengths, and better illuminate the nature of contemporary problems. Whether the historian has been successful in these endeavors is left, in critical educational history, for the reader to judge. Karier invited his readers to consider the assumptions of the author with respect to the author's present, the significance of the questions asked, and to examine the key documents upon which the interpretation is based.[43]

During the post-World War II years, what some recognize as the central feature of traditional historical interpretation, faith in progress, fell under critical examination. Following worldwide warfare, massive destruction in Europe and Asia, the horrors of the Holocaust, the beginning of the Cold War, and amid human and civil rights violations in the United States, John Higham noted the shift in historical thinking. "Few [historians] became prophets of doom, but fewer still remained oracles of hope."[44] Karier documented the dismal condition of twentieth-century humanity with such force and logic that some misread him as a prophet of doom. This thinking was too simplistic. Historical truth, Karier explained, was not to be found in the extremes of an optimistic, consensus history or a pessimistic, conflict-oriented theory. Some historical events, e.g., slavery, had no "bright side." And, history was not totally devoid of progress. It has always been bad practice to force interpretations of events, or historians, into such narrow boxes of thought.

Karier set the standard for critical realistic historians, those who seek "what really happened" without apology to cherished myths, as they work to understand our inescapable past and present. It should be clear to one who has read Karier's work that this search is a continual process; findings remain open to alteration in light of new scholarship.[45] Some suggest that one should not criticize established systems without proposing a viable alternative. This thinking, whether from the right or the left, Karier responds, places a heavy burden on the historian. In practice, such a policy is likely to stifle the most serious criticism. While indeed more comforting, specific alternatives are simply not necessary for historical analysis.[46]

Critical realistic history, as defined by Karier, rests on three assumptions: the world under study was not the best of all possible worlds; people are more or less free to choose their courses of action and, therefore, bear responsibility; and moral and causal criticism help determine "what really happened," which is a first step toward creating a better world.[47] Taken together, the assumptions that frame Karier's study denote a scholarly perspective that has not succumbed to despair. The primary reason for such careful, critical analysis of "what really happened" is, after all, to understand our past more clearly in order to illuminate our present strivings for a more just future. The nonalienated read in Karier's work of the significance of human intentions and the importance of human action. In Karier's history, humanity is not caught between the whim of an "unseen hand at work directing lemming-like creatures down to the sea" or "sinking into a meaningless nihilistic world."[48] With reference to the Renaissance scholar, Giovanni Pico Della Mirandola, Karier locates human dignity in the free choice of men and women. This, I submit, is as true in our present as it was in our past. Because we have free choice, we are responsible for our actions, but we are not bound to predetermined ends. Through his writing, Karier teaches that our destiny is not predetermined by our history. Understanding our history as clearly as possible, however, is crucial.[49] For the nonalienated, critical realistic history is vital to the work that is to be done. Clarence Karier's scholarship remains foremost among this work in the field of the history of education.

IV

Dewey's student, Randolph Bourne, articulated the role of the twentieth-century intellectual as dissenter in his essays on the liberal stance advocating U.S. involvement in World War I.

Bourne called on democrats to resist the emerging ideology that held technical intelligence above ethics, despite political and professional consequences, and despite the apparent hopelessness of the cause.[50] In large part, Clarence Karier's career has been one of intellectual dissent. Like Bourne, Karier experienced a degree of professional ostracism as a result of his uncompromising commitment to report the historical truth as he found it.[51] But Karier had found his work in critical realistic history, and he kept at it.

Karier's example of scholarly and personal integrity remains, for me, his greatest legacy. My appreciation for the importance of critical inquiry to the educational process, and its function in a democratic society, emanate, in large part, from study with Clarence. Teaching undergraduates in a liberal arts college, I explore this core lesson with students. Critical inquiry is an essential skill for navigating through our shared historical moment.

From a contemporary vantage point, how do Karier's concerns regarding the elements of New Liberal philosophy measure up? What has the individual gained as a result of social policy built on Eliot's dictum, confidence in experts and a willingness to abide by their advice? What do we know of individual freedom, human dignity, and well-being as evidenced in the United States today?

In 1998 the average CEO made 419 times the average yearly wage of a blue-collar worker. That's a 36 percent pay increase for the CEO over 1997; the average worker made 2.7 percent more. Incidentally, the average CEO pay of $10.6 million was a fraction of Walt Disney CEO Michael Eisner's 1998 compensation of $575,592,000.[52] Not surprisingly, given these figures, the income differential between rich and poor in the United States continued to exceed that of any other developed nation. The top 1 percent of households had more wealth than the bottom 95 percent. The minimum wage, lower in 1998 than in 1979 when adjusted for inflation, became a poverty wage. A 1998 survey of 30 major cities for the U.S. Conference of Mayors found that requests for emergency food and emergency shelter increased by 14 and 15 percent, respectively, over the previous year. Twenty percent of the food requests and 30 percent of the housing requests were unmet. Over 20 percent of the urban homeless were employed. Estimates projected that, for the fiscal year ending 30 September 1999, government aid for home ownership, much of it going to high-income families, will outpace the total 1998 federal spending by the Department of Housing and Urban Development by $23 billion.[53]

On 1 July 1999, *The Washington Post* reported that "Bush's Fund-Raising Opens Huge Disparity: Unprecedented Edge May Limit Rivals." George W. Bush's $36.25 million, raised in about six months, tops the list of campaign funds ever raised in the history of presidential campaigns, and had some Republican party leaders concluding, a year in advance, that the 2000 GOP nomination was all but sewn up.[54] Although the size of Governor Bush's cache has stunned the American public, the point that a moneyed elite buys influence in U.S. politics has become a truism. Investigations into the Democratic Party's fund-raising activity indicated that this problem is not owned exclusively by either major party. As Marlin Fitzwater, spokesman for President Bush, noted in 1992, attending fund-raising events marked by exorbitant fees amounted to buying access to the political system. People who didn't have so much money, Fitzwater stated, "have to demand access in other ways."[55]

Protest, a traditional means of political participation for the poor and oppressed, has become increasingly difficult, however, in the continued buildup of a national police state. Christian Parenti reports, at present, 30,000 armed militarily trained police units in the United States, and a fourfold increase in the mobilization of paramilitary police units between 1980 and 1995; between 1995 and 1997, the Department of Defense provided local police departments with more than 3,800 M-16 automatic assault rifles, 2,185 M-14 semiautomatic rifles, 73 M-79 grenade launchers, and 112 armored personnel carriers.[56] An article in the 28 January 1999, *New York Times* notes favorable White House reception of a request from the Pentagon for the power to appoint a military leader for the continental United States. Supporters argue that such a step is necessary due to threats of terrorism. The U.S. already leads all other industrialized nations in percentage of population imprisoned.[57] Yet, protests continue—as the nationwide marches against police brutality showed in spring 1999, and as the world looked on in Seattle the following December—in spite of imposition of a militarized "no protest zone" and in spite of police violence that has claimed the attention of Amnesty International. A review of the contemporary U.S. political economy includes the ongoing assault on Affirmative Action, bilingual education, and ethnic studies programs; the anti-immigrant sentiment fueling the adoption of repressive local, state, and national law; and lynchings and other expressions of virulent hatred, forever inscribed on our collective memory. It is clear that the well-being of the U.S. citizenry is severely threatened. Karier's plea for a philosophy of humanity is needed now as desperately as before.

Karier's students know him as an exemplar of one ever vigilant in the interests of democracy, his unaffected protests notwithstanding. His work is of critical import to the nonalienated among us, those who can still, for whatever reason, muster strength and energy in the struggle for justice. It is work in the spirit of Professor Rudy Acuña, who filed suit against the University of California regents in 1992 for discrimination based on his political work, race, and age—and won. Acuña's response to those who asked how he could expect to win against such tremendous odds is key in weighing the significance of Karier's scholarship.

> I can't lose. You empower people by giving them historical memory. Even if we lose this case, knowledge is gained. Memory is established. You can show why we lost, if we do. You can expose what happened.[58]

Clarence Karier's critical realistic history has broadened our knowledge of New Liberal ideology and its impact on schools and the practice of education in the United States. Without apology, he applies a moral compass to the study of history. He dares to write in defense of democracy. Seeds of empowerment lie in this historical memory.

6

An Audacious Analysis of Power and Control: The Significance of *Roots of Crisis* and *Shaping the American Educational State* for Current Critiques of American Bureaucratic Educational Systems

Stuart McAninch

I

When writing *Man, Society, and Education*, which was published in 1967, Clarence Karier was primarily interested in analyzing great debates in American history regarding the good society, human nature, and the education best suited to developing both.[1] The ontological stance assumed by the author was idealist: his analysis focused on the debates among great thinkers, which he perceived as being characteristic of eras and on the intellectual climates which informed those debates. Competition among ideas was treated as being of primary importance. In contrast, the political-economic context of ideas and debates and the impact of those ideas and debates on social ideologies and on institutional organizations, cultures, and behaviors either were not addressed or else were addressed in cursory fashion. American society in its historical development was for the most part presented indirectly by Karier through the social ideas of those thinkers he analyzed; it apparently was not his intention to construct a direct analysis of institutional and ideological change as a means to place those ideas into perspective.

The enduring value of *Man, Society, and Education* is Karier's systematic, occasionally brilliant discussion of ideological formulations by selected intellectuals of the good society and of the education which corresponds to it. It is still a book which is well worth reading. The most important problem, however, lies in a largely reified treatment of society, the state, and the economy—which lie on the margins of the analysis, and which are occasionally referenced (largely in passing), but which are never systematically addressed.

By 1972 when Karier published "Liberal Ideology and the Quest for Orderly Change" and "Testing for Order and Control in the Corporate Liberal State," his analysis had undergone a stunningly rapid and thorough theoretical reorientation.[2] Gone was the idealist stance. Society, the state, and the economy were no longer on the margins of analysis: their historical development was now at the center. While still assigning importance—and even at least limited causal agency—to ideas and debates of intellectuals, Karier now worked systematically to frame those ideas and debates by explaining their origin within a particular political-economic context and their subsequent influences on social ideologies and on institutional organizations, cultures, and behaviors.

Moreover, many ideas of intellectuals which had been presented by Karier in *Man, Society, and Education* as socially benign were critically reassessed in his two essays of 1972 and in "Business Values and the Educational State," all three of which he included in *Roots of Crisis,* which he coauthored with Joel Spring and Paul Violas.[3] He then elaborated on that critical reassessment in *Shaping the American Educational State.*[4] Informing the reassessment was an analysis of the relationship between university-based intellectuals, on the one hand, and the "educational state" emerging during the early-twentieth century, on the other. What had been presented as relatively benign, or in many cases commendable, in the social and educational thought of John Dewey or James B. Conant within his primarily philosophical and rhetorical analysis of their work in *Man, Society, and Education*, for instance, was now recast by Karier in his subsequent work as malignant when analyzed within the context of the distinctly antidemocratic educational state legitimated and rationalized by their thought. This educational state was developed and refined during the early- and mid-twentieth century in no small part through the work of university academics funded by corporate philanthropies and linked through an intricate network of government, quasi-public, and professional organizations. It was integrated into a larger "corporate liberal state" and was structured to meet the needs of that stratified corporate liberal state for tractable workers, consumers, and citizens, on the one hand, and for leaders and expert administrators and planners, on the other. Consequently, analysis of the educational state needed to focus not only on institutions of higher education and school systems, it also needed to identify how those institutions interconnected with corporate and governmental institutions. At the center of the educational state were systems of standardized testing and differentiated curricula which sorted students, largely on the basis of social class and race, for entry into the different strata of the corporate liberal economy and society. Also at its center were various mechanisms of myth creation and dissemination, socialization, and coercion by which thought was manipulated, managed, and circumscribed within the corporate liberal state, which during the Cold War had become increasingly militarized, repressive, and violent. Hence, Karier had come to argue that intellectuals like John Dewey and James B. Conant had established niches for themselves within an educational state and larger corporate liberal state—which were antidemocratic, racist and classist, repressive, and violent—and had played substantial roles in legitimating and strengthening those states.

But why such an abrupt theoretical change within such a relatively short period of time? Karier likely gave the key in the preface to *Shaping the American Educational State*. Historical interpretation, he maintained there, is inevitably shaped in important respects by perspective of the present. It is from their existential present that historians draw the concepts, questions, issues, and value positions which frame their work. Moreover, if their historical interpretations are to have value for the present, those interpretations must help explain the pressing social problems of the present and help inform the search for solutions. Hence, historical interpretations need to pass the test of social usefulness as well as the test of empirical credibility.[5] It would be warranted to assume that by 1972, the kind of intellectual history that Karier wrote in *Man, Society, and Education* no longer fit his own tests of either social usefulness or empirical credibility. On the one hand, it certainly did not help one understand the present problems which Karier especially emphasized in his work of the 1970s: the demonstrated capacity of a highly militarized state for implementing large-scale violence internationally and subversion of freedom domestically; the failure of the civil rights movement to achieve political and economic reforms or social changes fundamental enough to dismantle the institutional practices and cultures which perpetuate systemic inequality; or the cooptation of scientists and intellectuals so that they commonly serve as servants of power rather than pursuers of truth and/or teachers promoting freedom through their work. On the other hand, interpreting the ideas of intellectuals through the lens of the historical development of the "educational state" required Karier to rethink and significantly revise many of his interpretations of the documents he analyzed. What had appeared to be valid interpretation of texts in an idealist narrative largely devoid of political-economic context evidently often appeared to him to not be warranted when ideas were critically examined within the political-economic contexts in which they were generated.

In his work during the first half of the 1970s, Karier addressed very different questions than he did when writing *Man, Society, and Education*: What is the structure of decision making in the educational state? What are the political and cultural processes through which the educational state was built? What is the dominant ideology which came to govern decision making and institutional cultures within that educational state and to legitimate it? How did the educational state become integral to the perpetuation of inequality and large-scale violence within the larger and militarized corporate liberal state?

Reading today Karier's work from this period, one would be hard pressed to deny the sheer audacity of the project he undertook. Not engaging in the writing of monographic studies, he sought instead to identify and critically evaluate salient organizational and cultural characteristics of an educational system at the national level and to further identify and critically evaluate the relationship of that system to economic, governmental, and cultural institutions which directed the broader corporate liberal state. This project was partly derivative (drawing from the research of others) and partly grounded in his own earlier work in American intellectual history. It also was partly based on his working backward from a careful reading of present-day documents to identify a history which would place them into a comprehensible and defensible context. Yet, the audacity was not merely a matter of the broad scope of his analysis. It also lay in the challenge he presented to historians to identify and assume a public responsibility as researchers and teachers at a time of problems which cumulatively represented a crisis in American society: to research, write, and teach in such ways as to openly and critically analyze rather than perpetuate those myths which legitimate systemic inequality, injustice, and violence.

II

It is not my primary purpose, however, to engage in a historiographic exploration of the interpretive structure and importance in the historical field of Karier's work. Rather, what interests me here is the significance of Karier's historical analyses described above for American school and university teachers and administrators seeking to understand the bureaucratic educational systems in which they currently work and the problems and contradictions inherent in those systems. A wide range of research literature documents that the impact of bureaucratic systems has been absolutely disastrous on public schooling in poor urban and suburban communities.[6] Other literature indicates that, while the contradictions and problems inherent in bureaucratic systems may in many respects be less severe in public schools than in more affluent communities, they nevertheless still exist—and they seriously impede education and equality of educational opportunity within those communities.[7] Hence, while unevenly experienced, the dysfunctionality of bureaucratic educational systems is nevertheless general in the United States in its impact on public schooling.

How, then, might Karier's historical analyses help teachers and administrators identify the organizational and cultural characteristics of bureaucratic educational systems—and the broader political-economic and ideological contexts for those systems? How might his historical analyses help them to understand the dysfunctions with which they struggle in their own work, and develop strategies for addressing dysfunctions? In response to these questions, three related themes in Karier's writing of the early 1970s seem especially important: 1) the educational system as an interlocking network of institutions; 2) his critique of reflective thinking as it has been defined by John Dewey and as it had been practiced historically in twentieth-century universities and other educational settings; and 3) the need for reflective thinking, in order to promote democratic institutional practice and culture, to be guided by a clear and nonauthoritarian vision of democracy.

Karier persuasively rested his analysis on a premise which is of vital importance for educators seeking to transform or reform bureaucratic educational systems: the focus of analysis for those seeking to change dysfunctional systems cannot be strictly on schools or on the relationship between school districts and state departments of education. Rather, analysis of educational systems, as Karier's work strongly suggested, must identify the relationships between universities and school districts. In *Shaping the American Educational State* in particular, he worked to document the influence of institutions of higher education on ideologies legitimating sorting on the basis of social class and race and on the technical means for conducting that sorting. Focusing on conservative German academic influences and the unwillingness of American professors themselves to name and face issues concerning corporate and state influence on teaching and research, he also sought to explore the delimiting impact that circumscribed conceptions of academic freedom (which came to predominate in institutions of higher education and in the American Association of University Professors and other professional organizations) had on educational critique within colleges and universities. One can easily infer from Karier's work that educational systems can only be meaningfully understood as school **and** higher educational systems. Certainly, this is the broad analytic perspective that students in both higher educational administration and school administration programs need to take.

Karier's work also vividly illustrated that educational systems do not exist in a political-economic vacuum—or even in a loosely coupled relationship which permits an unsystematic and/or merely technicist focus strictly on immediately pertinent legislation, governmental policy, and corporate influences. Rather, his work during the early 1970s—with its central focus on the relationship between the educational state and the corporate liberal state—powerfully suggested that analysis must systematically identify relationships between school districts, universities, and the range of political, economic, and cultural institutions which directly and indirectly influence educational policy and practice in both. Moreover, such analysis is even more complex since such institutions can exist at the metropolitan, state, national, or international levels. An expansive analysis of the kind modeled by Karier ultimately requires attention, for instance, to such issues as the impact of United States military interventions abroad or of programs administered by such international economic agencies as the World Trade Organization, World Bank, or International Monetary Fund on curricula, practices, and ideologies in universities and schools. Such an expansive analysis on a metropolitan, state, national, and international level is a formidable task—and it is not easily structured within educational administration curricula. Analysis of this magnitude cannot be compartmentalized successfully in one or two social foundations courses but must instead be integrated into other courses as well in order to provide fuller opportunity to develop it—and also, overtly, to place the study of educational policies, programs, and practice into full context.

Reading today Karier's work written during the first half of the 1970s, one is not likely to perceive it as being theoretically definitive—which is hardly surprising given the relatively short time that he had been developing this line of theoretical analysis through his writing. Rather, his work from this period reads as a preliminary effort to identify salient organizational and cultural characteristics of educational systems as well as the ways by which those characteristics are shaped by political, economic, and cultural institutions. This preliminary nature of his work can itself be used as a model for educational administration students who may themselves be at preliminary stages of systematic reflection on the nature and political-economic context of educational systems. Understood within the framework of Karier's effort to write a history which explained the crises of the late 1960s and early 1970s, his essays included in *Roots of Crisis* and his subsequent book, *Shaping the American Educational State*, provide a case study on how to frame reflection on the history of educational systems and their contexts: integrated analysis of ideologies, programs, and institutional structure in higher education and in schools; the pursuit of connections between the educational and the political-economic; and the balancing of analysis and critique.

In this regard, Karier's work is significant for school administration and higher educational administration programs because it raises the vitally important issue of what kind of reflective thinking is sufficient for that analysis and closely related critique of complex educational systems which can serve as the basis for positively changing those systems. In particular, Karier's critique of the social implications of—and social-philosophical assumptions underlying—Dewey's model of reflective thinking serves as an important warning for those university educators engaged in facilitating such analysis and critique, that not all forms of critical thinking are necessarily suited for those tasks. In "Liberal Ideology and the Quest for Orderly Change," Karier criticized Dewey's model of reflective thinking as being governed by a vague and inadequate conception of political democracy which masked an elitist commitment on Dewey's part to "flexible, experimentally managed, orderly social change that included a high degree of manipulation."[8] Karier argued in that essay that Dewey's pragmatist social philosophy ultimately legitimated direction of social change by experts making use of scientific procedure and knowledge—and furthermore legitimated manipulation of the masses in order to maintain what such experts defined as orderly social change.

Committed to scientifically guided orderly change of the corporate liberal state, pragmatists like Dewey also ultimately eschewed conflict as a valid means for social change and adopted survival of that state as the primary value during times of crisis. Hence, reflective thinking for Dewey and other "new liberals" (as distinguished by Karier from classical liberals grounded in *laissez-faire* conceptions of freedom and the proper relationship between state and individual) became grounded in an unwarranted faith in the power of science and technology to affect the incremental ameliorative change in the corporate liberal state necessary to develop a benign, rationally planned and managed welfare state. Karier's analysis suggests a second, perhaps even worse, grounding for reflective thinking in practice in the corporate liberal state: a grounding in the cynical opportunism of managers, planners, and intellectuals who designed, legitimated, and maintained that state—and whose strictly private goals (devoid of even a naïve public faith in science and the welfare state) were to rise in career paths in the process of designing, legitimating, and maintaining it.

Karier's analysis thereby provides a strong cautionary note concerning current emphases on cultivating reflective thinking and reflective practice among school teachers and administrators. Reflective thinking and practice, when guided by naïve public values or a strictly private careerism, have historically played a vital role in legitimating and perpetuating inequality in educational institutions—and the involvement of those institutions in the ideological mystification and technological support of domestic and international violence. His analysis strongly suggests the responsibility for programs in the social foundations of education to facilitate development or strengthening among teachers and administrators (as well as among ourselves as university and college faculties) of public values which are clearly and defensibly democratic and not mystified. Three decades later, Karier's work from the 1960s and early 1970s still provides the means to stimulate rich dialogue on what constitutes clear and defensible democratic public values (which, for him, arise from classical liberal influences as well as from his critique of the corporate liberal state).

The grounds for such dialogue lie in the still seminal issues which he raised regarding equality of educational opportunity, the nature of an informed and rational citizenry and of its roles in establishing a more free society, the nature of academic freedom and the appropriate roles for the professoriate, the proper relationship between individual citizen and the state, forms of violence exercised by the state, and the relationship between capitalism and education. Potential for dialogue lies in reflective examination, in the light of historical and current evidence and counterarguments, of his denunciations as antidemocratic of prevalent sorting and testing devices and practices in schools, of objectification of human beings in capitalist schools and economies, and of militarization of education and government in the United States. That potential also lies in consideration of his analysis of the ideological and institutional points of commonality between the Fascist state and the bureaucratically structured modern liberal nation-state and corporate economy—and of his closely related analysis of the failure of progressive education and pragmatist philosophy to provide an effective alternative to authoritarian ideology and structuring of institutional decision making in the United States.

Karier's own normative vision of democracy (one which emphasizes a marketplace of ideas, an informed and vigilant citizenry, an open government respectful of civil liberties and restrained in its uses of violence, an economy which meets human needs rather than profiting on human alienation, and schools and universities which cultivate rationality and democratic and humane values and which provide equality of access to economic opportunity) certainly still deserves consideration as a set of public values. Perhaps even more important for discussion is the manner in which he refined his normative vision, which was only partly visible in *Man, Society, and Education*, through analysis and critique of institutional and ideological power and control in his subsequent works. That normative vision was expanded and deepened in the course of his analysis and critique of power and control in American education and in the corporate liberal state.

And it is precisely engagement in this kind of complex analysis and critique of power and control within educational systems—and ultimately within the broader state and economy—which affords educators the only real opportunity to clarify public democratic value positions which are not grounded in mystified or incoherent social belief. In sum, these clear democratic value positions coupled with an analysis and critique of the culture in which they are emerging are prerequisites for the development of potentially viable alternatives to America's current bureaucratic organization and culture.

7

Freud, Karier, and the Therapeutic State

Joseph L. DeVitis

Introduction

According to Kingsley Davis, the psychotherapist "enforces in a secular way and under the guise of science, the standards of the entire society."[1] For over three decades, Clarence Karier has sought to penetrate beyond commonly held assumptions so that he could help uncover, and thus demystify, dehumanized features in American social life. His realistic goal has been that personal development, in the form of unique individuation, might ensue in the recognition of those discoveries. But he has also understood a larger lesson: that individual change requires wide and deep sociopolitical transformation.

Unlike the universalized, essentialist foundations undergirding psychoanalysis, Karier writes "from a perspective that is invariably shaped out of one's existential present."[2] Indeed, the main difference between Karier and Sigmund Freud has been in the paths of their intellectual arrows.

Freud's journey ultimately led to enlightened self-interest, social adjustment, and stoical resignation to cultural constraints. Karier's quest has been more akin to a Marxian/Sartrean call to change the social structure in accord with the individual's newly found self-knowledge.

Furthermore, Karier's existential humanism, enjoined with critical social theory, aligns him against both the theologians who were threatened by modern psychology and the latter-day scientistic "authorities" who presumed to guide us toward their own versions of human nature and conduct. Freud saw himself as the Moses of that movement.

Culture and Its Discontents

In his psychic balancing act, Freud points to an optimal realization of self-control through an almost stoical exertion of rationality. He invokes such individual self-restraint because he believes that a substantial measure of repression is necessary to balance one's psychological apparatus, especially Id (animal-like) impulses, with the demands of culture. Freud thus employs the concept of repression to regulate the seemingly irreconcilable conflict between personal autonomy and cultural constraint.

Repression expresses that most general, largely unconscious, defense mechanism which enables us to keep out of consciousness those thoughts, wishes, and desires too dangerous to one's mental processes. A form of repression, sublimation refers to that specific defense mechanism which transforms id-like excitations into more socially acceptable patterns of behavior. Indeed, sublimation serves to build culture in the form of art, literature, religion, etc. Accordingly, Freud calls on human beings to sublimate what he assumes to be primary aggressive sex instincts with what he deems necessary to constitute civilization.

Thus, in Freud's scheme, the demands of civilized life require us to struggle with repression, i.e., to practice a frustrated form of individualism. In Karier's words,

> To Freud happiness was not attainable, for ultimately the fault did not lie with society nor with the individual, but was inherent in the very unchanging nature of man himself.... Most therapists ... made peace with the world by helping their clients adjust, if only in a suffering way, to the existing world.[3]

Karier's analysis closely resembles Herbert Marcuse's incisive critique of Freud's portrait of the individual, culture, and society. In Marcuse's view, human knowledge is historically conditioned, and therefore amenable to social change. With Marx, he claims that growing intellectual and material resources increasingly allow us to expunge irrationality and repression from existence.[4] Karier puts the case in more existential language:

> What, then, are the functions of knowledge, and to what extent are the producers of that knowledge accountable for the ways that knowledge is used to shape our social destiny?[5]

For Marcuse, like Karier, the Freudian model ushers in the "repressive idea of the person or personality who can 'fulfill himself' without making excessive demands on the world, by practicing the socially required degree of resignation."[6]

Though not sympathetic to Carl Jung's countervision as a whole, Karier acknowledges that Jung at least "offered a welcome relief for those in revolt against the repressive character of a patriarchal society which undergirded Freud's world view."[7] Jung is also more akin to the creative artist, and Karier notes that some artistic personalities, such as Waldo Frank, gravitated to Jung's psychospiritual insights as the "anchorage that would free him to express a variety of socially radical causes."[8] Frank is well known for his antitherapeutic sentiments, especially toward those therapies and therapists that "helped" people resign themselves to their social problems:

> Most of the ills of personal maladjustment which Freudian analysis may cure are the symptoms of the disorder, economic, social, cultural of the contemporary world.[9]

Theologians and Therapists

Factors basic to psychotherapy have also been found in most historic forms of "primitive healing, religious conversion, and even so-called brainwashing."[10] Thomas Szasz has been quick to point out that modern psychiatry has precursors in such superstitions and aberrations as demonology, witchcraft, witch-hunts, and the Inquisition.[11] In this sense, then, psychotherapy can be viewed as an interpretive reflection of the larger sociocultural environment—its mores, traditions, prejudices, and underlying value structure.

Though the goal of Freudian therapy is self-insight by the patient, the latter ascends that province only through the watchful eyes of the therapist—a substitute for pure self-enlightenment filtered by the conventions, methods, and mystifying language of psychoanalysis. This insight into Freud may be gleaned, in part, from his acceptance of social institutions as providing standards for both mental and moral well-being:

> All our social institutions are cut to the pattern of people with a unified, normal Ego, which one can classify as good or bad, and which either fulfills its function or is disabled by an overpowering influence. [12]

The further irony of Freudian therapy is that its foundational principle, i.e., the analysis and treatment of the individual patient, tends to separate thought and practice from those wider social and historical contexts which it unwittingly accepts as givens. Borrowing one of Freud's own terms, this separation amounts to a curious kind of displacement, whereby an internal, intrapsychic paradigm (Freud's self-contained analytic ideal) sets human beings apart from larger social reality. In practice, such a model compels patients to "blame" themselves, rather than any external social constraints, for anything they cannot overcome.

In his *Blaming the Victim* (1976), William Ryan has explored the enormous, often egregious, ramifications in public policy generated by such internal paradigms in social science.[13] In terms of therapy itself, Kenneth Benne has postulated:

> Counseling and therapy have traditionally sought to facilitate change in persons with little or no assumption of responsibility for facilitating changes in the cultural environment in which people function outside the counseling or therapeutic setting. This tends to place the entire burden of behavioral [change] upon the individual.[14]

In a similar vein, it has been said that "American religion has an individualistic emphasis. Much Protestant teaching has been exclusively concerned with the virtues, activities, and relationships of individuals rather than of groups and institutions."[15] The church has also been expected to act as guardian of societal norms, and churchmen have been accused of dysfunctional individual and social impact:

> [The church] tends to endow prevailing customs and doctrines with divine sanctions and to repress new ideas and usages almost as if its primary task is to prevent change. . . . It may be an "escape from freedom" for the neurotic personality. It sometimes contributes to arrested intellectual development and self-deception. . . . As a refuge from the stark realities of life and an outlet for discontent, it has supported servility in the working class. Otherworldliness . . . has often hindered social progress.[16]

Indeed, theorists as dissimilar as Karl Marx and Karl Menninger have pointed to religion's propensity to exacerbate mental illness and social escapism in all manner of repressions, cultural stereotypes, and ritualistic self-denials. Karier distinguishes therapeutic and religious practitioners in this fashion:

> The life of the therapeutic man . . . is dominated by an impulse for feeling, dispensing curative remedies in order to gain a sense of well-being, whereas the life of the theological man has been most often dominated by an impulse for salvation.[17]

The church has thus been characterized as "that institution which furnishes the salvation from suffering to other institutions."[18]

While Freud compares the Catholic Church to the army (he views both as authoritarian), he nonetheless proposes science and psychoanalysis as an alternative remedy. Freud conjectures, in materialist terms, that "all that is true of man—his motives, behavior, self-image—is ultimately reducible to biochemistry."[19] While noting that Freud sees science as proffering "only a limited redemption," Karier is fond of citing Freud's remarks about science and illusion: "No, our science is no illusion. But an illusion it would be to suppose that what science cannot give us we can get elsewhere."[20] Needless to say, both Freud and Karier view the natural order from the vantage point of the nonbeliever. [21]

According to the cultural historian Christopher Lasch, Karier contends that psychiatry "became a secular religion, designed like the old religion, to reconcile the people to social conditions that need to be changed through an aggressive 'revolutionary' politics."[22] Lasch is not paying Karier a compliment; rather he is asking to what extent is being a reflection of one's own time (i.e., being bound by certain traditions) not only understandable but also even good?

In his critical rebuttal to Karier's book, *Scientists of the Mind*, Lasch problematizes his habit of finding fault with those religious and psychological thinkers who were apparently unable, or unwilling, to override and overcome their sociohistoric situations. At the same time, Karier appears to argue that they should have evolved more unbiased world views than they did. As he puts it:

> It is clear that wherever we look in the human sciences of the twentieth century, we find the field riddled with unexamined philosophical and religious assumptions about human nature and the "good" society. From my perspective, the human sciences ought to be more scientific.[23]

As a critical social and intellectual historian, Karier's vision did not stop with science. Unlike Freud, a child of the secular Enlightenment, Karier posits an interlocking connection between the misuse of science and social oppression. He locates culpability in those men and women who could, or would, not transcend their cultural boundaries in order to criticize, and thus seek to alter, the sociohistoric bondage that they, as cultural leaders, helped to create. Karier is utterly straightforward on this point: "Science and social meliorism did not necessarily lead to a better future, but they could lead to a Hiroshima or a death camp."[24] With Jean-Paul Sartre (as well as Wilhelm Reich, Waldo Frank, and R. D. Laing), Karier urges theologians and therapists to become "social revolutionaries" who would abolish the social ills endemic to capitalist society.[25]

Unlike Freud, Karier is continually grappling with gritty existential and political questions, challenging the status quo and the creative imaginations of thoughtful, engaged intellectuals. Indeed, his constant admonitions to theologians and therapists are remindful of C. Wright Mills' sobering rejoinder to historian Richard Hofstadter in 1948:

> Political analysis today involves continual self-observation as well as observation of events. You cannot have a secure self-location in a period where every movement is half-assed and not deep going into the corruption of this society of which we are sensitive. . . . I believe that the

reason for our ambiguity has to do with the uneasiness of self-location and insecurity—which make[s] us strive to be politically happy when we know in our souls that [t]his is not the answer to anything we are really interested in on the political sphere.[26]

The Walls of Social Control

Much of Karier's academic career can be interpreted as a persistent quest to tear down the walls of social control. He consistently warns against the oftentimes unsavory relationship between intellectuals and policymakers. (In this, he is at times remindful of Randolph Bourne's heroic battle against John Dewey and government officials at the dawn of the First World War.) At its zenith, this unseemly alliance can be seen in Harold Lasswell's political adaptation of the psychiatric model:

> The permanent removal of the tensions of the personality depend upon the reconstruction of the individual's view of the world, and not upon belligerent crusades to change the world.[27]

Lasswell further urges policymakers, psychiatrists, and social scientists to band together to become "social engineers" for a presumably unbalanced culture:

> [The] most far-reaching way to reduce disease is for the psychiatrist to cultivate closer contact with the rulers of society, in the hope of finding the means of inducing them to overcome the symbolic limitations which prevent them from utilizing their influence for the prompt rearrangement of insanity producing routines.[28]

Lasswell recapitulates and extends Freud's vision of "knowledge through science" as a vehicle to harmonize inevitable tensions and conflicts between individuals and the state. The major problems with Lasswell's analysis are twofold: (1) to what extent therapeutic knowledge is indeed "scientific" (a question Karier would surely pose); and (2) whether that knowledge would become a handmaiden for "mutual understanding" or an instrument for social control (an issue Karier would never let us forget).

Peter Sedgwick's social constructivist view of mental illness sheds ample light on the above questions. For Sedgwick, concepts of mental health are culturally laden and culturally relative: what one culture condones may be condemned and stamped out in another culture.[29] Sociologist Thomas Schaff's "social deviance," or labeling, model resembles Sedgwick's position. According to Schaff, those designated "mentally ill" are so labeled because they transgress social norms and standards. He argues that we are thus dealing in *ideology*, not science, when making such judgments.[30] In a word, Karier would roundly applaud that analysis and its conclusions.

The lack of "objective" truth and the presence of countless semantic penumbrum in psychiatric models of mental health have spawned a countercultural movement known as "anti-psychiatry." By now a cottage industry, it is perhaps still best represented, in academic circles, in the work of Thomas Szasz, himself a psychiatrist and professor of medicine. As Szasz sees it, mental illness is a mythical notion in that it has no literal, extant objectivity, or "thingness." As such, it "exists" or functions much in the manner of other mere theoretical constructs.[31]

Yet Szasz's own solution to the dilemma of mental illness also seems to be problematic at best. He proffers that it can be explained in terms of "problems of living" for his patients. The rub with this explanation is that Szasz himself does not avoid the issue of asking clients to (a) internalize their own problems (consonant with the psychiatric model that he condemns) and then proceeding to (b) judge whether they have "externalized" enough to meet the pressures of their social world. In a sense, he may have unknowingly erected his own kind of "double bind" for mental health. Moreover, Szasz adopts an "ethical" stance for psychic well-being that falls back on individualistic notions of "freedom" and "liberty." That is, he seems committed to a form of Freudianism without realizing it: a self-contained, analytic ideal which he had portrayed as the fundamental weakness of traditional therapy.

Karier captures these "inner" and "outer" themes in his view of alienation in the modern age:

... as twentieth-century man pursued the Enlightenment idea of social meliorism and gained objective freedom through the creation of bureaucratic structure, he lost his subjective freedom at the hands of the very institutions giving him the greater objective freedom.[32]

Like Marx and Sartre before him, Karier is vitally concerned with social alienation in a sense unknown to Freud (whose social psychology was limited despite the presence of Emile Durkheim). Karier challenges repressive social forces in a manner unheard of in Freud's unswerving rendition of an intractable human nature.

The distinctions in human nature raised by Karier are once again similar to those originated by Marcuse, one of Freud's major modern-day revisionists. Marcuse uses the concepts "basic" versus "surplus" repression to clarify those kinds of repressive measures that are necessary and unnecessary. Basic repression refers to that modification of the "instincts necessary for the perpetuation of the human race in civilization," e.g., provision of food and shelter and combating of disease. Surplus repression refers to those additive "restrictions necessitated by social domination," i.e., extra-layered forms of social constraint over and above that which is needed for the maintenance of civilized life. According to Marcuse, surplus repression has been caused by sociohistoric conditions, which are amenable to social change.[33]

Thus did Marcuse, and later Karier, seek to explode Freud's increasingly antiquated reality principle. Karier bluntly summarizes this intellectual transformation: "Freud's rationalism ... went too far. It excised 'the cosmic connection' and ... proved the irrationality of the rationalist dogma."[34] In the end, Freud's essential theoretical egocentrism focuses primarily on internal, individualist, and universal measures of human nature and conduct. Freud established a certain set of preconceptions about any possibilities for social change. On the other hand, Karier seems to have cherished independent thinking and freedom as important sociopolitical goods in ways which eluded Freudian analysis. In Karier's words, "Freud's own quest to make the irrational rational was the ultimate in rationality.... Against the irrationality of religion [he] posed his own God of Reason."[35]

Postscript

It is perhaps noteworthy that Karier's obvious personal favorite among the psychological giants in his *Scientists of the Mind* turns out to be William James. Karier is critical of James' failure to develop a thoroughgoing critique of larger social structures. However, he seems at one with his ardent dedication to freedom of thought amidst the flux and exigencies of choice in an unfixed universe. Karier always sought to underscore the deeper significance in James' subtle view of "psychology as a natural science," to wit:

> . . . we must not assume that that means a sort of psychology that stands at last on solid ground. It means just the reverse: it means a psychology particularly fragile, and into which the waters of metaphysical criticism leak at every joint, a psychology all of whose elementary assumptions and data must be reconsidered in wider connections and translated into other terms. [36]

8

Clarence Karier on War, Race, and Other Dynamics at the Intersection of Economics and Education

Ronald Rochon and Paul Theobald

Clarence Karier, like Bernard Bailyn and Lawrence Cremin, was an articulate spokesman of the view that the history of education was in no way synonymous with the mere history of schooling.[1] In some way all three of these luminary intellectuals were curious to learn about and expose the variety of phenomena through which Americans learned to be what and who they are. To be sure, schools and schooling had a role to play in the shaping of an American identity—all three agreed on that—but Karier pushed his exploration much further than the others. Karier searched for, and tried to expose, the shapers of beliefs about the world. Toward this end, no "source" was off limits, no institution was sacred. The General Accounting Office of Congress, the Pentagon, the CIA were all mined by Karier for whatever he could turn up.

The shapers of beliefs about the world, or, as he sometimes referred to them, the "servants of power," had the wherewithal necessary to rationalize and legitimize public policy.[2] The effects of public policy were, for Karier, the best measure of justice and injustice in a democratic society. As a nation consciously created in the image of liberal ideals, one would expect American public policy to distribute justice far more regularly than injustice. Consider the rhetoric amid which the nation was formed. We were to be a free democratic republic. We were to be peace-loving, self-governing, and capable of raising the common good above our own self-interest. We were to be solid community members, sharing our rights and responsibilities with equally solid neighbors. Such a description resonated with federalist and antifederalist alike. And why not? It's an attractive picture. In such a world, clearly, justice would serve as the primary criterion for all policy matters.

In some ways, the corpus of Karier's work in educational history can be described as a long search for an answer to the question, "how can a society that defines itself with the highest of human ideals propagate injustice year after year, decade after decade?" In short, with such good intentions, how can there be so much injustice in America? How can a nation which gave the vote to blacks in 1867 take it back by 1905 and then continue to withhold it until 1965? How could a nation which gave women the right to vote in 1919 declare twelve years later that they could be expatriated by marriage to a racially inappropriate foreigner? Or that a state could legally sterilize them if they were deemed to be "feebleminded?" How can the wealthiest nation on earth tolerate the fact that children represent the largest segment of the American population living in poverty?

Karier argued that there are enormously powerful educational efforts being exerted in the interest of legitimizing the great American paradox: a nation defined by justice in theory, yet marked by injustice in practice. These efforts enabled the distortion of liberal ideals over time and their subsequent sale to the American public. For Clarence Karier, chronicling these educational efforts was the job of the educational historian and he dedicated his professional life to the task.

In broad strokes, the distortion of liberal ideals has taken place in three phases. The first is the creation and dissemination of what Karier came to call "corporate liberal" ideals. The second phase came with the creation and dissemination of ideals that culminated in what Karier called the "warfare state." The last, most recent, phase could be called the consolidation of power, for it has been marked by a kind of totalitarianism, or elite decision making, that has all but destroyed an ethic of citizenship, community membership, the desire for mutual prosperity, and several other original liberal ideals upon which the nation was built.

The Corporate Liberal State

In Karier's analysis, Thomas Jefferson and Benjamin Franklin most precisely set the liberal standard to which Americans would strive for the largest part of the nineteenth century.[3] It was a radical democratic vision. Indeed, Clarence Karier is one among a relatively small group of American historians to recognize the "radical" nature of Jefferson's vision, given the distance American society has moved away from Enlightenment ideals.[4] Jefferson and Franklin both possessed tremendous faith in the common man, both believed that education would enable enlightened self-government, that a nation could be diverse yet tolerant, and that prosperity could be widely shared.

More than a few historians have noted the differences between the *Declaration of Independence* and the *Constitution*. One set us on a path toward Jefferson's radical participatory republic. The other curbed the democratic radicalism of the earlier document by severely limiting the political participation of the common man, to say nothing of the unfortunate history it set in motion for blacks, Native Americans, and women. Still, the possibility that lay in front of the new nation as the eighteenth century turned into the nineteenth was fairly unprecedented. The United States successfully separated the feudal power of church and state, it successfully adopted the concept of free public schools, it dramatically increased the white male franchise, and it set in motion so many democratic institutions that lastingly impressed the famous French visitor, Alexis de Tocqueville.

The flaws of the *Constitution*, however, exacerbated the problems surrounding the issue of chattel slavery in America. Though a decisive clash was avoided for decades due to the efforts of "compromisers" like Henry Clay, it eventually came. When the Civil War ended, the *Constitution* was amended in ways that made it a decidedly more democratic document. But other developments were taking shape that would make the democratic constitutional gains of relatively little importance. In fact, the forces that would move America from an embrace of democratic liberalism to an embrace of what Karier and other historians refer to as "corporate liberalism" were largely in place by the war's end.

High on Karier's list in this regard was Comtean positivism and Spencerian evolutionary theory.[5] Both legitimated the idea of cultural evolution—from primitive to advanced—and in so doing gave added fuel to an emerging capitalist system. The new science of society that these men heralded seemed to suggest that America was on the right evolutionary track, thus reducing the need for the kind of moral surveillance of self-interested commercial transactions advised by the likes of John Locke and Adam Smith.

Auguste Comte was convinced that certain natural *social* laws existed alongside natural physical laws. Using the scientific method, the social scientist could discern and validate these laws. The end result, Comte predicted, was that order could be brought to a chaotic world. Ceaseless debate in the policy arena would become a thing of the past as policymakers simply adopted what was suggested by natural law. As the father of sociology, Comte spread the idea that science would increasingly supply the solutions to society's ills.

When Comtean positivism was combined with the seductive, self-congratulatory theory of social evolution advanced by Herbert Spencer and William Graham Sumner, an enormous blow was dealt to the original liberal tenets of shared community membership, mutual prosperity, and the conviction that the common man was up to the business of statecraft. Spencer believed that a society premised on these ideals could not possibly act in accordance with natural law. Such a society would allow the weak to survive, a circumstance that Spencer believed would significantly impair the evolution of American society toward more advanced levels. Natural law maintained that the weak must be allowed to die. Good government, according to Spencer, would allow these natural processes to unfold.

America's elite learned to think in evolutionary terms. Karier brilliantly described how they acted on their new knowledge in a 1972 journal article entitled "Testing for Order and Control in the

Corporate State." In this extended essay, Karier demonstrated the degree to which leading intellectuals legitimized meritocracy at the expense of earlier democratic ideals. Due to the popularity of evolutionary social science, American elites began to equate poverty and other social ills with racial degeneracy and, consequently, they saw no reason to alleviate them.

Trained within a positivistic, evolutionary framework, scientists of the mind,[6] the new psychologists of the turn-of-the-century era, all emphasized the *nonrational* nature of the human mind, thus legitimating elite decision making throughout society. These men even created the standardized tests to identify those who would ascend to policymaking power.

The educational agenda of America during the Progressive era became tightly connected to the business interests of the nationally consolidated industrial houses and, in particular, the philanthropic foundations they created. John D. Rockefeller's General Education Board and Andrew Carnegie's Foundation for the Advancement of Teaching represent two excellent examples of corporate contributions to the education of Americans. They touted a differentiated school system analogous to the differentiated labor required at their parent firms. The tests they supported empirically "confirmed" the elite belief in the validity of the correlation between race and intelligence.

The corporate leaders who sat on bodies like the National Civic Federation, the foundation presidents that represented corporate America, and the intellectuals trained in the academic milieu set by Comte and Spencer all became shapers of beliefs about the world that have influenced American social thought throughout the twentieth century. Karier cogently described America's circumstances once the corporate liberal state secured its ideologically dominant position and established itself beyond the pale of the once worrisome threats of populism, socialism, and trade unionism. "Henceforth most social change would be institutionally controlled and the interest of government, corporate wealth, and labor more securely managed. The state which thus emerged included a mass system of public schools which served the manpower needs of the state."[7] Completely lost amid the ascendance of corporate liberal ideology were the liberal ideas of Franklin and Jefferson, most notably, the notion that public schools be designed to equip citizens for the burden of self-government.

The Welfare State

The Progressive era and its new corporate version of liberalism ended as the United States entered World War I. Things would never again be quite the same. Prior to the war, America supported a small military force. By the war's end, and ever since, it has supported the world's largest military force. Much of this circumstance was due to the fact that for most of the twentieth century we have never been too distant from the spectre of war. Indeed, as Karier put it, we live in a time "when war became indistinguishable from peace." The end result of this, for Karier, was that "the corporate liberal state became the welfare state."[8] For example, we fought the Great War to make the world safe for democracy. Then we fought to make the world safe from fascism. Later we entered into "a stalemated war to make the world safe from communism."[9] Now we engage in relatively safe, quick, easy wars to protect "American interests," although this trend differs substantially from warfare efforts through Vietnam. We'll come back to this phenomenon in the next section of this chapter.

It is doubtful that a people claiming democracy as a watchword could be induced to support a war-ready military force year after year, decade after decade, without a social philosophy that legitimates the expense. Where this social philosophy came from, and how the American public came to learn and embrace it is, for Karier, a crucial piece of twentieth-century educational history.

The first ingredient in this twentieth-century philosophy was the mythos surrounding our nineteenth-century frontier experience. In a kind of romanticism that grew out of westward expansion, Karier saw the beginning of a powerful rationale for twentieth-century imperialism. In his words, "the frontier mythos was the thread out of which much of America's twentieth-century ideological fabric was woven."[10] Karier went on to connect the romantic and neo-romantic movements in both Germany and the

United States to the escalating national chauvinism that contributed to the creation of the warfare state. Part of this, to be sure, had to do with scientific claims concerning racial superiority, but another part was due to what Karier has called a "peculiar romanticism" that was part American manifest destiny, part German volkishness.[11]

Just as Auguste Comte and Herbert Spencer contributed to an intellectual milieu conducive to the ascendancy of corporate liberal ideals, Karier sees certain key twentieth-century intellectuals as crucial shapers of the beliefs that have supported our "corporate militarized state."[12] Among them he counts the likes of Walter Lippmann, Herbert Croly, and surprisingly, John Dewey.

At the end of the twentieth century it is easy to see the tight connection between massive defense spending and huge corporate profits. As the debate whether or not to enter the Great War proceeded, however, the business and industrial interests were far from enamored by the prospect of heightening the powers of the state through entry into a world war (although their reservations were nonexistent by the time the second world war came around). This is because we had not yet witnessed the completion of what President Eisenhower would later call the "industrial-military complex." The appropriate social philosophy was not yet in place. Quoting *The New Republic* from 1917, Karier argues that "the effective and decisive work on behalf of war has been accomplished by an entirely different class [than the industrial and business interests]—a class which must be comprehensively but loosely described as the 'intellectuals.'"[13]

Analyzing Croly's arguments in *The Promise of American Life*, Karier weaves together the various ideological strands that went into the creation of the social philosophy undergirding the warfare state. Consider this passage:

> At this point, when the peculiar self image of innocence and virtue combined with that long-standing Puritan sense of duty and destiny, the new nationalism of Croly's America became the new internationalism of [President] Wilson. America's "manifest destiny" was to make the "world safe for democracy." The American ideal of democracy was to be exported to build a better

world of peace and order in the form of the League of Nations. America then had an international program expressed as a national purpose.[14]

While this agenda of the intellectuals may have been well intentioned, Karier is quick to note that its persuasive power and longevity have had more to do with the ability of the nation's elite financial interests to maintain their hegemony over the state. This is exemplified by their rejection of America's participation in the League of Nations.

Karier counts John Dewey among the intellectuals who underestimated the power of the nation's financial interests to control policy directions. On the other hand, Dewey's faith in the ability of the scientific method to bring solutions to societal shortcomings merely complemented the efforts of America's business leaders to legitimate militarism and the warfare state through the vocal espousal of our national duty to make international contributions to democracy. Said Karier, "Dewey's notion of industrial democracy did not involve an equalitarian distribution of power or wealth, but rather a distribution based on a steady developing pragmatic use of intelligence and scientific method."[15]

The trouble with the pragmatic use of the scientific method is that it ignores moral and ethical dilemmas, or solves them on the basis of business and scientific principles such as efficiency. Such a pragmatic philosophy, Karier argues, has been a great boon to the warfare state. Though Dewey felt that war might be a catalyst to production in the interest of meeting social needs rather than private profit, war's end inevitably proved him wrong. In the meantime, however, his intellectual rationale in support of war made him a key shaper of public beliefs about the world.

Karier poignantly described how the reality of the warfare state has fallen far short of the expectations taught to Americans by the likes of Lippmann, Croly, and Dewey. During the last half of the twentieth century, the American record has been incredibly bleak with respect to the extension of democracy through the world. "We have repeatedly expended the great wealth of this country . . . on supporting and creating military dictators who maintain their power by terror tactics. We have stood against the freedom and independence of people, either economically or politically and have been most effective at deterring democracy through the world."[16]

The warfare state has indeed been perpetuated for undemocratic ends and at enormous cost. As Karier observed, "One of the very obvious and direct legacies of war has been the growing inability of our local and state governments to support a viable educational system."[17] And in response, as many Americans begin to look toward the huge, untaxed profits of multinational corporations, the CEOs of these institutions take every opportunity they can to spread privatization propaganda in an effort to protect corporations from the burden of contributing to the public good. But this educational activity brings us close to the present and to the final phase of distorting the liberal democratic ideals common at our nation's founding.

The Consolidation of Power

The social philosophy that undergirded the warfare state is no longer palatable to many Americans, largely because of the huge discrepancy between the intentions suggested by our philosophy and the reality of our actions. Though the news media hinted ceaselessly about all manner of atrocities perpetrated by Serbians on the Kosovars during the first half of 1999, the American public showed little interest in entering into war once again. This is why the most recent American engagements have been short and fast. While the Pentagon continues to issue media releases that speak of grave military dangers, the American public, by and large, has lost interest.

This has precipitated a new strategy espoused by corporate leaders designed to legitimate and rationalize the status quo. The enemy, it turns out, according to new arguments designed to educate all Americans, is not so much external as internal. It consists of those responsible for a mediocre public school system, or those responsible for an expensive social safety net that grows welfare queens, or those responsible for early parole prisoners like Willie Horton, not to mention dangerously liberal intellectuals like Martin Luther King, Jr.

Karier took careful aim at the creation of this new social philosophy in an extended review of David J. Garrow's 1986 book, *Bearing the Cross: Martin Luther King, Jr., and the Southern Christian Leadership Conference*. In this review, Karier documented FBI attempts to discredit King because he had become, in the words of an FBI document presumably referring to King, "the most dangerous and effective Negro leader in the country."[18] Delineating the range of activities undertaken by the FBI to accomplish their nefarious goal—planting prostitutes around King as he traveled away from home, issuing false reports about his connections to communist groups, persuading universities not to extend honorary doctoral degrees—Karier revealed the extent of the "educational" efforts undertaken by the power brokers of the status quo.

Civil and economic justice, the twin goals for which King gave his life, were simply ideas that the power elite could not allow to flourish, despite their obvious resonance with the foundational virtues upon which the nation was built. As an earlier King biographer noted, it didn't cost the nation anything to extend the franchise to blacks or to open up public accommodations; this talk of economic justice was another thing altogether. It explains the wire-tapped phones, the attempts at entrapment, the FBI intelligence extended to Southern police departments. But more important, this also explains why the attempts to discredit King have gone on after his death. What the FBI has done, according to Karier, is engage in a wholesale effort to teach the masses in America how to respond to an icon that stood for civil and economic justice. In order to protect the present parameters bounding the distribution of justice, the discrediting effort had to go on after King's death so that people continue to harbor suspicions regarding King, his intentions, and what well-distributed economic justice might cost them.

The character assassination of King, and the reassassination after his death, probably would not have been successful had it not been for what the nation's schools had become. In short, Karier argues, schools have facilitated mass adaptation to the existing social system, almost a complete reversal of an originally stated mission of providing widespread intellectual wherewithal for the burden of self-government. Focusing on the provision of economic utility, school curricula have left Americans ill equipped for grassroots participation in public policy. In the absence of meaningful democratic practices at the local level, the surveillance of power has been left to the multinational corporations who control the print and broadcast media. This is, of course, a little like the fox guarding the henhouse. It has enabled the ascendancy of the "industrial-military complex" that Eisenhower warned Americans about near the end of his presidency. The interconnections of military, industrial, and governmental power have become so entrenched that Karier sees them as elements of a coming fascism in America.

Conclusion

Clarence Karier has been an articulate critic of the current distribution of social and economic justice. More than any other educational historian, he has documented the myriad ways that the American public has "learned" to accept the status quo. Karier has shown that war and race have been the public "curriculum," so to speak, that has been used to legitimate our wholesale rejection of the Enlightenment ideals upon which the nation was founded, ideals such as peace, tolerance, self-rule, mutual prosperity, and good neighborship.

The scholarly trajectory Karier took during his working life left him at the margins of the educational research community, even at the margins of the smaller community of educational historians. Despite this, he never wavered, he never took the path that leads to ample research funding and highly lauded scholarship. That is, he never became an apologist or defender of the status quo. Other scholars effectively become pedagogical agents in the educational efforts of corporate America. A critique of these efforts has been Clarence Karier's most significant scholarly legacy.

9

Clarence Karier's Influence on Two Careers in Native American Policy Studies

Mark W. Sorensen and Guy Senese

Introduction

This piece is a blend of influences and reminiscences regarding the influence of Clarence Karier and his work in the research and practice of Mark Sorensen and Guy Senese. Both of us were students in the Department of Educational Policy Studies during the early 1980s and late 1970s respectively. It was Clarence who first facilitated our mutual interests, and who along with Professor James Anderson, have had a significant influence on each of us, as our paths have crossed many times in the past twenty years. This project has offered us the opportunity to reflect with gratitude on a shared indebtedness as we began to trace our association with Clarence Karier. We have pursued different career paths, and the following article attempts to provide a retrospective description of our careers and the ways in which Clarence Karier's influence and encouragement have shaped and continue to shape our work.

"Twenty-Four Years in Navajo Community Education"—
Mark Sorensen

When I reflect on why I have spent the last twenty-three years as an educator and school leader in tribally controlled schools on the

Navajo Nation, I inevitably begin to reflect upon the powerful influence that Clarence Karier, my advisor and mentor, had on me during my graduate education at the University of Illinois during the 1970s. Clarence's gentle manner, but passionate commitment to unmask the subtle control mechanisms in mainstream educational thought, helped to give an intellectual discipline and honesty to my own historical investigations. In my own thinking, I was struck by the disharmony between the democratic ideals of American public education and the day-to-day realities of minority youth and youth culture in American schools today.

I began my graduate studies at the University of Illinois in 1972. I had just been awarded a Danforth Fellowship to pursue and complete my doctorate and to eventually become a professor. The Danforth allowed me to go to any university of my choice, and I had chosen the Department of Educational Psychology at the University of Illinois, Urbana-Champaign. However, during my first semester, I was so disappointed with the lack of intellectual responsiveness by the educational psychology faculty to what I considered to be pressing social issues (such as racism, class conflict, and antidemocratic institutions), that I began to look toward other universities that had constructed their mandated advanced degrees programs to better address these issues. Fortunately, it was then that I took my first course from Clarence. I remember it felt like I had crossed a dry and barren desert to find an oasis—with enough water for me and for many others to drink to our satisfaction.

Soon, I transferred into the Department of Educational Policy Studies and became immersed in unraveling the knotty problems of how access to knowledge in American educational institutions was restricted by issues of race, class, and social control. Clarence Karier and the intellectuals he attracted to the department, intellectuals like Jim Anderson, treated the graduate students as fellow explorers on a very important mission. This was a great opportunity for me because I wanted not only to discover all I could about the roots of the problems that bothered me, but also to do something about the hidden elements of social control and individual oppression. I was struck by how Clarence and other professors in that shop were willing to listen to and consider the intellectual basis of a myriad assortment of alternatives to mainstream educational thought, giving each movement the same thorough critique. Less committed academic researchers oftentimes reserve their attention and time only for their own favorite stalking horses. From the bottom of my heart I thank Clarence Karier, and Jim Anderson, for providing me with the challenge (and, for living that challenge themselves) to never be timid or afraid about going to the root of each educational problem as it was experienced and researched. I came to understand during my graduate years that the real meaning and challenge of being a radical was hidden in the process of searching for the root of any problem through a combination of critical historical study and democratic social action.

I took that challenge. My master's thesis, under Clarence's guidance, was focused on the educational policies of Francis Leupp, a turn-of-the-century Commissioner of Indian Affairs. In my research, I uncovered within his ostensibly pro-Indian posturing, a carefully crafted plan for the demise of Native culture through the development of a network of federal government–operated "progressive" day schools. I became focused on the similarities and differences between the educational policies toward African Americans and Native Americans over the past hundred years. I found Clarence both willing and eager to respect and challenge my research in these areas.

The desire to really see and understand the root of the problems in Native American education led me in 1976, to interrupt my studies and head for the heart of the Navajo Nation in northern Arizona. I took a position as a curriculum coordinator for Rough Rock Demonstration School—the first bilingual, bicultural Native American–controlled school in the country. Since its inception in the late 1960s, Rough Rock was then and has been the inspiration for a largely tribal movement to actualize the democratic promise of local community control with minimal interference from traditional controls by administrative elites in the Bureau of Indian Affairs (BIA). My intent was to learn directly from the Navajo people who had recently mobilized an indigenous leadership. I wanted to hear and learn from them what pressing issues they most wanted to have addressed in the historical research I was doing as part of my graduate studies. Now, some twenty years later, it is ironic that I can be proud of my participation in the development of a legitimately community-controlled Navajo elementary and middle school, along with a community-controlled Wellness Center, governed by Navajo people and largely staffed by Navajo teachers. This school, Little Singer Tribal School, named for a local religious leader of the previous generation, is located just outside the community of Leupp, Arizona, fifty miles from Flagstaff (i.e., it was named for the very Francis Leupp, educator and internal colonist, that had been the topic of my master's thesis).

I must admit I became so thoroughly involved in the actual application of community control approaches for education in the Navajo community where I lived that the completion of my doctoral program seemed for many years as but a pale shadow of the struggle I was directly involved in at the community level. Nevertheless, Clarence encouraged me to return to complete the doctorate when I felt I had a handle on the issues needing to be addressed in Native American education. He remembered my research and recommended my thesis to another graduate student in the department, Guy Senese, who was serious about exploring the same set of issues. We struck up a correspondence and Guy too, came out to Rough Rock to observe and to teach high school. I had just become principal of the local elementary school, and our friendship and collaboration began.

Over the years, I have met several of Clarence's students and have always been impressed by the struggles many expressed in trying to balance their own internal search for truth in academia with more subtle pressures to submit to an agenda of antidemocratic manipulation from school bureaucracies and mass culture. My own choices have led me to work at the grassroots level in an effort to help empower Native American communities to determine their own futures in education. Throughout the years, it has been my purpose to work in collaboration with Native American community leaders to realize the democratic promise of community action and localized control. An honest critique of government, whether it be the BIA or tribal governments, has been at the heart of this process. My earlier studies with Clarence and Jim, as well as my own experience, have shown me the importance of "critical history." I have certainly not been alone in the effort to critique governmental intrusion and manipulation in Native American education, but Clarence's research and teaching encouraged and validated my own research agenda. I came to understand that the language of reform can be misleading. It can lull you to sleep, and, as a result, you can find yourself with less power and promise than if you had been alert to the subtle deceptions that have been a part of antidemocratic bureaucracies throughout Indian country.

In 1993, I completed my dissertation, but I did it at "home" at Northern Arizona University, working with Navajo educators and community members. My Ph.D. dissertation, entitled "Navajo Parents' Perceptions of Their Tribally Controlled Grant School," was an in-depth study focusing not just on the ideology of community control but on how "those most nearly touched" by the school have responded to its operation and development.[1] For the past eight years, while I have been the Executive Director of Little Singer and the Wellness Center there, I founded (and currently direct) the activities of the Native American Grant School Association. My activities range from organizing Native parents to speak of their concerns in tribal schools across Arizona, to helping craft national and state legislation affecting tribal community–controlled schools. These activities have been the expression of my desire, first articulated by Clarence, to go to the root of the problem and not be afraid of what I see. In my mind, Clarence Karier stands for the best of our intellectual heritage, for while he taught us to challenge all our assumptions, he also encouraged us to hold the educational institutions and persons responsible accountable for upholding democratic ideals of freedom, justice, and equality for all citizens.

The Critique of New Liberalism and Native American Social and Education Policy—Guy Senese

Clarence Karier's labor as a critical historian helped provide an intellectual home for all the teaching and writing I have done in my career. And for that I am grateful. A lot of water has passed under my personal bridge since 1985, when I received my Ph.D. in Educational Policy Studies from the University of Ilinois at Urbana-Champaign. As I read Mark Sorensen's contribution to our work here, I think back twenty years, and remember how Clarence responded to my own inquiries about the history of Progressive-era Native American education. I was interested in critical democratic theory, and wanted to know more about educational experiments in tribal schools that were developed as a response to the ambiguous Progressive-era legacy. He did something remarkable. He helped guide me to resources that would sharpen a critique of those developments. He also encouraged me to read Mark's thesis, to correspond with him about these issues, and finally gave me the encouragement to work, teach, and study at Rough Rock Demonstration School. Here, ideas of democratic self-determination were being employed, and Mark had found his place working with these same ideas there. Eventually, after teaching at Rough Rock, and conducting two years of research, I completed my dissertation under Jim Anderson, and went through the tough process of dissertation drafts, revisions, and finally, dissertation defense. The result of this process was the eventual publication of my research as a book entitled *Self-Determination and the Social Education of Native Americas* in 1991.[2] In this paper, I would like to focus on the legacy of John Collier, who was instrumental in making great changes in Indian policy, and is often given credit for all the democratic reforms in Indian Country that followed his reign. It was through the influence of Clarence Karier and the faculty in the Department of Educational Policy Studies at the University of Illinois that I began to look differently at the efforts of progressive liberals in relationship to the Native American Self-Determination Movement as it has evolved through its various historical stages. All my subsequent observations on schooling in Indian Country have been conditioned by these influences.

Liberal intellectuals, such as Collier, Commissioner of Indian Affairs, during the New Deal, were indeed at the heart of the most influential changes in Indian educational policy during the twentieth century. Collier, along with W. Carson Ryan, Lewis Merriam, Willard Beatty, as well as men like Leupp from an earlier generation, have received enormous intellectual scrutiny from academics and liberal intellectuals for their role in redirecting the offensive and punishing effects of a variety of pre-Progressive-era Indian policies.[3] In particular, they have been cited for their work in regard to land allotment (i.e., work that helped reduce the holdings of the tribes by some 150 million acres); the boarding schools (i.e., with their policies of student labor); monoculturalism; and health care. In doing critical research on these issues, the most important thing that I grappled with was Karier's own critique of administrative expertise, with special attention to his documentation of the shift in liberal social psychology from the earlier more overt and coercive forms of assimilation to the newer and more subtle forms of ideological and intellectual hegemony.

I have been interested in the democratic doctrines of self-determination articulated by John Collier, the Progressive administrator who had begun to legitimize tribal governance as part of the Indian Reorganization Act. To liberal scholars studying these theories, Collier's actions appeared as the crucial watershed events preparing the way for legitimate tribal self-government. It would have been easy to follow the academic parade of Collier bromides to a respectable, tenable position on American Indian education. Indeed, along with supporting a return of power to tribal governments, Collier had been instrumental in supporting a shift away from boarding schools toward day schools, where students could study near home. This appeared to many as the beginning of community control and self-determination, and has been the source for the well-known, comfortable, and often repeated scholarly position: without Collier, no community tribal schools, no Native bilingual education, no democratic reform. I was encouraged by Clarence and my other mentors, Terry Denny and Jim Anderson, to ask the same questions of these changes as were being asked about the "administrative progressives" working in the urban schools of the Progressive era.

Indeed, Clarence's leadership in the department provided me with an intellectual home where I could work with philosophers and historians like Ralph Page, Steve Tozer, James Anderson, and Paul Violas who encouraged rigorous and thorough scholarly exploration by a close critical reading of primary documents. Equally important, they emphasized the importance of keeping an open ear for contemporary problems and developments in Indian Country, which might shed light on these historical issues. We were encouraged to honor and understand contemporary movements and the way they reflected on the lived meaning of history (i.e., we were near enough to the early 1970's Red Power movement and the struggles at Wounded Knee). Clarence's active work on government secrecy and FBI skullduggery gave encouragement to my own sense that one could make new sense of the legacy of Collier's tribal "governments" by watching the "goons" of tribal chairman Dick Wilson work in tandem with the FBI to establish a reign of terror and intimidation in Lakota country, against resistors and the traditional Lakota people. This was powerful, hegemonic, antidemocratic action coming from within an alliance between "tribal" governments and federal secret police. The rest of the story is history, and the legacy of America's most famous political prisoner, Leonard Peltier, has left our democratic life with an indelible stain. It was Clarence's example that gave support to the notion that a "revision" of history is correct when we are led to our data by the demands of the historical search for truth rather than academic comfort or bureaucratic convenience.

The influence of progressive social theory on the development of Native American social policy between World Ward I and II has been well documented by Kelly (1983),[4] Philp (1976),[5] and others. There is an important element missing from most interpretations of progressive reform; most interpretations tend to emphasize the influence of social pragmatism in developing policy initiatives. Philp argued that Indian New Deal reform achieved its great expression in the development of tribal government as the outgrowth of an ethic of community democracy. Most histories have identified the spirit of progressive reform working in opposition to the more oppressive and inefficient school and social programming run through the Bureau of Indian Affairs (BIA). Progressive school reforms, such as the day schools, bilingual programs, and programs of religious tolerance have been described chiefly as part of an evolution toward a more harmonious and sound progressive pedagogy allied with the scientific credibility of modern social theory.

Each of these interpretations underrepresents the powerful ideological dimensions influencing these drives for reform. This error contributes to a notion that it was political and ethical concerns in progressive reforms that were paramount. This historical interpretation served to strengthen arguments that progressive reforms were nothing more than a long overdue movement toward tribal cultural and political sovereignty, now expressed in reformed social and educational policy. This historical error also functions to establish a greater connection between liberal progressive reform and meaningful shifts in Indian political power and social self-determination than is revealed by a more critical look at the historical data. Instead, the ideological character of these reforms is better understood as a symptom of an ethereal pluralist ideology—a pluralism supported not for its juridical legitimacy but for its cultural-aesthetic appeal. It would have been too much to depict progressive reformers of this period, and particularly the most influential reformer, John Collier, as mere aesthetics. But to underrepresent this dimension as part of an explanation for progressive reform is to impute an ethic of pluralist counterassimilationism that is equally undeserved. This research was stimulated by my talks with Clarence and by my reading of his research on the liberalism of John Dewey, a Collier contemporary, correspondent, and ideological mate.

The important impact of John Collier's work on the shape of reform is misunderstood without an emphasis on the degree to which he was influenced by an aesthetic of tribal life. Indeed, one of the changes which distinguishes the shift in modern social reform from nineteenth-century Christian reforms is the developing aesthetic of Indian cultural life. This aestheticism is part of the reason Indian cultural and political sovereignty remains threatened today after two generations (i.e., in the 1930s and the 1970s) of social reformism. Hunting and fishing rights, free religious expression, community school development, bicultural education and self-determination—in general—have each been ideologically justified as much by culturally aesthetic arguments as they have been by juridical, trust/treaty-based protections. One recent example (one of the many possible that comes to mind) is the recent case in Wisconsin where temporary abrogation of Chippewa fishing rights was considered seriously by officials in the Interior Department as a way to avoid confrontation with sportfishers and their supporters. One may fairly ask whether these rights are established by the full force of the Constitution and treaty law, or whether they merely inhabit the minds of federal policymakers as a sort of cultural-aesthetic netherworld—relics of the reformers' interest in the preservation of primitive, tribal cultural forms. "Ideological aestheticism" has been an underlying component of tribal social and educational reform structures (especially during times of stress), but it provides poor glue for the preservation of a more rational, legalistically grounded argument for Native American sovereignty.

Progressive Social Management

Progressive social study and management are exemplified best by the eighteen-month study of the U.S. Indian Service carried out by the Brookings Institution's Institute for Government Research under the direction of Lewis Merriam in 1926. Published in 1928 as "Problem of Indian Administration" (hereafter referred to as "the Merriam Report"), the report concluded that the reform of the Indian Service must not be a simple overhaul of Bureau management but rather a revision of the philosophy of cultural assimilation (i.e., a philosophy that had previously been expressed in BIA policies in regard to boarding schools and land allotments).[6] In effect, this study argued that more, not less government administration would be required to effect needed policy changes. It furthermore stated that education was the most fundamental concern of the Bureau. Through education, the Indian could begin to better understand the demands of modern culture and technology. This concern had been implicit throughout the federal government's control over Indian educational policy, but with the Merriam reform efforts, they began to apply pressure for a different policy approach to these issues. The report concluded that it was important, in light of the most modern anthropological and social science research, that the Indian be allowed to retain his or her cultural wisdom (or, at least that a benevolent policy of noninterference be instituted). While the Indian school was not directed to teach Indian culture, it was also directed not to interfere with tribal lifeways. Through the influence of the anthropologist and the new cultural sciences, antitribal, pro-Anglo indoctrination in the schools began, in principle, if not always in practice. Indian culture became a value heretofore unrecognized by federal governance administration. No one had more to do with the beginning of this subtle shift in attitude than John Collier.

Karier's critical history shows how important it is to look at the "ideas" that shaped the work of an influential policymaker. Therefore, it is important to sketch a clear outline of Collier's intellectual thinking as it developed over his lifetime. More than any other figure, Collier evolved from a more traditional reformer's stance on several key issues in regard to Indian welfare and land policy, to become the main architect of a new age in federal government—Indian affairs. As a young social worker in New York, Collier was one of the early reform-minded intelligentsia who reflected a concern with the maintenance of indigenous culture. Collier's pluralism, however, was a carefully managed one. Lawrence Kelly's research has emphasized the modern managerial liberalism that became the signature of Collier's work. As social reformer and future Commissioner of Indian Affairs, Collier would influence the development of twentieth-century Native American social and educational policy more than any other individual in American governmental life.

During my studies in the Department of Educational Policy Studies at the University of Illinois, Urbana-Champaign, I was encouraged to take seriously the antidemocratic impulse of social meliorism, which typically was ignored by scholars blinded by the liberal humanitarianism of progressive reform. Thereafter, I was drawn deeply into Lawrence Kelly's depiction of Collier's efforts to regulate the growing film industry. Kelly analyzed Collier's belief in the social impact of the new and growing film industry and the necessity to control it for social betterment. I was encouraged to go beyond a superficial analysis of this effort. It was a beginning for my ongoing efforts to get at the root of the ideological underpinnings of Native American educational policies that has since taken me so far afield. Through the People's Institute, Collier established a number of social centers, which unlike the school social centers, were independent of public school control. Collier believed that the work of the public school, while important, had been sacrificed to important ethical and civic virtues to the greater good of the community. The social centers would replace what the secularized public school had left out—citizenship, ethics, social good will, play, and aesthetics.[7]

For Collier, motion pictures would be an essential component in the "curriculum" of the social center. Yet, like the centers themselves, the character of these films would be strictly controlled. Between 1908 and 1914, Collier was active in the first organized effort to censor motion pictures, and began as a "roving critic" in his capacity of Civic Secretary to the People's Institute. In 1909, a Collier report submitted to the Institute's Board of Directors called for a film regulation board to preview all films shown in the New York City area. Upon this recommendation, Charles Sprague Smith, the People's Institute director, established the National Board of Censorship of Motion Pictures, and named Collier General-Secretary. Characteristically, Collier saw censorship in the soft light of social amelioration, that is, as "assisting" film producers in the gradual moral and artistic improvement of films. Throughout, Collier's social judgment was tempered by an aesthetic appeal to social and cultural harmony.

"Socialized" amusement is wedded here to a philosophy where art and culture retain great power to rehabilitate and harmonize social life. The Indian Defense Association formulated the major goals that became keystones of later social policy. Just as the Christian reforms of the 1880s and 1890s culminated in the Dawes Allotment Act, the new reforms were associated with 'the Bursum issue" (i.e., a beginning struggle for the repeal of land allotment). As the earlier reforms had sought to Americanize the Indian through land, social, and educational changes, the new reforms attempted to revitalize traditional tribal community ideals.

The Indian Defense Association articulated a variety of policies to rejuvenate Indian culture, traditional manufacture, and tribal ownership of land. These newer goals were reflective of the progressive thought that John Collier would later formulate for the Indian Bureau. The idea of tribal solidarity that Collier developed was consistent with his emphasis on reform managerialism and social melioration, and was developed against a template of "the idealized community" in much the same way Collier had built immigrant community solidarity in New York. He favored an image of orderly community, exhibiting high social and religious cohesion. Tribal autonomy developed this same kind of aesthetic and ethical conservation, fortifying his belief in the power of indigenous culture to reform the dominant white culture.

During the years that Collier worked with the Indian Defense Association there was little evidence of any great change in Bureau policy toward Indian tribal solidarity. The Bureau reported in 1925 that the future well-being of the Indian people lay in their ability to adapt; Native people would absorb European civilization with school or without it.[8] As late as 1932, one year before Collier's appointment to the Office of Commissioner of Indian Affairs, the Secretary of the Interior announced his aim to terminate the relationship between Indian people and the federal government. The Interior Department leadership must have felt fierce economic pressure, both from the financial burden of Indian social welfare and educational programs, as well as from its knowledge of the great (and, as-yet unexploited) natural resources embedded within Indian land holdings and reservations.

Collier continued to implement his new social programs, increasingly turning his attention to the development of Indian cultural rebirth. During these early years of Collier's term, the land battles never ceased, but Collier still found time to keep alive his push for Indian cultural rebirth. For example, in 1935 the Indian Arts and Crafts Board was founded as a way to develop indigenous cottage industries and create price controls and label protections for the Indian artist. Here, Collier's aestheticism was consistent with a renaissance in artistic sensibility which had developed and been nurtured in the Southwest since the first

World War. Artists such as Robert Henri, and Lewis Aiken, among others, had discovered the beauty of the New Mexico Highlands and the power of Indian art. Some of these artists had also been with Collier as a part of the Mabel Dodge salon in New York City.[9] These New Deal programs were promoted as ones having the potential for increasing the economic independence of the Indian tribes, and the Interior Department reported enthusiastically in regard to the "effectiveness" and "practicality" of such programs as the Indian Arts and Crafts Board.

Just as indigenous art became a means of boosting Indian self-sufficiency, so did the Indian linguistic aesthetic become a new touchstone for the social meliorists. Bilingual-bicultural education programs were proposed as a way to effect a recovery in Indian self-awareness and to increase educational success. Tribal language deterioration was a fact that could not be ignored by Collier's administration. This new tribal language emphasis did not take place as an argument for native cultural and language acquisition, but rather as an argument for more rapid acquisition of English language skills. This educational policy, like land reform, was developed ostensibly so that the Indian could become "bilingual, literate . . . proud of their racial heritage, [and] completely self-supporting."[10]

Many of these progressive cultural programs have been described as part of an enlightened attitude toward Indian culture. Yet, a more careful investigation of their roots reveals that they were institutionalized as part of a more sophisticated program of social engineering, not as ends in themselves. They were accepted into policy because they were offered as both cost-effective and sound methods for rebuilding the morale of Indian people and ushering in a hoped-for future era of cultural rebirth and economic resurgence. The dreams of these new reformers (and, in particular, of Collier) were themselves altered to fit the social planning of the Great Depression-era recovery efforts. They also worked to provide an approach to social reform that would be more compatible with the aesthetic sensibilities of these new liberal reformers (and at least to some of the Indian people).[11]

These progressive reforms, inspired by Collier, carry several strong themes, each of which was expressed in specific social and educational policies. The ethic of efficiency was wedded to a concept of democratic localism that emphasized day school over boarding school arrangements. The day school movement was not only more socially desirable but an efficient mechanism in creating a more carefully managed model of acculturation than the earlier, more radically assimilationist model that preceded it. Social hygiene replaced Calvinist Christian moralism. A new model of tribalism, highlighted by its ethos of cultural and religious toleration, replaced rapid cultural assimilation and more dogmatic concepts of religious suppression. The harsh, punitive character of the boarding school was replaced in theory and limited practice by the softer, Deweyan, child-centered curriculum and living arrangements of the day school. Harsh Social Darwinism gave way to Lester Frank Ward's vision of planned social change. This new reform model was characterized by combining elements of the older managerial liberalism with a newer, more romanticized aesthetic; unfortunately, this did not result in any increased tribal control or political hegemony by indigenous peoples. The mere fact that this new reform ethos became fashionable as a part of a "new tyranny in aesthetic sensibilities," rather than as a result of any real advances in treaty negotiations or resource or land reclamation, is a reminder not of the weakness of tribal cultural forms, but of the misplaced faith that many had (including many indigenous peoples themselves) in the power of these new aesthetic sensibilities. Like Collier, many believed that a return to these primitive aesthetic forms could provide the basis for a renewed indigenous sovereignty and more legitimate democratic models of self-determination.

Collier's genius was to transform "the Indian problem" from a civic sore to a vision of tribal life as an aesthetic resource. Certainly this is not an inconsiderable accomplishment. Yet by grounding these rights so exclusively in "a language of aesthetic sensibilities," concepts of Native American sovereignty and resource management were also enmeshed in the same aesthetic yearning for a futuristic world, largely romantic and rather Volkish in its conceptualization. As a result, leaders in Native American communities who have tried to strengthen tribal sovereignty, have been forced, as no other Americans, to articulate the moral, ethical, and legal arguments with a discourse premised upon and embedded in arguments largely governed by more aesthetic concerns.[12]

Conclusion

The process of writing and defending this line of reasoning gave me a hint of the fortitude it takes to defend critical history to liberal audiences. I remember two times especially well: one, at the beginning of my work on this project, and the second, near the end when the manuscript was at the publisher. First, I remember giving a presentation of my research, which implicated the venerable Collier within the intellectual traditions of a generation of educational policies whose community and democratic legacies I argued were ambiguous at best, and subtly hegemonic at worst. I was in Moorhead, Minnesota, a broke graduate student, staying at the Coleman hotel (my two-person tent). After giving my paper, an audience member bluntly challenged me. She said, "How dare you criticize John Collier in that way! Without Collier, you wouldn't be standing here talking about Indian education. In fact, this whole conference (she motioned to the room, referring to the assembled academics, here talking about multicultural Indian education) wouldn't be here, either!" I've never been too smooth in these kinds of situations, and I remember saying something like, "So what! . . . none of us would be here if it wasn't for Columbus either!" While I got a big laugh, I remember the guy who wanted to talk to me about a job in North Dakota . . . he never showed up in the lobby that night. That was one thing about Clarence that never rubbed off on me. He always had a soft-spoken dignity and was very difficult to ruffle.

Clarence once referred to me as a "March Hare," and I remember being grateful that he put up with me, despite the big differences in our styles. Through Clarence and the Department of Educational Policy Studies he crafted, I have always felt like I had a home, even when in hostile territory many years later. This has stood me in good stead, including while in my present job at Northern Arizona University. Many of the issues I deal with confront the realities of Native American life in the Southwest. It was a lot easier to pontificate about this during my eleven years at Northern Illinois University. The audiences can be a lot tougher out here, both Native and non-Native. During a guest lecture here, I got criticism for "bashing the public education which this university stands for" and for "only presenting a dry outline of the failings" of Navajo education. This can be unnerving for a committed scholar and social activist that I consider myself to be. A rereading of Clarence's published works on issues of academic freedom in American institutions of higher education during these periods of personal crisis have always given me a sense of balance and purpose in my life, as I sensed his own anguish and unsolved moral dilemmas. When the book which developed from this line of thought was under review, I remember receiving a scathing critique from Vine Deloria, the Lakota legal scholar and writer. The support I received from the house that Clarence built helped me weather a virtual rewrite, which made the final manuscript much stronger.

Along with the sense of dignity and purpose that characterized Clarence and his "shop," there was a sense of compassion and warmth, which helped confirm the sincerity of the work that went on there. Despite the numerous demands on his time, and many students working directly under his supervision, as the years went by, on the rare occasions I got to visit, he always would remember my family, and to ask about my daughter's health. It was that sort of concern that impressed me about Clarence. It's the sort of thing that is of a single piece in his character—this basic human concern that is the underpinning of all our human values and responsibilities. He held to that standard where I was concerned and where "the ideas" were concerned. I'm sort of a September Hare now . . . and a thankful one at that! As I work here in Northern Arizona, along with my friend and colleague Mark Sorensen, with all its challenges, he and I both still have energy to spare, and we credit a lot of that to the influence that Professor Karier continues to have on our lives. He and the department he built taught us the value of the honest democratic critic and the endurance required of the critical gadfly. Thanks Clarence!

10

The Preparation of School Practitioners: Social Foundations of Education, Critical History of Education, and Educational Change

Steve Tozer

Clarence Karier's most evident legacy, as this volume makes clear, is his contribution to the scholarship of history of education. Less obvious, but also evident in a volume edited and written by his students, is Karier's role as an educator—not only of doctoral students who would become historians, but of school teachers and administrators. He does not write history simply for other historians, but for purposes of making a difference in educational practice. His work has distinct pedagogical purposes, and, as a university professor in a college of education, he situated his scholarship in institutional settings preparing professionals for the field of education.

Karier's first book was a textbook, rooted in his teaching at the University of Rochester and intended to reach audiences of teachers and administrators as well as teacher and administrator candidates throughout the nation via publication with Scott Foresman, a leading textbook publisher. Karier believed that students should read primary sources, but he also saw the pedagogical need for textbooks.

> With the increased availability of excellent primary sources in paperbacks, it is apparent that one could teach the history of American education through the use of primary sources alone. Yet students often

seem to need a model which gives some sense of continuity and perspective without presuming to tell the whole story. In this sense, *Man, Society, and Education* was conceived as a stimulant for further reading in the primary sources in history of education.[1]

This belief that textbooks were an important vehicle for scholarship was sustained throughout Karier's academic career, from *Man, Society, and Education* in 1967, to *Roots of Crisis* with Paul Violas and Joel Spring in 1973, to *Shaping the American Educational State* in 1975, to the 1986 revision of his first book, retitled *The Individual, Society, and Education*.[2]

Even the early *Man, Society, and Education*, while less critical of the dominant ideology than Karier's later scholarship, can be described as a critical inquiry into historical relations between schools and their social contexts. This approach aligned Karier with a tradition of social foundations of education that had been instrumental in shaping the department that he joined at the University of Illinois at Urbana-Champaign in 1969, and with which he was intimately familiar.

That social foundations tradition, self-consciously developed at Teachers College Columbia in the 1930s, was committed to a critical, cross-disciplinary analysis of the relations between schools and their social contexts.[3] Kenneth Benne, R. Freeman Butts, and Harold Rugg, three of the cofounders of the social foundations curriculum at Teachers College, have each written separate accounts of the faculty study group from various different "foundational disciplines" that met for over a decade to discuss how the relationships between schools, education, and the wider culture should be taught to educators. For example, Benne wrote:

> They came to believe that all teachers should become students of the issues of contemporary society and culture and of the relations of these issues to questions of educational aims, methods, and programs. They also believed that a cross-disciplinary approach was conducive to adequate treatment of these issues. In keeping with this thinking, they brought the psychological, sociological, economic, historical, and philosophical perspectives together into a division of educational foundations.[4]

Social Foundations in Historical Perspective

Before the 1930s, if teacher and administrator candidates took foundations courses, they tended to be of two kinds. One was single-discipline coursework such as philosophy of education, history of education, or sociology of education. Scholars like R. M. MacIver in sociology, Elwood Cubberly in history, and W.H. Kilpatrick in philosophy used the lenses of the social sciences and humanities to study and teach about education in cultural context. The other kind of foundations course at the turn of the century used a different meaning of foundations: more akin to "fundamentals" or "basics." Thus, New Jersey State Normal School Professor Levi Seeley's 1901 text, *The Foundations of Education*, was really more an introduction to teaching practice than an effort to use foundational disciplines to study school and society.[5]

In the 1930s, however, George S. Counts published *The Social Foundations of Education*, which focused not on teaching or schools at all, but on the cultural context in which education in the United States takes place. During this same period the previously mentioned multidisciplinary group of faculty at Teachers College Columbia began meeting regularly to devise a two-semester curriculum, culminating in *Readings in the Foundations of Education* (1941).[6] These two efforts shared a common approach to foundational study in professional preparation: they sought to provide a critical, cross-disciplinary study of education, including schooling, as a cultural process grounded in the social institutions, processes, and ideals that characterize particular cultures. The metaphor "foundations," then, was not intended by Counts, Rugg, and others to represent the "fundamentals" of education or the "bedrock" component of teacher preparation programs, but rather it was conceived as one of the two fundamental bases of all teaching and learning. One of these two bases was the human learning organism, and the other was the cultural and organizational context in which any human organism must always reside. The first base, then, emerged in professional study as the psychological foundations of education, and the second as the cultural or social foundations of education.[7] It was this critical, cross-disciplinary view of social foundations of education, not the "introduction to teaching" approach, nor the single-discipline study of history or philosophy of education, that marked the development of the field from the 1940s onward—and that led to the founding of the American Educational Studies Association (AESA) in the 1960s and the Council of Learned Societies in Education (CLSE) in the 1970s. These social foundations (clearly not psychological foundations) organizations had by 1978 published the *Standards* for the nature and quality of social foundations study in professional preparation programs.[8] Today, CLSE is the official voice of other foundational organizations (e.g., History of Education Society, Philosophy of Education Society, AESA) in the governing structure of the National Council for Accreditation of Teacher Education (NCATE). That is, what began as a distinctly *pedagogical* scholarly enterprise at Teachers College, Columbia, the founding of a social foundations division and social foundations curriculum for the preparation of teachers and administrators, has developed over the last seventy years into new organizational forms to sustain the original pedagogical and professional vision developed by Counts, Kilpatrick, Benne, Rugg, Butts, and others.

The CLSE *Standards*, like the Foundations Division at Teachers College in the 1930s, present an explicit rationale for the role of social foundations of education in the professional preparation of educators: that social foundations uses the lenses of the social sciences and humanities to help teacher candidates develop "interpretive, normative, and critical perspectives on education" and that such perspectives are important to interpreting educational practice in both cultural and organizational contexts.[9] The knowledge, skills, and dispositions indicated in the standards are explicitly intended to help teachers develop the sociocultural understandings, critical skills, and habits of mind to interpret and evaluate educational aims, practices, and problems in their institutional and cultural contexts.

On the one hand, Karier's work was, disciplinarily, history of education; however, it extended that tradition in its critical, cross-disciplinary treatment of intellectual history, ideology, psychological history, and political-economic history as the social contexts of education and schools. In these ways, and in its explicitly critical, pedagogical approach, his scholarship stood squarely in the social foundations tradition developed at Teachers College and transplanted to University of Illinois by Benne, Archibald Anderson, William O. Stanley, and others who preceded Karier there. But Karier deepened and extended that critical tradition by engaging in ideology critique that was nondogmatically attentive to economic sources of cultural and educational change. By 1967 he had developed a three-part analytic and pedagogical framework that emphasized a construct of ideology that was more Mannheimian shared belief and values than Marxian false consciousness, but applied in new ways to the understanding of education in cultural context:

> A student of history of education invariably finds that his inquiry takes him through at least a three-dimensional view of education. First, he is concerned with the major ideas and values which seem to predominate in any given period; second, he is concerned with the material conditions of life which seem to influence educational practice as well as ideology [defined by Karier in a footnote as that system of ideas and values by which men profess to live]; and third, he is concerned with actual practices in both formal and informal education of the young . . ..
> . . . the major emphasis of this book [*Man, Society, and Education*], then, is on ideology, which is used here as only one factor in a possible constellation of factors at work in any process of educational change. . . . While a strong case can be made for economic determinism in American formal educational institutions, the thesis breaks down when applied to individuals. The ideology one holds seems related to personality, and personality undoubtedly is markedly affected by child-rearing practices, which, in turn, seem as much related to ideological factors as to economic forces. Any single determinant can render only partial truth and partial insight.[10]

From Social Foundations to Cultural Studies of Education

It was later, particularly in *Roots of Crisis*, that Karier began to find the most critical potential of ideology critique. In so doing, he began to create a bridge between a relatively moribund textbook literature in social foundations of education, which had become significantly diluted and deranged during the postwar McCarthy years, and an American version of the field of cultural studies that had begun to emerge in England in the mid-1960s.[11] Cultural studies in education had not yet developed as a distinct tradition in scholarship in England or the United States at this time, and there is no need to try to gauge Karier's contribution to the emergence of that field in the 1980s and 1990s. However, his sharp ideology-critique, his attention to the interactions of politics, economics, cultural values and practices, power, media, and education, all prefigured prominent components of cultural studies in education. At the very least, Karier contributed groundwork for the field of cultural studies in education with a critical vocabulary that would be found in the work of others who would follow with ideas of education as "contested terrain" and a site of cultural conflict. Karier wrote in 1967:

> Sometimes the major ideas of a particular period have reached such a consensus that the answers to the questions about human nature and society are merely assumed, or taken for granted. At other times, when a current ideology is threatened, conflicting answers to these questions can usually be found behind the dust and smoke of battle. Indeed, when education becomes a battleground, it often does so for reasons far deeper than the usual problem of determining the most efficient method of educating children. . . . From one perspective, the ideology of one period can be viewed as a reaction to another; but from another perspective, the same ideology may be viewed as a consequence of economic and social conditions.[12]

In "Liberal Ideology and the Quest for Orderly Change," for example, or in "Testing for Order and Control in the Corporate Liberal State," Karier showed how modern liberalism, while rooted in a democratic history, provided an ideological justification for those in power to protect their positions of privilege through antidemocratic and racist means—including use of the schools to do so.[13]

Like the founding authors of social foundations of education before him and the cultural studies authors who would come later, Karier took the notion of culture seriously, analyzing it from a consistently critical perspective that foregrounded relations of power in contemporary life.[14] Admittedly, cultural studies, or cultural studies in education, are difficult to define. Tony Bennett describes it "largely as a term of convenience for a fairly dispersed array of theoretical and political positions which, however widely divergent they might be in other respects, share a commitment to examining cultural practices from the point of view of their intrication (sic) with, and within, relations of power."[15] Karier's concern for relations of domination and subordination in contemporary capitalist culture provided a focus for whatever aspect of that culture he focused on, often prefiguring the concerns of later cultural studies scholars. For example, even today, the concept of "youth culture" is underexamined in the cultural studies literature. In "Business Values and the Educational State," Karier situated youth culture in the larger capitalist order, writing, "Youth culture, with its unique psychology, sociology, economic needs, and tastes, is largely a by-product of the social conditions used to delay entrance into adult life."[16] Similar insights recur, and are still being worked out in, the cultural studies literature today.[17]

A Postmodern Lesson for Students: Interpretation and Validity

Cultural studies, in its attention to the interpretation of text, its rejection of grand narratives, and its concern for power relations in the constitution of knowledge, is closely aligned with the emergence of postmodern scholarship.[18] Karier's critical approach to history of education went beyond pragmatist antifoundationalism to a postmodern critique of the power inherent in pragmatism—while at the same time admitting the interpretive, constructed, and incomplete nature of his own historical narrative. "History is not the story of man's past," he wrote, "but rather that which certain men have come to think of as their past. One may read a particular interpretation of a historic period but never *the* history of that period."[19] While pragmatism, too, could accommodate such a provisionalist approach, Karier distanced himself from pragmatism's failure to challenge prevailing power relations. "If we had critically analyzed pragmatic liberal thought within the context of the corporate state," he wrote, "we might have understood the fascist flirtation as a logical and reasonable outcome of certain characteristics of liberal thought."[20]

Karier's textbooks stand as early examples of postmodernism in questioning the enlightenment faith in reason while at the same time relying on reason as the vehicle through which his readers, the majority of whom would be teachers and administrators, might come to recognize and resist the antihuman dimensions of contemporary education. Karier wrestles with the constructed nature of educational history and yet his belief in its validity in the Preface to *Shaping the American Educational State*:

> History is an imaginative art in which pictures of the past are painted in the contemporary world by the historian out of artifacts of the past. Much of what the historian creates, including chronology itself, is a consciously developed illusion. . . . History, however, is more than pure fiction and illusion. A picture of the past leaves the world of fictional writers when the historian insists on documentary evidence to establish the validity of his story. Here, context, documentation and fair use of documents are important criteria for establishing the validity of his particular view of the past. . . . Historical analysis, thus, involves both addressing the important problems of the present and past in such a way that the story of the past is functionally useful in understanding those problems, and the process of critically establishing the validity of the interpretation through documentary evidence. Historical writing must ultimately pass the test not only of social usefulness, but also of empirical credibility. Neither test, however, leads to certitude with respect to historical judgments.[21]

Karier intends to let the student know that historical interpretation is not unassailably true, but that it may be more or less valid methodologically—a view that is, paradoxically, closer to Dewey's "warranted assertability" than to a postmodern valuing of multiple, conflicting narratives. It is this methodological "validity" that Karier believes will make plausible a critique like the following:

> The author writes from a perspective of the present which holds that American society is not structured to enhance the dignity of man but unfortunately, is structured to foster a dehumanizing quest for status, power, and wealth. We live, I believe, in a fundamentally racist, materialistic society which, through a process of rewards and punishments, cultivates the quest for status, power and wealth in such a way as to use people and institutions effectively to protect vested interests.[22]

Lest that perspective seem too relentlessly pessimistic for students seeking to bring about change through their chosen profession, Karier tempers this somewhat in "Business Values and the Educational State":

> So we have both dilemma and promise in the present age. American Society may yet move from the materialistic spirit of capitalism to a transformation of values. There might be the time and the possibility in the affluent cybernated age of the future to usher in a human age that will enhance the dignity of man.[23]

Language of Critique, Practice of Possibility

Although that passage begins to suggest a language of possibility in Karier's work—a pointing to ways to bring about change in an unjust situation—there are precious few hopeful notes in his textbooks. Karier's is not a scholarship of paralysis or pessimism, however. He conducted his scholarship of critique not so much with a *language* of possibility, but embedded in a *practice* of possibility. As an author, he wrote extensively for a practitioner audience. As a teacher, he consistently taught in professional preparation and development programs for teachers and administrators throughout his career. As an administrator of a social foundations department at Illinois for a total of over twenty years, he doggedly protected the curricular space for social foundations in all degree programs at all undergraduate and graduate levels throughout the college of education. He was known, further, for allocating unusual resources—a large cadre of hand-picked doctoral students, high-incentive salaries to professors—to the required social foundations course for undergraduates that engaged them in critical examination of school and society. He maintained the largest faculty of philosophers and historians of education in the country while increasing the number of sociologists of education, engaging all of them in the teaching of practitioners as well as aspiring researchers. He made these pedagogical commitments as if they mattered; as if he believed that teachers and administrators who understood the critical history that Karier and his colleagues generated would be likely to practice differently than if they did not understand it.

This commitment to social and educational critique in professional programs are about as close to a theory of social and educational change as one might glean from observing Karier's practice of possibility. Sure, doctoral students who came under Karier's influence went on to write textbooks of their own for practitioners (a number of those students are contributing to this volume). But how would all of this amount to any kind of practical challenge to the racist, dehumanizing system Karier documented? On the one hand, he leaned sometimes toward a kind of economic determinism that would hold out little promise for mere professors having much effect at all:

> The moral demand system premised on scarcity cannot survive in an affluent age. To whatever extent capitalist economics demands a value system premised on scarcity, one is forced to conclude, paradoxically, that the success of capitalism will be responsible for its demise. The possibility of such a demise represents the real danger as well as the promise for the last third of this century—danger, because out of fear or panic those in power may erect a repressive regime against those who threaten the security of those holding the traditional value system; promise, because of the possibility of developing an economic and social system that enhances something other than men's materialistic competitiveness. [24]

On the other hand, economic determinism does not explain Karier's career-long commitment to engaging school practitioners in the study of critical history of education, which can't readily be understood apart from an account that links their understanding to potentially changed practice. Karier was not explicit, however, about any kind of change theory with respect to how historical critique can be linked to educational change. Taken together with his concern that those in power cannot be trusted to bring about meaningful change, as will soon be addressed, this lacuna represents a potential problem in Karier's pedagogy—one that will also be addressed in the next section.

Critical History, Educational Problems, and Educational Change

Karier did not pursue history of education simply for the sake of doing history of education. He quoted Hayden White: "The contemporary historian has to establish the value of the study of the past, not as 'an end in itself' but as a way of providing perspective on the present that contributes to the solution of problems peculiar to our own times."[25] What Karier took to be the problems that were peculiar to the present was made clear in the introduction to *Roots of Crisis*:

> If one starts with the assumption that this society is in fact racist, fundamentally materialistic, and institutionally structured to protect vested interests, the past takes on vastly different meanings.[26]

These were the problems that Karier took to be "peculiar to the present," that needed solutions, and about which he taught his students in his textbooks and his classes. Thus far, therefore, I have situated his critical scholarship in history of education loosely in the context of three academic traditions in education. I have done so in part because his work shares something with each of these traditions, in part because his work has contributed to each, and finally because limitations in these traditions alert us to potential limitations in Karier's work as well. I will also argue that his cultural critique provides valuable perspectives on those limitations and offers possible ways of interpreting our contemporary educational situation.

Karier's work shares much with social foundations of education because, in part, history of education is one of the primary disciplinary lenses with which social foundations scholarship is conducted. Additionally, like the avowedly pedagogical intent of the original social foundations scholars, Karier's work was an effort to have an impact on school teachers and school leaders. I have mentioned cultural studies because Karier's work prefigured the literature in cultural studies in education that began to take seriously the critical study of cultural contexts of educational practices. I find it interesting also to examine Karier's work loosely in the context of postmodern scholarship that displays a tension between a suspicion of master narratives, including a master narrative of scientific reason and, on the other hand, the extensive use of reasoned argument and evidence to establish its critique of the cultural power that is served by established narratives of science and reason. In addition to these commonalties, Karier's work shares something else in common with these traditions: a more sustained commitment to academic scholarship than to an explicit agenda for educational or social change. Of the three interrelated traditions—and there is a sense, as Patti Lather has pointed out, in which postmodernism is not a tradition but a disruption of tradition[27]—only social foundations of education has had an explicit agenda for change through educational practitioners. The term "educational statesmen" was used by the founders of social foundations at Teachers College, Columbia, to articulate how practitioners could become intelligent about educational policies affecting them, and in turn seek to change policy and practice to accord with democratic ideals.[28] They believed that critical cross-disciplinary analysis of social contexts of education would equip practitioners with the understanding necessary to foster change agency.

> This means that the educator fails in his line of duty if he refuses to look beyond the walls of academy and laboratory, reject the irresponsible role of disinterested spectator, make ethical and aesthetic choices, and operate under the guidance of some recognized conception of social welfare and policy. . . . The task of utilizing the findings of research is the responsibility of men of action.[29]

It is fair to say, however, that the social foundations tradition in scholarship has more effectively reflected its social sciences and humanities roots than it has reflected anything like a recognizable agenda for institutional change in schools in the United States. In fact, the division of labors reflected in the passage above is a convenient one for those who would prefer to do the high-status and relatively easier work of institutional critique than engage in the lower-status, more difficult work of engaging in institutional change. Scholars in social foundations tend, like Karier, to become committed to the scholarship of their field—history of education, philosophy of education, gender studies in education, or cultural studies in education—in ways that are at their best a search for truth but that most often do not reflect an engagement in institutional change practices—other than the effects that their scholarship may have on school practitioners such as teachers and administrators. That their scholarship may have such an effect is more clearly a hope than a well-developed account of how practitioners' insights gained through coursework translate into institutional change.

Not only has Karier's work been most notable for its commitment first and foremost to academic scholarship, but Karier is explicit about the dangers of intellectuals trying to bring about educational reform. Karier argued that professors doing "applied science" are in a role that is "hardly neutral." This is interesting because Karier clearly was committed to scholarship as a dispassionate endeavor—that scholarship should be a search for truth, within the limitations of a discipline's ability to construct valid interpretations.

> Traditionally the role of the intellectual, or at least his self-image, has been that of a dispassionate critic. Insofar as that role has been lost, the relation of the schools to intellectuals should, in fact, be one of self-defense.[30]

Karier recognized that for academics to work toward educational change most often meant having to work with those in power and thus risk becoming "servants of power [who] fail to question" the power that they serve.[31]

On the other hand, Karier did not believe, as his pedagogical practice makes clear, that his history of education scholarship should not be relevant to the problems of education—that it should make no difference. As his use of Hayden White indicates, for Karier, history would help us understand our present problems, and this is where his implicit change theory becomes most evident. The role of the historian is to "get it right" so that practitioners could resist oppression with the best available understanding of the nature of power and how it has operated to benefit some at the expense of others in educational institutions in the United States.

Whether that is enough of a change agenda to genuinely matter in practice leads one to question whether there is an important disjuncture between Karier's concern to start with the educational problems of the present and his demonstrated belief that it is important for school practitioners to understand those problems so they could act in accord with that understanding.

One can argue that it was enough for Karier to do the scholarship, to get the story right, to shed the historical light of understanding on contemporary relations of domination and subordination and the agency of teachers and principals in their institutional relationships. And this is especially so when one recognizes that a good number of his students also went on to write textbooks, reaching still more practitioners in schools with a scholarship of critique. Yet, given that such a historical critique has now been prominent for 35 years, it raises the question of how we are to interpret the current movement in educational reform. Does Karier's scholarship help us understand this movement; and how does this movement contribute to our understanding of the value of Karier's work?

The Contemporary, Standards-based Movement in Teacher Quality

In asking these questions, it is useful to focus on one particular component of the current school reform movement—one that might be described as the teacher quality component. The *current* attention to teacher quality as an essential ingredient in school reform originated in the mid-1980's reports by the Carnegie Foundation and the Holmes Group. These foundation-funded manifestos focused on high standards for the preparation, certification, and development of teachers as one route to educational reform. Since that time, a great deal of activity has taken place nationwide, involving all fifty states and a number of national agencies, with respect to the establishment of teaching standards. This activity includes the National Board for Professional Teaching Standards (NBPTS), which Carnegie called for in 1985; the involvement of every state in the national board certification efforts; the efforts of state boards of education and state legislatures to adopt professional teaching standards and assessments of teachers that would establish clear expectations for what professionals know and are able to do in their teaching practice. Moreover, four interlocking national organizations have been working closely on this agenda for several years: (1) the National Council for Accreditation of Teacher Education (NCATE), which focuses on standards and assessments for the preparation of teachers; (2) the Interstate New Teacher Assessment and Support Consortium (INTASC), which focuses on early career teacher standards and assessments; (3) NBPTS, which focuses on standards and assessments of experienced teachers; (4) and finally, the National Commission on Teaching and America's Future, which published an influential report in 1996, *What Matters Most: Teaching for America's Future*, which looks at the entire professional continuum of teaching in terms of standards and assessments, arguing that the improvement of teaching is essential to the improvement of student learning in schools.[32]

A number of dimensions of this movement ring familiar to anyone acquainted with Karier's critiques of educational reform in the United States. One prominent feature is the role of philanthropic foundations in this effort. For example, the National Commission on Teaching and America's Future, which works closely with NCATE, INTASC, and NBPTS, has been funded by the Rockefeller, Ford, Carnegie, and DeWitt Wallace Foundations. Karier long ago alerted us to the extent to which philanthropic foundations tend to serve the interests of power. He wrote:

> The fourth branch of government born in the progressive era and representing liberal corporate interest—that is, the foundations—has flexibly and effectively served to maintain the interests of corporate wealth through the support and maintenance of the liberal state. . . . Foundation trustees and executives were intelligent men who recognized their own interests in what they viewed as a progressively developing society. . . . Whether it was Terman calling for special education for the gifted, or Conant calling for "national educational assessment," or ETS striving to develop, in the name of "accountability," performance-based teacher tests, all served as part of a broader efficiency movement to classify, standardize, and rationalize human beings to serve the productive interests of a society essentially controlled by wealth, privilege, and status.[33]

Within that remark, we see the issues of assessment and accountability, as well as performance-based teacher assessments, all as objects of Karier's critique. We recognize that these are significant elements in the current teacher quality initiative. Secondly, it is important to recognize that university faculty play important roles in this reform agenda. Whether on the National Board, NCATE, or National Commission, university professors play prominent roles in policy formation and implementation. Karier cautioned us about the extent to which university scholars could participate in educational reform movements without ultimately serving the ideology of the privileged. He wrote:

> Under the guise of a meritocratic system, the "professional" experts served to stabilize and rationalize a class system based on privilege, status and economic power. These experts . . . invariably worked as servants of power within the educational state. . . . Was it possible to serve truth and power without a conflict of interest or were there times when as a moral person the expert as advisor to those who wield power would be required to choose the hemlock? This was the dilemma of the university professor in the educational state.[34]

Given these familiar notes that are being struck in the current teacher quality movement, it is important to ask whether this philanthropic foundation-driven movement toward standardizing and systemizing teaching is any more than what Karier disparaged as having emerged throughout the twentieth century. In today's period of progressive reform of teaching through changing state certification requirements and new state level standards and assessments, Karier's remarks hold special significance:

> The major impetus of progressive reform, whether political or educational, was to make the system work efficiently and effectively, and progressives would use the compulsory power of the state to achieve that end. Progressive reform, was, without question, conservative.[35]

This ought to be of special concern to those of us who participate in the many different arenas in which these efforts are supported; either by working toward NCATE accreditation in our own institutions, working with teachers on national board certification, or working at the state level to try to establish teacher assessments that are more rigorous. In these activities, are we also participating in what Karier called, "the defanging of the American professor"?[36] This perspective, in fact, is suggested by Lanny Beyer's concern that the various national teacher standards initiatives and the teacher assessment movement have ushered in a "new orthodoxy" in teacher preparation and development.[37]

Alternatively, is there a different perspective one can take on all of this: that the current movement is not reducible to its most conservative tendencies, like the competency-based teacher education movement of the 1970s, but that this current effort is in fact reflective of the success of Karier's critique of power and privilege in contemporary educational thought? On this reading, several features of the dominant ideology that prevailed earlier in the century are discredited. One important example is the rejection of both genetic deficit and cultural deficit theory as explanations for the low achievement levels of low-income and minority students in schools. One premise of the current teacher quality movement is that children in low-income families are limited neither by native ability nor by cultural inferiority, but rather the burden is on the educator to develop the considerable talents of young people, regardless of ethnicity or economic class. One of the prevailing themes of Karier's scholarship—reflected, for example, throughout *Shaping the American Educational State*—was that the failure of children from low-income and minority backgrounds to learn in school should not be attributed to the children themselves but rather to how these children were treated in schools that were not designed for their success. This point of view is reflected throughout the work of the National Commission on Teaching and America's Future.

Conclusion: Making a Difference

These two perspectives on contemporary teacher quality reform—that it is simply more of what Karier warned against versus that it is informed by critical scholarship—represent different views on whether history of education scholarship is ultimately anything more than marginal to contemporary schooling efforts. This difference in interpretation is important because what motivates many people to go into the field of education in the first place is the desire to make a difference in the lives of others. This, I believe, is one of the reasons that Karier engaged in history of education as opposed to some other noneducational history focus. It also helps explain Karier's embracing of Hayden White's view that one doesn't do history simply for its own sake. On the other hand, if the current reform movement constitutes the same kind of justification of the status quo and its relations of oppression that Karier identified as characterizing the reform movements that shaped the American educational state throughout the twentieth century, then it would suggest that critical scholarship of the kind that Karier pursued is actually marginal to the development of educational practice and policy. It suggests that the many thousands of teachers and administrators who have been exposed to Karier's critique over the past 35 years—through his textbooks and through the teaching and textbooks of many professors who once studied with Karier and whose work reflects his critical scholarship—have not yet been enough to create a critical mass of resistance in the face of the concentration of power in the hands of government, business, and philanthropic foundations. Or it suggests that such scholarship could never create such a critical mass.

However, if one sees the contemporary teacher quality movement as illuminated by perspectives such as Karier's, then different interpretations of the role of such scholarship in institutional change may be warranted. It is possible that the "new orthodoxy" in teacher quality reform is not at all like the competency-based teacher education movement of the 1970s, for example, but is instead a much more critically oriented consensus about what is needed for low-income and minority youth to succeed in schools. If this new critically oriented consensus can be characterized as one that rejects genetic-deficit and cultural-deficit theories of school failure, and if it is one that rejects a simple assimilationist view of school success for minority and immigrant children, and if it is one that holds school structures, funding, ideology, and practices accountable for the failure of low-income and minority children, then it is hard to believe that Karier's work has made no contribution to this consensus.

It does seem clear that Karier's critique of power in education and society should be taken into account by any scholar who seeks to make an impact on practice beyond the uncertain practical consequences of academic scholarship itself. It seems fair to say that Karier dedicated his professional life to the search for the truth as he was able to determine it, and to the critical engagement with students who themselves would become school practitioners and academic scholars. He believed that this search should be guided by a disciplined adherence to historical methodology. It was not enough for Karier to achieve "empirical credibility," but "social usefulness" as well.[38] For the scholar who seeks to construct a social reform program grounded in one's academic research, however, Karier's work offers the caution that to work with those in power potentially corrupts the efforts of those who would use that power even for the most democratic of intentions.

Whether one takes the position that the current teacher quality movement is more of the same or is informed by historical critique, the ability to think about that question is informed by Karier's scholarship. It gives us some of the categories with which to think about contemporary educational change and provides warnings to the scholar who makes choices about how best to make a difference. Karier sought to make his difference by conducting scholarship that was socially useful and empirically credible. Whether that constitutes an unsupported optimism about how truth will serve democratic impulses or whether it is simply recognition of the scholar's only moral choices is an important question. We can again return to Karier's remarks: "Was it possible to serve truth and power without a conflict of interest or were there times when as a moral person the expert as advisor to those who wield power would be required to choose the hemlock? This was the dilemma of the university professor in the educational state."[39] It remains a dilemma for professors today who wish to align themselves with the oppressed by working for educational change. Formulating an understanding of how our work can and/or should address the unequal power relations that we identify—in scholarship, in teaching, or in collaborative practice with school practitioners—remains a future challenge for each scholar-practitioner in academia.

11

Democratic Agitations: Transformation of a Critical Historian

James D. Anderson

Historian Clarence J. Karier's distinguished career as a critical voice in American education and democracy is divided into two eras—before and after the publication of his classic study in 1967, *Man, Society, and Education: A History of American Educational Ideas*. The publication of this important book was well received by the academy of historians of American education. Six years later he coauthored with Paul Violas and Joel Spring a book that would forever change his standing within the field of educational history, *Roots of Crisis: American Education in the Twentieth Century*. As *Man, Society, and Education* was received as a thorough and comprehensive treatment of the history of American educational ideas, *Roots of Crisis* was received as a collection of original essays that sparked a heated and intense debate regarding the meaning of education and democracy in twentieth-century America. The sharply different receptions that these two publications received raise an important question. What transformation occurred in Karier's scholarship between 1967 and 1973 that compelled such radically different responses to his history of American education?

The aim of this essay is to examine the transformation in Karier's historical scholarship, both in terms of his own evolution and of the emergence of a wider field of new historiography in American education. Karier's view of the mainstream of American education and the larger field of American educational history changed significantly at the end of the 1960s. Undoubtedly, the new questions that were raised as well as the new approaches to history were influenced by the problems in education and democracy that were exposed by the various movements of the 1960s. The decade generated a critical reading of society and education. Prior to that time the history of American public education was chronicled as the genesis, rise, and triumph of the nation's great democratic institution, one that provided a golden door for the children of immigrants, ethnic minorities, and working-class families to enter the middle class. To be sure, there were elements of truth in this story, but it fell far short of capturing the complexity of educational opportunity over time and it occupied a disproportionate place in the historiography of American education. Although particular histories of American education differed on major issues, taken together the traditional histories of American education were rarely critical of public education or its major champions such as Horace Mann, Henry Barnard, William T. Harris, and John Dewey. Historical criticism was reserved primarily for the enemies of public education. This all changed at the end of the 1960s. Then the public school and its leading champions were examined in a critical mode unprecedented in American history.

Karier played a central role in shaping the new and more critical historiography of American education. This examination of his particular evolution within the general transformation of educational history is only one story within the broader emergence of a new and different historiography of American education. In retrospect, the changes that occurred in Karier's historical scholarship were less a fundamental departure from his earlier analyses than the extension of a particular kind of democratic critique to the full range of American education and democracy. The basic underpinnings of his critical analysis were clearly evident in *Man, Society, and Education*, except for one core dimension; he did not extend it to the liberal center of American social and educational ideas. Indeed, Karier's emergence as a critical historian of American education is marked by an increasing commitment and determination to subject the liberal center of American social and educational thought to the same critical lens that he focused on neo-Enlightenment, elitist humanists; conservative psychologists; fascists; and communists in *Man, Society, and Education*. What is apparent in his first book is a mode of criticism informed by a deep concern for grassroots democracy. Karier's critics were often puzzled as to his own views and the reasoning behind his historical criticisms. Many simply labeled him a "Revisionist," which placed him in an amorphous category of historians with sharply different social theories, methodological approaches, and interpretive frameworks. Others mistakenly assumed that his criticisms flowed from a Marxist framework. A careful reading of his scholarship, however, reveals a pointed and persistent concern with the democratic and antidemocratic assumptions embedded in individual conceptions of human nature, views of the good society, and the role of education in realizing the good society. Thus his critical history is informed mainly by a consciousness of radical individualism, a sense of grassroots democracy predisposed to restructuring foundations of antidemocratic thought and practice. It is democracy with a small "d,"—participatory as opposed to representative democracy—individual autonomy in contradistinction to institutional dominance and control by experts.

In *Man, Society, and Education*, Karier articulated particular conceptions of American educational history that would shape his intellectual interests over the course of his career. His focus on the history of educational ideas marked a preference for intellectual history, and a focus on individual actors and human agency in the process change over time. Although Karier insists that ideas be analyzed within their social context, his analysis focuses primarily on a study of individual social and educational thought as opposed to a study of such structural forces as industrialization, economics, labor markets, or bureaucracy. Within the realm of intellectual history, three interrelated and unresolved problems form the core of his histories of American education and democracy. These interrelated themes are different conceptions of human nature, views of the good society, different criteria and bases for truth, and the implications they all hold for educational thought and practice. Without question, he believes that ideas ultimately have a great impact on social actions. He takes ideas seriously, as things to be treated in their own right, and not as mere reflections of objective social structures. Indeed, inherent in Karier's treatment of educational ideas is the notion that human beings have a considerable amount of freedom to construct their own conceptions of human nature and society and are not mere reflectors of underlying economic and political contradictions. Thus, to Karier, educational conflict in twentieth-century America is not merely a reflection of the contradictions of economic life, but is also contested ideological terrain over the meaning of human nature, social order, truth, and the role of education in shaping imagined societies. Although he concedes that one can make a strong case for economics-based critiques of schooling, ultimately he held that economic theories, as all structural analyses, broke down when applied to individuals. Individual ideologies, he maintains, are related to such factors as personality, religion, psychology, and metaphysics as much as they are related to and informed by economic forces. Although he argues that any single explanation of educational change over time renders only partial truth and partial insight, he is much more focused on the history of individual and ideological difference than with economic and bureaucratic structures. Nonetheless, his emphasis on the history of ideas is not meant as an alternative to the great impact of economic and political forces, but instead as a means to understand and bridge the gulf between structural analyses and human agency.

Although structural explanations define the limits of human agency, inherent in Karier's approach to history is a belief that at any given moment in history, individuals, within the bounds of structural economic and political constraints, face a wide range of choices, however difficult those choices may be. Moreover, he believes that individuals, as well as the choices they make, are as much influenced by ideology or economic consciousness as they are shaped and reshaped by objective social relations. Further, he assumes that individuals should be appraised critically for the choices they make, in spite of the fact that such choices are routinely constrained by structural forces. Historians of the late 1960s and 1970s emphasized the multiplicity of structural forces that shaped twentieth-century social and educational thought, such as economic restructuring, labor and housing markets, urban workplaces, and bureaucratic institutions. In contrast to the emphasis on structural constraints, Karier focused on the critical contributions of powerful individuals and the ways in which they shaped the main currents of social and educational thought. Believing that individual intellectuals make important differences in shaping educational and democratic thought, he takes ideas more seriously than most of his contemporaries and places greater emphasis on individual choice and responsibility. Karier maintains that religion, philosophy, literature, psychology, and metaphysics have a significant impact on the development of key intellectuals and by extension on the shape of twentieth-century American education and democracy.

Most of the aforementioned ideas and conceptions are evident in *Man, Society and Education*. Agreeing with R. Freeman Butts and Lawrence Cremin, he maintains that "the history of education must record the history of ideas as instruments of educational change as well as social conditions that serve to accelerate or thwart educational change."[1] Arguing that much of the discord in twentieth-century American education lay in conflicting concepts of human nature and conflicting bases for truth, the book focuses mainly on different views of human nature, the good society, and education. Though generally critical of conservative humanists, fascists, communists, psychologists, and neo-Enlightenment thinkers, Karier is protective, if not openly praiseworthy, of pragmatic liberals; this is consistent with traditional educational historiography. Contrasting the differences between European nihilism and existentialism, on the one hand, and American pragmatism, on the other, he emphasized the optimism, sense of progress and social meliorism, and the basic rationality of America's "native philosophy."

Initially, Karier was favorably impressed with the scientific, rational, liberal, and democratic character of pragmatism. However, this impression is formed through a view of pragmatic liberals against the conservative and reactionary thought of the nineteenth century. Leading pragmatists such as Charles Sanders Peirce, William James, and John Dewey rejected the metaphysical absolutes, utopias, and ultimate truths that crossed the Atlantic from Europe, and instead developed an American philosophy that stressed progress and the application of rational intelligence to the process of social amelioration. Human nature, according to the pragmatists, was neither bad nor good but largely a product of cultural evolution. The stress, then, was not on inherited characteristics, cultural determinism, or the survival of the fittest, but rather on the social environment that could develop and enhance the most valued human traits. Karier argues that Dewey saw the function of the school as a vehicle for reforming society by producing critical thinkers who as adults would make their own decisions. Further, in Karier's view, Dewey consistently refused to provide a blueprint for the new social order because such direct action on the part of education implied a control and direction of learning in conflict with his conception of free and continuous growth. Agreeing with George Herbert Mead, Karier defined Dewey as "the philosopher of America." Pragmatism varied according to the philosophies of particular individuals, but taken together the various forms of pragmatic liberalism represented a fairly broad picture of the mainstream of twentieth-century American intellectual life. In Karier's view, pragmatism reflected the practical temper of American culture and, therefore, American democracy. Pragmatists advocated the application of science to shape and control change for human progress, conceived of human nature as plastic, and the good society as pluralistic. Unlike the European nihilist who denied any possibility for truth, American pragmatists accepted the tentative nature of truth and assumed enough faith in the reasoned intelligence of humans to shape their destiny significantly.

Although the critical perspective that shapes this analysis is not made explicit in the book, one cannot help but notice the democratic assumptions underlying Karier's critical appraisal of different intellectuals and their conceptions of human nature, the good society and education. And democratic assumptions, one quickly finds, carry much evaluative freight in Karier's critical perspectives on Puritan thought, the Enlightenment, neo-Enlightenment, humanists, pragmatism, conservative psychology, communism, and fascism. These assumptions are most apparent in *Man, Society, and Education* in his critical analysis of psychological conceptions of human nature and the good society.

He reasserts William James' point that the psychological sciences, which are inescapably involved in philosophical and religious assumptions, make inevitable assumptions regarding human nature and the kind of society most fitting for that nature, and, hence, require a critical analysis of their implications for education and democracy. Different psychological conceptions of human nature lead inexorably to very different social and educational implications. In the social thought of G. Stanley Hall, the first American to receive a Ph.D. in psychology, and founder of the American Psychological Association, Karier discovered the religious, philosophical, and social foundations not only of an undemocratic society but also the key elements of fascism. Karier contends that Hall's views on religious mysticism, a collective unconscious, the primitive nature of humans, and the necessity of charismatic leadership to manipulate the instincts of the human herd, ushered in an antidemocratic social philosophy. In point of fact, Karier writes, "Hall, with almost uncanny prophetic vision, blueprinted National Socialism at least a decade before it was realized in Germany."[2] Karier draws a fundamental distinction between the metaphysical assumptions of a conservative like William T. Harris and those of an "extreme conservative or fascist" like G. Stanley Hall. The major difference between the two lies to a considerable extent in Harris's view of humans as reasoning beings and Hall's view of humans as nonreasoning, instinct-driven beings.

Against the backdrop of Hall and other conservatives, Karier emphasizes the constructive influence of John Dewey's work at Chicago and the general reluctance of American social scientists to construct the past as a cosmic determiner of the future. Dewey and Mead, in particular, contributed to the rapid decline of Hall's ideas and influence. Increasingly, American social scientists looked to the cultural environment for an understanding of human behavior rather than to the anthropological past. Nonetheless, Karier cautions that the antidemocratic values of such influential psychologists as Edward L. Thorndike and others were essentially compatible with the elitism of a business-minded, conservative, middle-class America. In Karier's view, business-minded conservatives found much comfort in Thorndike's assertion that science had substantiated the fact that the abler persons in the world in the long run are the more clean, decent, just, and kind. Thorndike's positive correlation of wealth, morality, intelligence, and social power appeased business-minded America and opened up for him a vast influence on the shape of American educational practice during the first half of the twentieth century.

Karier's first book contained an emergent critique of antidemocratic thought in the social ideas of American educators and social scientists, but, on balance, offered a brighter future for democratic thought and practice in the philosophy of John Dewey and the psychology of George Herbert Mead. Although he cautioned that pragmatism was not a system, that it left many loose ends, and that it was expressed in different ways in vastly different areas, he closed the chapter on pragmatic conceptions of the individual and society with an analysis of "the pragmatic consensus." He concluded that Dewey was the main representative of pragmatism and that pragmatism represented the mainstream of American intellectual life in the twentieth century. Still, there was an undercurrent of concern about yet unexplained implications of pragmatism. He underscored Peirce's pragmatic quest for order, James's quest for freedom, and Dewey's quest for unity, but failed to explore the ultimate meaning of order and unity for individual thought and freedom in a democratic society. This critical analysis would come later and represented a significant shift in Karier's perspective on the pragmatic consensus in American social thought. In the long run, changes in the larger society and paradigmatic shifts in educational and intellectual historiography compelled him to question, and ultimately alter, the analysis of pragmatic liberalism that he presented in his first book.

In October of 1970, just three years after the publication of *Man, Society, and Education,* Karier presented a paper before the Midwest History of Education Society's annual meeting in Chicago entitled "The Quest for Orderly Change." Joe Burnett, a philosopher of education who was also a faculty member in the Department of Educational Policy Studies at the University of Illinois at Urbana-Champaign (UIUC), presented the first paper in the session, entitled "Schooling as a Subordinate Institution." In his analysis, Karier argued that John Dewey was the key to understanding the basic ideological structure of twentieth-century American liberalism. Further, he maintained that the ideology of pragmatic liberalism was the key to understanding how the dominant class managed to maintain ideological hegemony over the political economy. Finally, he concluded that if and when the American social order was threatened by a crisis of conflict between the left and right, many liberals could be expected to move to the right rather than to the left of the political spectrum. This interpretation represented the emergence of a whole new area of critical history. In contrast to his analysis in the first book, Karier expanded his critical analysis of American educational ideas to interrogate the role of liberalism in twentieth-century America and held it accountable for much of the educational policy and practice that developed during the first half of the century.

As graduate students at UIUC, we had read and critiqued drafts of both papers prior to their presentation in Chicago. To the graduate students, steeped in the social criticisms of Jonathan Kozol, Ivan Illich, Franz Fanon, Malcolm X, Paul Goodman, Jacques Ellul, Marshall McLuhan, Herbert Marcuse, Alvin Toffler, Charles Reich, Charles Silberman, Eldridge Cleaver, Angela Davis, and James Baldwin, the perspectives of both papers seemed critical, but not particularly radical. Little did we know that Karier's interrogation of the liberal center of American social thought would produce a firestorm. Following the presentation of Karier's paper, we got our first clue as to the critical nature of his emerging perspective on American liberalism. For what seemed to be an inordinate amount of time, no member of the audience asked a question, which was both unusual and unnerving for an audience of historians. Finally, an elderly gentleman arose to make the following comment: "I began teaching 36 years ago and all I had to guide me was John Dewey; he couldn't have been all that bad." This marked the beginning of the kind of response that Karier would frequently receive as he embarked upon a career of analyzing critically the key assumptions of liberal philosophy, which in his view had occupied the center stage of American social and educational reform throughout the twentieth century. As Karier's paper was published (*History of Education Quarterly*, Spring 1972) and republished (*Roots of Crisis*, 1973), it became the centerpiece of a growing debate over the meaning of American education in the twentieth century.[3] That period is remembered for the debate over "Revisionism." More importantly, however, it was the beginning of a new and exciting historiography of American education, one that would change forever our views of education and democracy in the late-nineteenth and twentieth centuries. Karier's transformation was part and parcel of the larger transformation of American educational history.

Several factors account for this particular transformation in Karier's historical scholarship. First, his sense of the past in *Man, Society, and Education* was significantly shaped by the consensus historiography of the 1950s and early 1960s. By 1970, however, the critical historiography of the late 1960s reshaped his views of the American past in general, and the educational past in particular. For example, in *Man, Society, and Education*, most of the suggested readings at the end of the chapter on pragmatic conceptions of man and society were published prior to 1960. The critical history of the 1960s represented a significant paradigmatic shift from the consensus interpretation of earlier decades. Karier was especially influenced by the writings of Robert Paul Wolff (*The Poverty of Liberalism*), Isaiah Berlin (*Four Essays on Liberty*), Gabriel Kolko (*The Triumph of Conservatism*), James Weinstein (*The Corporate Ideal in the Liberal State*), and C. Wright Mills (*Sociology and Pragmatism*).[4] Such historical, sociological, and philosophical studies shifted Karier's interpretations of America's past, especially interpretations of the role of liberal thought and practice in American culture and institutional life.

A second transformation in Karier's scholarship was the shift to a greater reliance on primary sources. By the time he published "Making the World Safe for Democracy: An Historical Critique of John Dewey's Pragmatic Liberal Philosophy in the Warfare State" (*Educational Theory*, Winter 1977), his evidential base was very largely one of primary sources.[5] Indeed, upon reading his scholarship from the late 1960s to the late 1970s one cannot help but be struck by the overwhelming shift to primary sources.

Increasingly, as he relied heavily on primary sources, and in light of the new historiography on American social thought, Karier found that his interpretations of pragmatic liberalism in *Man, Society, and Education* proved inadequate. If, as he consistently claimed, liberal philosophy had occupied the center stage of American social and educational reform, then to what extent was liberalism accountable for many of the nation's shortcomings?

Social problems were all too apparent at the end of the 1960s. The burning cities, collapsing urban schools, widespread poverty, government assaults on privacy and individual rights, the Vietnam War, deeply entrenched racial inequality, sexism, and the assassinations and harassment of radical leaders raised fundamental questions about the democratic nature of liberal thought and practice. In the face of apparent contradictions between liberal philosophy and the structure of social reality, Karier called for a critical analysis of the social implications of liberal philosophy. Hence, the paradigmatic shifts in the new historiography, the increasing reliance on primary sources, and his assessment of his own social context compelled him to ask new questions and to search for new evidence. There was also a fourth transformation in Karier's historical scholarship and this, too, resulted in a more critical reading of the nation's past. In *Man, Society and Education*, Karier interpreted American social and educational thought mainly by juxtaposing the ideas of different individual thinkers. In "The Quest for Orderly Change" and the writings that followed, he critically evaluated Dewey's liberal philosophy in terms of how Dewey applied his thought to practice over time. Karier came to view Dewey as one who changed the meaning of terms like democracy, freedom, and equality, and, therefore, the meaning of such concepts for Dewey could only be understood in terms of the practical consequences of his philosophy. This approach, which began with a critical analysis of Dewey, was extended to the mainstream of American liberal thought as Karier argued that Dewey constructed the operational philosophy for America's liberal center. To be sure, he understood that many liberals did not follow Dewey's philosophy of pragmatism. But he agreed with Edward Shils's assessment that Dewey's liberalism had been assimilated into the modern mainstream of American social sciences. Hence, Karier's critical history of the role John Dewey played in shaping American pragmatism developed into a critical analysis of the basic assumptions of liberal philosophy.

Many historians recoiled at Karier's focus on individual liberal philosophers and particulary his assessment of their political motivations and deliberate intentions as historical actors. This reaction was due in part to the increasing emphasis on social history and the attendant views that intellectual historians placed too much emphasis on the role of ideas in shaping social reality. Consistent with his perspective in *Man, Society, and Education*, Karier insists that the study of individual motivations and intentions was an important part of history and deserving of the same attention as studies of structural forces. To do otherwise, he insisted, is to sever the human actor from purposeful action and from history itself. Karier's own faith in democracy is tied closely to his belief in the dignity of human beings and his conception of human beings as creatures whose lives, however constrained by structural forces, are determined largely by their own free choice. Thus throughout an era characterized by the ascendancy of social history, Karier championed the cause of intellectual history and the belief that ideas and ideology make a real and important difference in intellectual and social life.

His work in this area contributed significantly to closing the gap between structural analyses and the particular role of human agency in shaping educational reforms. Many conceptions of the structural relationship between the economy and educational change were, and are, pitched at the most general level of abstraction. That is to say, they are, at best, conceptions that enable us to grasp and understand the broad processes that organize and structure school reform. As soon as these broad conceptions are applied to specific changes we are required to move from the level of general abstraction (e.g., industrial relations, labor markets, bureaucratic structures) to a more concrete level of application. This shift requires not simply more detailed historical specification but additional concepts and paradigms to guide us from the skeletal frame of structural economic changes to the context of ideology, politics, reform movements, education, and the state. To be sure, social historians are on solid ground when emphasizing the powerful role that the economic foundations of social order play in shaping and structuring the whole edifice of social life, including the broad reform of its educational system. Still, there are important and necessary passageways between structural economic changes in society and the actual social or political forces that become decisive in a particular historical moment. Moreover, structural economic changes, while setting some fundamental limits and conditions for the whole shape of historical development, do not fully determine the content of educational, political, and ideological struggles, much less do they determine the outcome of such struggles.

Karier's study of religion, literature, psychology, metaphysics, and general ideology contributed to a fuller accounting of the means that enabled one group to exercise leadership and its ultimate domination in American educational reform. The basis of the pragmatic liberal leadership and domination in societal and school reform throughout the twentieth century was not an automatic one, or a reflex action to fundamental shifts in the economy. Rather, it resulted from a system of alliances; the establishment of a profound measure of intellectual, social, and moral authority; a substantial degree of popular consent; and the allegiances of segments of the dominant economic and political class. Understanding the passageways between structural economic changes and specific educational changes require additional concepts and interpretive schemes to render comprehensible the process by which pragmatic liberalism encompassed the critical domains of cultural, moral, ethical, and intellectual leadership.

That is to say, how did the pragmatists, in contradistinction to the humanists, fascists, communists, neo-Enlightenment thinkers, and such psychologists as G. Stanley Hall become capable of enlisting the positive participation of different and broad segments of society? Clearly, this was a long-term, hard-fought, major victory for the pragmatists. While they may have capitalized on changes in the economy, these structural changes do not account for the means that enabled them to exercise leadership and domination in American social and intellectual life. Presumably, major shifts in the economy influenced the pragmatists in much the same way as it did the humanists, fascists, communists, and neo-Enlightenment thinkers. But how did the pragmatists' understanding of the political economy, their construction of the educational implications of economic changes, their interests in particular economic restructuring, and their ideology of educational reform prevail over others? The effective leadership by pragmatic liberals during the first half of the twentieth century was not imposed merely by fundamental economic shifts; it was necessarily complex. And it had to be produced, constructed, and created as a result of specific political, ideological, and organizational practices. Karier's study of new liberal philosophy contributed to our understanding of the passageways between structural forces and the emergent ideological dominance of particular social and educational reforms. In so doing he helped to reinforce the inextricable relationship between social and intellectual history.

Clearly, we need concepts and interpretive schemes to render comprehensible the triumph of the liberals over their opposition. Since all groups came from the ranks of the same social class what accounts for the intrasocial class differences and conflicts? Further, since fundamental shifts in the economy influenced each group in roughly the same manner, what accounts for the struggles against each other and their different conceptions of human nature, the good society, and the role of education in shaping the good society? From the vantage of some theoretical frameworks, the various reform movements could be construed as dominant class self-reformations, at once conservative in their attempt to preserve the social order, yet liberal to reactionary depending on their rigidity or flexible response to fundamental shifts in the economic foundations of society. Thus each group faced the challenge of convincing a cross section of the dominant class that its conception of social life and education would strengthen rather than weaken the social order.

Finally, the abstract notion that fundamental shifts in the economy ushered in particular reform movements proposes an economically rational explanation of social and educational changes. Karier's study of the humanists, fascists, and, particularly, the psychologists, underscored the irrational nature of human beings. Therefore, he approached history with the understanding that not all human beliefs and behavior are economically rational. On the contrary, in some instances reforms pitted rational or objective economic interests against racism, sexism, and ethnocentrism and other irrational and hysterical beliefs. Indeed, particular reformers won support in some corners simply because their proposed reforms for women, ethnic minorities, and immigrants allayed the fears and suspicions of those who feared that a broader inclusion represented social dynamite. The history of the South provides ample evidence of the ways in which dominant groups often pit economic interests against racism and the ways in which appeals to racial hysteria can solidify people in behalf of social causes that, in fact, undermine their objective economic interests. This further emphasizes the need to develop and explain the passageways between shifts in the economy and the actual social or political forces, including school reform movements, which become decisive in a particular historical moment. The fact that pragmatic liberalism dominated most of the twentieth century, through very different economic shifts, only underscores the need to explain how it encompassed the critical domains of political, cultural, moral, ethical, and intellectual leadership. In such works as *Man, Society, and Education* (1967), *Roots of Crisis* (1972), "Business Values and the Educational State" (1973), *The Individual, Society, and Education* (1986), and *Scientists of the Mind* (1986), Karier developed the kind of intellectual history that offered insightful analysis of the relationship between structural forces and human agency.[6]

October 2000 will mark the thirtieth anniversary of Karier's presentation of "The Quest for Orderly Change." Undoubtedly, this historical fact will go unnoticed by the Midwest History of Education Society. But the central theme of his essay is far more difficult to forget and virtually impossible to ignore. In October 1970, Karier speculated that, given the nature of liberal ideology, "in times of severe crisis, most liberals can be relied on to move to the right rather than to the left of the political spectrum."[7]

Following the turbulent political crisis of the 1960s, the nation experienced the severe economic downturns of the 1970s and 1980s. During this period America's liberal center moved decisively to the right, to the point that Senator Edward Kennedy now represents for many media experts and social critics the "left wing" of American politics. What happened to the liberals? One could easily dismiss Karier's prediction as an almost uncanny prophetic vision. But this would underestimate his broad and deep knowledge of America's past, the power of his historical imagination, and his courage to advance a reasoned speculation based on the best available historical evidence. His analysis was on the mark. It reminds us that his arguments are provocative yet balanced. It also demonstrates the excitement and continued relevance of his scholarship and of the tradition of critical history that he helped to launch. He authored some of the finest works in American educational history and we are all in his debt.

Part Three

Implications for Future Scholarship

12

Resistance to Standardized Testing: From Issues of Validity to "Testing for Order and Control"

Timothy Glander

"The history of education knows of no single educational movement that has had such a vast sweep and range as the present one, the process whereby numerical values and ratings are affixed to mental endowments and mental efforts."[1] So wrote Upsala College's P. H. Pearson, a critic of standardized testing, in March of 1929. A school superintendent was less restrained when he wrote in 1932 that the movement toward standardized testing represented "one of the worst pieces of asinine nonsense ever perpetuated on an innocent and defenseless public."[2] The rapid growth of standardized testing in the early decades of the twentieth century—including intelligence, achievement, licensure, personality, and diagnostic testing—caused considerable consternation among a significant number of people in the United States. Responding to the large-scale development of group testing during World War I and special aptitude testing during World War II, the growth of a variety of testing procedures in industries and schools, and the pervasive ideology that sought to manage behavior and adjust people to an emerging mass society, many people in the first half of the twentieth century found ways to voice their discontent about an increasingly powerful standardized testing movement. A few schools banned the use of standardized tests outright, while many individuals expounded on the negative implications of these tests in popular and scholarly journals alike.[3] Perceptive critiques of standardized testing were made from a variety of ideological vantage points throughout the twentieth century.

Today, most educators recognize the shortcomings and dangers of standardized testing and advocate for more authentic forms of assessment. However, there is a general lack of awareness of the significant criticism of standardized testing that occurred in previous decades. This ahistorical viewpoint has led to overly optimistic views about the anticipated demise of standardized testing, as if these tests will just wither away now that we have examined them and found them lacking. This historical myopia has also tended to discourage understanding of the larger economic, political, and ideological forces that continue to support and profit from this central educational practice. An increased awareness of this pervasive early criticism, then, helps us to deepen our own critique of standardized testing by moving us beyond the mere theoretical critique to considering these larger (and, some may say, more concrete) dimensions. Becoming aware of this history also enables us to both recover forms of criticism that have been lost in the current analysis and situate our criticism within a legacy of resistance to standardized testing. Finally, it can be said that this early criticism compelled testers into an even more deceptive practice of their work; recalling this early criticism, then, would be a necessary precondition to understanding contemporary practices in standardized testing which are, at least in part, a response to this early criticism.

The purpose of this paper is to review some of the dominant strands of criticism of standardized testing in the United States from the 1920s to Clarence Karier's landmark 1972 study, "Testing for Order and Control in the Corporate Liberal State."As a preliminary analysis, this paper can merely identify the prevailing themes around which this criticism came to cohere during certain historical periods. For convenience sake early criticism of standardized testing is organized around three central themes, and the paper is thus divided into three sections: 1) Issues of Validity; 2) Pedagogical Implications; and 3) Social Implications. These three themes are in no way distinct, and there is significant overlap among them. However, it is clear that some early criticism of standardized testing suffered from the inability to tie these various strands of criticism into a unifying whole. What is needed today, it seems to me, is a critique of standardized testing that connects criticism of the validity of standardized testing to an understanding of its pedagogical and social implications, and which makes clear the ideological, economic, and political forces that support the use of standardized tests. It is here that Karier's 1972 investigation remains so timely today. A concluding section raises such issues and points to areas that might be fruitful for future research.

Issues of Validity

The guiding definition of validity used by the Educational Testing Service is "the extent to which inferences and actions made on the basis of test scores are appropriate and justified by the evidence."[4] More generally, the term *validity* refers to the extent to which an examination measures what it purports to measure. Questions regarding the validity of standardized examinations, then, hinge not only on the character of these examinations, but also on the very possibility of measuring the phenomena under consideration. If an examination utilizes a passing point, or cut-off score, the method employed to determine this passing point is also at the center of any claims of validity. The twentieth century has seen numerous and continual attacks on the claims of validity made by the standardized testers.

Early twentieth-century criticisms of examination validity centered on intelligence tests and the arguments that these tests measured innate intelligence and offered predictability with respect to future academic and social achievement. Perhaps the most famous of these critiques was launched by Walter Lippmann in a series of six articles appearing in *The New Republic* in October and November of 1922.[5] Lippmann focused his argument on the still contemporary position that there has been no agreed upon definition of intelligence even among those testers who maintain they are able to measure its magnitude and amount. Lippmann could understand the confusion promoted by the testers, given the success with which people have been able to quantify other aspects of the world. Human intelligence, however, represented a much different order of phenomena than that which would yield to quantitative measure: ". . . length and weight are qualities which men have learned how to isolate no matter whether they are found in an army of soldiers, a heap of bricks, or a collection of chlorine molecules. Provided the footrule and the scales agree with the arbitrarily accepted standard foot and standard pound in the Bureau of Standards at Washington they can be used with confidence. But 'intelligence' is not an abstraction like length and weight; it is an exceedingly complicated notion which nobody has as yet succeeded in defining."[6] Lippmann called into question many of the prevailing assumptions of the testers at that time, including the concept of "mental age," which he referred to as "nonsense," and he even pointed to some of the social implications of these tests, noting that "the propaganda based on intelligence testing is to treat people with low intelligence quotients as congenitally and hopelessly inferior."[7] While no great believer in democracy, Lippmann noted the singular and one-dimensional way standardized tests define talent and punish those who do not thrive in "testing" situations:

> The tests are all a good deal alike. They all derive from a common stock, and it is entirely possible that they measure only a certain kind of ability. The type of mind which is very apt in solving Sunday newspaper puzzles, or even in playing chess, may be specially favored by these tests. The fact that the same people always do well with puzzles would in itself be no evidence that the solving of puzzles was a general test of intelligence. We must remember, too, that the emotional setting plays a large role in any examination. To some temperaments the atmosphere of the examination room is highly stimulating. Such people "outdo themselves" when they feel they are being tested; other people "cannot do themselves justice" under the same conditions.[8]

If there was a contemporary quality to Lippmann's criticism of standardized testing in 1922, he could not have been more mistaken about the future of standardized testing when he characterized it as a "fad" that would soon pass out of existence like "phrenology and palmistry, and characterology."[9]

Lippmann's line of argument was extended by Harry Miles Johnson, a psychologist at the University of Pittsburgh, in his essay "Science and Sorcery in Mental Tests," which appeared in *The Forum* in December of 1929. "Certain professors of psychology at reputable institutions," he wrote, now "admit that they know how to determine the generosity of your boss, the submissiveness of your wife, the social intelligence of your salesman, and the smartness of your children."[10] Such claims, however, are fallacious, argued Johnson, since the claims violate two central tenets of measurement: 1) "For one property of a thing to serve as a genuine test of another property, it is necessary that the property to be tested should *exist*"; and 2) "The property to be tested must be capable of being observed and measured *independently* of the property by which one proposes to test it."[11] Words such as "General Intelligence," "Learning-Capacity," "Capacity for Leadership," "Social Adaptability," and so on, are premised on the assumption that these words reflect human traits that are "observable, definable, and measurable," which is itself a spurious assumption. Moreover, the testers have had to rely on indirect measurements since these traits do not yield to independent and direct assessments. "The educational psychologist proposes, since he cannot measure intelligence directly, to measure something that he is to *call* intelligence, and then treat it as if it is what the label should indicate."[12] And "whenever anyone tells you that he has measured something indirectly that has never been measured directly, you are justified in asking to be excused from further exposure to his nonsense."[13]

Johnson argued that the psychological testers' work would best be equated with the work of the sorcerer or magician who operates by sleight of hand, and he urged testers to "quiet down for a while, until the public has had time to forget the claims that certain members of their group have made." Johnson, too, pointed to some of the social implications that followed from the testers' exaggerated claims:

> ... these experts have obtained huge appropriations, which they have squandered in "research" on pseudo-problems. They have pronounced judgment on the "general intelligence," the "moral discernment," and the various "special abilities" of thousands of children, on grounds that warranted no judgment whatever; and they have allowed their pronouncements to be used as authority for abandonment of further

effort to develop those children in certain directions . . . . Their "tests'"are made salable, and at the same time worthless, by depending on the fallacy of equivocation. This is a far more powerful agent of deception than direct lying: it deceives the user as well as his readers and hearers.[14]

Similar criticisms of the validity of standardized testing continued apace through the 1930s and 1940s. In 1932 C. C. Grover, Assistant Director of Research and Guidance for Oakland (California) Public Schools, cautioned against the overuse of standardized assessment and reiterated the perception of many others when he wrote:

> There is no general agreement among psychologists as to the meaning of the "General Intelligence," or as to how it may be measured, or even to the fact that it exists. The modern intelligence test maker ignores the divergence of opinion as to the nature of intelligence, attacks the problem from a pragmatic angle, and says that a test is good if it serves the purposes for which it is intended regardless of *a priori* considerations.[15]

Writing for *Child Study* in 1934, Anna Gillingham encouraged circumspection with regard to the claims about what aspects of human experience are measurable. While suggesting that testing for diagnosis and achievement has its place, Gillingham pointed out that many "teachers, parents and children themselves not infrequently do protest when, upon the premises of test data, predictions are made of future progress, and practical action taken which closes the doors to future opportunities."[16] By 1935, Walter S. Monroe, from the University of Illinois, argued that "there is apparent a child-like faith in the efficacy of objective tests as instruments for measuring school achievement," and that this "present situation is hazardous."[17] Monroe sought to critically examine the principles undergirding standardized testing and argued that standardized "objective" tests did not provide an adequate means by which to measure educational achievement.

> . . . objectivity in scoring does not make a test a satisfactory instrument for measuring achievement, that a coefficient of reliability is an index of very limited significance, and that a high correlation with a criterion is not sufficient evidence to justify the use of the scores yielded by a test as

highly accurate measures of the achievement considered to be defined by the criterion. . . . The widespread acceptance of them (the principles undergirding standardized testing) which is apparent in current educational writings and educational practice creates serious hazards in educational measurement.[18]

In 1940, James Mursell, writing for *Harper's Magazine*, lodged a far-reaching protest against the rise of standardized testing. "The public has been regaled with ballyhoo about the 'uncanny accuracy' with which 'science' can measure this or that mental characteristic and predict the potentialities of young children, when often tea leaves would be a safer guide."[19] Mursell went to the heart of the matter when he argued that "ordinary experience and common sense" provide deeper insight into human experience than the statistical data provided the testers. In essence, the alleged validity of these standardized measures have not been proven:

> Tests by the score are turned out which expressly claim to measure all sorts of mental traits—prevailing interests, moral attitudes, introversion-extroversion, musical and mechanical aptitudes, and so forth, as well as general intelligence. *In not one single case can such claims be rigorously proved.* Yet they are made without a qualm by people who ought to know better, and swallowed whole by the public. The glaring weakness of the testing movement is the general absence of proof that tests really measure what they purport to measure, coupled with a general tendency to interpret them as though they certainly did so. This holds true of the best tests, as well as the worst.[20] (Emphasis in the original.)

John Wahlquist examined the various philosophical positions extant in the controversy over standardized examinations in 1940 and noted that those who argued for the validity of these examinations "naively accepted the realistic premise that the universe is composed of 'reals' that exist in and of themselves."[21] "Intelligence," from this perspective, was not unlike temperature, which could be determined via a thermometer. Wahlquist went on to explore the philosophical underpinnings of those idealists and pragmatists who found fault with the metaphysical assumptions of the testers. "Is it not possible," he asked in his conclusion, "that the philosophical problem (reflected in the measurement controversy) will remain with us always?"[22]

In 1955 the sociologist Pitirim Sorokin took up the issue of the validity of standardized testing in an article entitled "Testomania," which appeared in the *Harvard Educational Review*. "We are living in an *age of testocracy*," he wrote. "At the present time in the Western countries almost every individual is tested from the cradle to the grave, and before and after every important event in his life." Moreover, "this enormous influence of tests and of the testers is primarily due to the supposedly scientific and infallible character of these tests."[23] Sorokin surveyed the various kinds of intelligence, personality, and psychological tests that had come to dominate life in the United States, including tests that sought to quantify emotions, ethical judgments, aptitudes, preferences, adjustment, criminality, loyalty, and others. Arguing that some form of testing *"goes on incessantly in all differentiated, stratified, and long-living societies,"* Sorokin discriminated between *"continuous real institutional testing"* and *"artificial and magic tests."*[24] Agencies of "continuous real institutional testing" include the family, school, and religious, economic, and occupational organizations, among others. These institutions engage in a constant and ongoing process of sorting individuals into various ranks within the social order. "These continuous and lifelong tests and re-tests by the family, the school, the church, the social and occupational groups are of *a most rigorous calibre, being real-life tests of real mental and overt activities of the individual discharged in real life conditions."*[25]

In opposition to these real-life institutional tests, Sorokin argued, "artificial and magic tests rarely test the individual directly. Instead, they are based upon a belief of an existence of mysterious or causal relationship between certain events or objects and the tested characteristic of a person."[26] The modern paper and pencil, psychosocial tests that had come to prevail in the United States were largely "artificial and magic tests," which did not differ significantly from "playing card tests, tea-leaves tests, coffee-grounds tests" and other forms of "make-believe" tests. Like the artificial and magic tests, the modern psychosocial tests are generally "ad hoc tests, administered from time to time, and of a short duration."[27] In addition, Sorokin described several defects of these tests, including the artificial way in which they are administered, the arbitrariness of the time constraints placed on the testee, and the significant problems with the very structure of the questions posed on the tests. The questions frequently attempt to probe the emotional and subjective characteristics of the person taking the test, the questions often pose hypothetical questions, and they are frequently ambiguous and sometimes incorrectly keyed. Moreover, "questions ask mainly for various bits of information or for memorized terms, concepts, definitions, and theories," and this is particularly damaging in fields such as psychology, history, philosophy and others where "there are few generally accepted concepts, definitions, theories, methods, uniformities and values."[28] Finally, Sorokin argued that problems with these tests were "immeasurably magnified by the subsequent interpretation of the tests' results" and distorted further by their quantification.[29]

> Obsessed by metromania, our testers indefatigably measure their test-data and present them in an "exact" and "objective" form of numerical scores, indexes, statistical tables, marvelously decorated with impressively looking mathematical formulae and other simulacra of precise quantitative research. Manufacturing of these "quantitative movies" is done so artfully that many a logically and mathematically innocent onlooker seriously takes this sham-quantitative appearance for a genuine reality. A legion of psychosocial researchers sincerely believe that these impressively looking scores, indexes, rows of figures, coefficients of correlation, probable errors, standard deviations, coefficients of reliability, and so on, deliver the objectively studied and exactly measured "diamonds of a valid knowledge." As a matter of fact, the bulk of these "diamonds" are but arbitrary, subjective, often fantastic, assumptions of the testers dressed up in quantitative costumes and mathematical make-ups. Our testing numerologists have as far (a) relationship to real mathematics as had various numerologists and astrologers ("*mathematici*" as they were called) of ancient times and of the Middle Ages.[30]

Sorokin went on to point out that the data gleaned from the administration of tests were essentially qualitative and, therefore, could not be legitimately translated into quantitative terms. These psychosocial tests were of "doubtful validity," he argued, and he encouraged "a strongly sceptical [sic] attitude towards the scientific nature of these tests."

> All in all, such tests are hardly more scientific than the old-fashioned tea-leaves or coffee-grounds tests. The modern testomania is mainly a new form of the old beliefs in revealing omens, paper-pen magical operations, or vocal incantations dressed up in modern scientific garb. This verdict is well corroborated by a closer examination of the main modern tests and by inductive testing of the tests themselves.[31]

Banesh Hoffmann, a mathematician at Queens College in New York City, undertook such a close examination of modern multiple-choice testing in a series of articles that appeared in *The American Scholar* and *Harper's Magazine* in the late 1950s and early 1960s, and culminated in his 1962 book *The Tyranny of Testing*.[32] In these works, Hoffmann argued that standardized testing had "grave defects."[33] "The great question that the public must ask of the multiple-choice testing industry is not how quick and economical its products are but, simply, how good the tests are themselves," he wrote.

> Significant flaws in the tests we use so widely should certainly be of vital concern. The test-makers, by their impressive scientific ritual of psychological expertise, pretesting, and statistical analysis, have created a widespread impression that their products must surely be free of such flaws, an impression especially prevalent among people with unshakable confidence in scientific routines, no matter how or by whom.[34]

Noting that "test-making has developed into a large, lucrative, and increasingly competitive business," Hoffman pointed out that these "non-profit" organizations were able to stave off criticisms by arguing that their work required secrecy.[35] Hoffmann agreed with many commonly heard critiques of testing in the 1950s, including the arguments that these tests tended to stifle and punish creativity; that they penalize test takers who perceive "subtle points unnoticed by less able people"; that they are frequently "superficial and intellectually dishonest, with questions made artificially difficult by means of ambiguity because genuinely searching questions do no readily fit into the multiple-choice format"; that they discourage the development of skill in careful and articulate expression; and that "they often degenerate into subjective guessing games in which the candidate does not pick what he considers the best answer out of a bad lot but rather the one he believes the unknown examiner would consider best."[36] Hoffmann argued, however, that the testers have learned to deal with this kind of criticism by assuming the posture of the reasonable scientific expert, shrouded by "such an aura of scientific infallibility that few people realize that they have avoided answering the criticism aimed at them." Therefore, Hoffmann encouraged the analysis of specific questions employed by the testers as a means of revealing their significant shortcomings. "Instead of making general criticisms, one should exhibit specific test questions . . . declare that they are defective; and challenge the test-makers to defend these questions specifically."[37]

Hoffmann's critique of the defects with individual questions was highly effective, even though he was severely constrained, by the testers' need for secrecy, to examine only those questions that had been published in test preparation and other such manuals. Henry Chauncey, President of ETS; John Stalnaker, President of National Merit Scholarship; and William Jovanovich, President of Harcourt, Brace, & World, Inc., all wrote letters to *Harper's Magazine* deriding Hoffmann's analysis. Chauncey argued that Hoffmann "dismisses evidence with amazing ease"; Stalnaker claimed that Hoffmann "exhibited ignorance both of the able youth and of the system of higher education in this country"; Jovanovich wrote that "almost any profession or group or object can be made to seem sinister by demonstrating how pervasive or ubiquitous it has become. . . . It is silly to suggest [as Hoffmann had] that educational test publishing has grown because it is unchecked."[38] Nevertheless, *Harper's Magazine* indicated that the "letters coming in from our readers are four to one in favor of Dr. Hoffmann."[39]

There were many other voices heard in the 1950s and early 1960s calling the validity of standardized testing into question and doing so from a wide variety of ideological perspectives.[40] Some of this criticism was subsumed under the larger critique of the emerging mass society during that period, and reflected a widespread concern about the standardization, homogenization, and bureaucratization of American culture. The testing companies were able to weather this recurring criticism, however, by continuing to adhere to the posture of the scientific expert Banesh Hoffmann noted nearly forty years ago.

Pedagogical Implications

In turning to the pedagogical implications of standardized testing one finds a long-standing concern about the way standardized testing forces upon the teacher certain educational approaches, narrows classroom activities, and deadens learning for both teacher and student. Again, this recognition of the negative pedagogical implications of standardized testing was widely held, and again this criticism cut across a variety of ideological perspectives. This is understandable when it is noted that standardized testing of school achievement has been premised essentially on a narrow positivist-connectionist-behaviorist perspective and driven by the efficiency movement, which is at odds with so many other educational philosophies. As Harl Douglass from the University of Minnesota wrote in 1934: "The national leaders in secondary education and in the philosophy of education are vigorously opposed to such uses of tests. Dewey, Kilpatrick, Proctor, Bode, Morrison, Counts, Newlon, Eikenberry, Judd, Jones, and Cox, among others, have expressed grave concern relative to the dangers of statewide achievement testing programs." Douglass went on to note that these educators "are fully aware of the retrogressive and narrowing effects of the New York Regents examinations and the College Board examinations upon the objectives and outcomes of secondary schools."[41]

One particularly important line of investigation concerned the likely impact of standardized testing on student motivation and its relationship to knowledge. A modified version of this perspective was offered in 1929, when Alfred North Whitehead railed against the stultifying effect of "inert" knowledge and argued that the "common external examination system is fatal to education."[42] Whitehead appreciated that in order for knowledge to be relevant and meaningful, which is to say "alive," learning activities had to be decided on within a local context. Common external examinations undercut this essential aspect of real learning by forcing student and teacher to attend to knowledge claims that frequently have no bearing on their lives. "No educational system is possible," he wrote, "unless every question directly asked of a pupil at any examination is either framed or modified by the actual teacher."[43] Also in 1929, Lorne Henry, of the Central Technical School in Toronto, pointed to the real danger that the use of "objective tests" placed too much importance "upon things that can be measured . . . to the exclusion of other considerations of greater significance."[44] Glenn Frank, President of West Virginia University, argued that "the examination mania turns students into professional witnesses instead of learners."[45] By 1932, H. H. Rigg, Superintendent of Otsego, Michigan, schools revealed that essay examinations had been entirely supplanted by "objective tests" in many school districts. "One can give serious thought," Rigg wrote, "to the fact that perhaps teachers are making blank fillers out of students."[46] Also in 1932, a survey of three hundred forty school superintendents indicated that "well over one-half . . . agree that tests have been over-emphasized."[47]

In 1933, H. A. Jeep of Ball State Teachers College, worried about the dogmatism that was both reflected in the testers' work and which resonated through the increasing use of "objective tests." Jeep observed two dominant modern trends in education that were diametrically opposed to each other. "One of these is the ever-increasing emphasis being placed upon the test, especially the objective test, and the second is the attempt to minimize dogmatism in instruction."[48] This presented a pervasive contradiction that could be observed in many classrooms in the 1930s:

> One of the greatest obstacles blocking the realization of the ambition of teachers to get away from dogmatism is the present trend in testing. Testing has not kept pace with teaching. Rather, it has become even more factual and dogmatic. The dilemma in which teachers find themselves is very evident. They are trying to improve their testing technique by making their tests more objective, factual, and dogmatic,

and at the same time they are attempting to avoid dogmatism in their instruction.[49]

The use of standardized tests to measure teacher effectiveness and instructional quality was being considered as early as the 1930s. "It has been frequently suggested that the teachers be rated by the tests scores of the pupils on standard tests," wrote Harl Douglass, of early accountability models. "One writer recently proposed a 'teaching quotient' based upon achievement quotients of pupils."[50] Douglass objected vigorously to this proposal and noted the "objectionable byproducts" of such a means of teacher evaluation: "the narrowing effects upon the teacher, and her methods of teaching, which more than offset any possible values of the use of tests for measuring the effectiveness of teachers."[51]

Throughout the 1940s Leon Nordau, a teacher at James Monroe High School in New York City, wrote a series of articles that raised questions about the pedagogical implications of standardized testing.[52] "Like so many gadgets adapted to the ends of mass production, the intelligence test has been converted into a mechanical toy whose lever anybody may crank and so get it to spin round by itself."[53] Nevertheless, Nordau argued, educators have not seriously questioned how the use of these tests influence how we think about student learning:

> Through furtive consideration of the individual we have gained "objective" results, considered reliable because we have chosen statistical records as our ultimate criterion without profoundly questioning the nature of the questions from which such records have been derived. What is their nature? Do they employ the intelligence of the pupil or do they rather reward his ability to memorize as the average actor memorizes his lines?[54]

Nordau noted that standardized testing tended to redefine what is meant by both intelligence and academic achievement and placed too much importance on the cognitive function of simple recall. "Success," he wrote, is "predicated upon what has been learned by rote and whose meaning is arrived at, not through tested thought, but blind acceptance."[55] Nordau understood that standardized testing was premised on faulty epistemological assumptions, where the accumulation of facts replaced genuine inquiry, and where a simplistic "right or wrong" format resonated to other areas of knowing. Standardized tests do not "teach what is connected, clear, and profoundly real for there is no question in existence which can be intelligently answered with the abruptness these so-called measures of intelligence insist upon," he wrote. "Who then can earn the highest score in these scales but he whose mind is crammed with antiquarian scholastic lore promiscuously mingled and unidentified, that is, unincorporated into an organic system of thought?"[56] Finally, Nordau pointed to the dangerousness of a method of assessment that was not tied to the lives and experience of students and teachers. Standardized tests, he wrote, "have only a superficially external application to the lives of students and instructors, (and) are not conducive to the linked function of living-teaching."[57]

Many educators echoed Nordau's concerns about the way in which standardized testing reinforced a faulty and simplistic view about student learning and reduced the complexity of knowledge claims made in various domains. Frank Freeman, in a 1946 article entitled "The Monopoly of Objective Tests," argued that the "use of objective examinations is greatly overdone in the present-day school and college in this country, and that this excessive use is bound to have a harmful effect on study and learning in America."[58] Freeman believed that "students were acquiring a wrong concept of what study means" and that the larger purposes of education were being "distorted" by these standardized examinations. "At the moment when the importance of seeing things in relation to each other and to the major concerns of human life is recognized," Freeman wrote, "our schools and colleges are dominated by a technique of examination that leaves this type of thinking out of account."[59]

Emerson Shideler, of Iowa State University, revisited these concerns in a 1960 article entitled "What Do Examinations Teach?"[60] Shideler argued that "knowledge does not consist in the quantity of one's facts."[61] While standardized tests "probably do an adequate job of testing the accumulation of facts or data" possessed by the student, they are unable to provide "evidence of capacity to integrate those facts into a meaningful comprehension of the subject matter, or of capacity to communicate the understanding one has achieved."[62] Shideler went on to point out that there was no domain of knowledge where the simple recall of bits of information reflected a coherent or competent understanding. Yet the increasing use of these tests has conditioned student and teacher alike to treat as sufficient this fact-based approach encouraged by standardized testing. The student so alienated from a field of study "does not see himself as a participant in the field of activity being studied. Instead, he is simply looking at a showcase—the textbook, or his notes on experiments and instructor's lectures—which exhibits a great many items which he hopes to remember in sufficient number to get a passing grade. He does not see himself as one taking part in the enterprise represented by the field of study."[63] The teacher so alienated comes to conceptualize his or her own discipline as static and fragmented, and tends to lose sight of the value and purpose of the domain: "One who thinks that mastery of a field consists only in ability for immediate recall of the discrete items in the catalogues of a field of knowledge, without reference to capacity for integration and communication, has lost all awareness of why his subject should be taught."[64] By using standardized examinations, argued Shideler, the teacher is relieved of the personal responsibility of making judgments of the students' achievement. Moreover, "a quantitative test capable of machine scoring is a great help to the teacher of large classes. . . . It saves him both time and emotional involvement."[65] Nevertheless, the widespread use of these tests has tended to diminish the essential human relationship that is at the core of the interchange between teacher and student. "There are enough barriers between teachers and students at best without interposing the barrier of unconcerned detachment" exemplified by standardized testing.[66]

In addition to the recognition that use of standardized testing forced a particular view of learning and knowledge on the teacher and student, there was increased awareness that the tests themselves were being forcefully necessitated by an educational system that promoted mass-like conformity in its overcrowded institutions. One Ohio University professor noted the irony in this situation: "At the very moment when many of us are coming to realize the shortcomings of multiple-choice questions, we are obliged to construct them ourselves—simply to survive—for the hordes of students rushing into our classrooms!"[67] With respect to those examinations created by the professional test-makers at the Educational Testing Service, Psychological Corporation, Professional Examination Service, and other testing companies and publishing entities, there was increased worry among educators that these distant corporate bodies were determining the content of the curricula that teachers were required to teach. The concern about "teaching to the test" was much in evidence in the first half of the twentieth century, and was reflected in Arthur Traxler's 1958 essay "Are the Professional Test-Makers Determining What We Teach?" Traxler, a supporter of standardized testing, argued that "practically everyone engaged in testing realizes that measurement may unduly influence the work of the schools, and practically everyone in this field wants to avoid this danger."[68] Traxler recognized that "tests are powerful instruments," and he argued that the best way to keep the test-makers from determining the content of the curriculum was to make sure that teachers and school administrators held these tests in check. "To prevent tests from encroaching on inappropriate areas," he wrote, "teachers and administrators will do well to avoid comparing test scores of classes and schools."[69] Traxler's advice, of course, was not well heeded as the National Assessment of Educational Progress and other testing programs began this comparison in earnest in the 1960s, and helped to deepen concerns about the social impact of these tests.

Social Implications

Early considerations of the social implications of standardized testing were in many ways derived from questions pertaining to examination validity and the educational consequences of these examinations. From the perspective of those who challenged the validity of standardized testing, for instance, the central question concerned the implications of utilizing a faulty technique to make important decisions of social discrimination. From the perspective of those who saw clearly the negative pedagogical implications of standardized testing, the degree to which these examinations encouraged narrow thinking, deadened authentic inquiry and critical citizenship, and disempowered teachers were of central importance. Interestingly, questions pertaining to the racial, gender, and socioeconomic status bias of these examinations, as well as questions about the larger meritocracy served by the sorting function of these examinations, were rather late in coming. There were relatively few published voices who raised these concerns during the first half of the century, although recognition of such bias was likely widespread among marginalized and largely voiceless groups.

Like the critique of the validity and pedagogical implications of standardized testing, the critique of the social implications came from a variety of ideological perspectives. Banesh Hoffmann, for instance, argued that the great danger of standardized testing was that it frequently punished those students who he regarded as being more able. Taking a classically conservative position with a belief in a natural hierarchy of intellectual talent, Hoffmann criticized standardized testing because it rewarded students who possessed a superficial understanding while penalizing the superior students who were sensitive to different shades of meaning and interpretation not captured by the testers. Hoffmann's social critique of standardized testing, then, did not call into question the system of sorting encouraged by Cold War human resource planners who supported the testing movement. Rather, his argument was with the tests themselves, which from his perspective did not adequately identify talent; they did not, to paraphrase Thomas Jefferson, provide a legitimate rake by which to clear away the rubbish.

There were others, however, who drew different conclusions regarding the likely social impact of the rise of standardized testing. As early as 1929, one writer tried to respond to the question "Are Mental Tests in the Schools Democratic?"[70] The writer answered in the affirmative, although the fact that the question was even posed indicates that many parents, teachers, and pupils did regard these tests to be undemocratic. Also in 1929, P. H. Pearson, of Upsala College, observed that standardized assessment was "a response to the social demand for efficiency."[71] This value of efficiency, however, restricted other educational values and significantly curtailed the recognition and development of individual differences. "More output in less time," he wrote, "is not the whole of life."[72] Standardized testing tended to routinize behaviors, restrict alternative and individual forms of experience, and make people apprehensive about the future. "To routinize a person from school days on will hasten the time when he does not want to look forward. Why? He is afraid of new things. Why? New things hurt him. They do not conform to the shape of his mould and he staves them off in self defense."[73]

In 1938, F. L. Wells of Harvard Medical School correlated the rise of multiple-choice testing with the increase in mass-like conformity characteristic of burgeoning authoritarian societies. "The mass education complex and the mass testing complex have gone hand in hand to encourage procedures of the multiple-choice sort," he wrote.[74] Multiple-choice tests create multiple-choice minds.

> Multiple choice presents the universe of discourse in either-or fashion, and it ought not to be necessary to remind [the reader] that a large part of the material of education (and of life) is subject to only very imperfect formulation in this way. Multiple choice formulations of such material commonly elicit negative reactions in students with a set towards independent thinking, and in general they diminish the tendency to independent thinking. This feature accordingly well adapts the multiple choice technique to authoritarian social and didactic patterns."[75]

Not only did standardized testing thwart the development of critical thinking, but it was also indicted as a significant means by which human beings were objectified and dehumanized. "The modern scientist and especially the modern educator have been guilty of a misapplication of principles and methods in the prevalent assumption that man, the human self, is but another object among an array of objects," Morley Mays wrote in 1955. Standardized testing, he pointed out, is premised on the belief that human beings "can be scrutinized, analyzed, and quantified like any other object; that he can be understood largely in terms of observable and measurable phenomena; that we can account for his behavior in terms of conditioning which is identifiable; that, in short, he is a thing not a person."[76] Standardized testing was understood, from this perspective, to be an important component of the radical dehumanization of life that occurred in the twentieth century. "Is it not obvious," Mays asked, that the practice of standardized testing "tend(s) to reduce the student to the status of a thing, to be manipulated in ways appropriate to things?"[77]

Harold C. Hand, of the University of Illinois, regarded national testing programs such as those promoted by the NAEP to be a "Recipe for Control by the Few," in a 1966 article that he wrote by that title. "Any national achievement testing program whose results are used to compare public schools," he wrote, "would prove coercive in respect to the public schools, because it would inevitably force teachers to teach for the tests."[78] Teachers would be compelled to tailor curricular decisions to the demands of the testers. The result would be a de facto national curriculum, where what is important to learn is decided by a few individuals who were not publicly elected and therefore not accountable to anyone. "Private conferees, private test makers, private test approvers, and a private financial angel—there is not a person among them who is in any way either legally responsible to or legally removable by the public in respect to what the consequences of the NAEP achievement tests would be in the public schools."[79]

The public outcry against the racial and cultural bias endemic to standardized testing was not generally manifest until the early 1960s, although this recognition was not unheard of in earlier decades. In James Mursell's 1940 essay "Mental Testing: A Protest," which appeared in *Harper's Magazine,* there is clear acknowledgment that standardized tests endorse experience clearly foreign to the experience of most minority children. "Tests furnish a most precarious basis for inter-racial comparison," Mursell wrote, "and for the simple reason that *they are built upon differences observed in White children.* An item which is highly significant with White Children may be meaningless or deceptive with those of different background and culture" (emphasis in the original).[80] By the time the New York City schools banned the use of group intelligence tests in the fall of 1964, there was pervasive awareness that the tests were "oriented to middle-class abilities both in experiences considered basic and in norms, with resulting discrimination against culturally disadvantaged children."[81] In the previous year, a poll taken by the National Opinion Research Center revealed that more than 40 percent of adults thought it was "unfair" to use these tests "in deciding who is to be admitted to college."[82] The significant problems with standardized testing were obvious to anyone who cared to look closely at them and think seriously about them, although their use continued to rise sharply throughout the ensuing decades.

There existed a strong legacy of criticism of standardized testing, then, by the time Clarence Karier took up his historical analysis of testing in 1972.[83] But unlike previous criticism that had more narrow aims and limited explanatory power, Karier's historical perspective encouraged a transcendent means of understanding both prevailing contemporary circumstances as well as the larger historical context in which testing was developed and thrived. Part of the critical historical and sociological scholarship that flourished in the late 1960s and early 1970s, Karier's study explicated further the discriminatory nature of standardized testing, even as it made clear the ideological and vast economic interests that undergirded the development of these tests.[84] Karier emphasized the confluence of corporate, governmental, and military interests that emerged early in the twentieth century that sought to use the social sciences and educational institutions to regulate producers and consumers, create willing soldiers and docile citizens. He probed critically the emergence of the phenomena of the philanthropic foundations that provided the funding and impetus for so much of the educational testing movement, as well as other central educational practices oriented around the seemingly benign value of efficiency. The dominance of these foundations in shaping educational policy, Karier accurately noted, "reflected a development of virtually a fourth branch of government, which effectively represented the interest of corporate wealth in America."[85] Recognizing the pernicious consequence of these developments in sustaining a system of domination and exploitation, Karier argued that the ideological commitment to the testing industry was rooted in "the American progressive temper, which combined a belief in progress, certain racial attitudes and faith in the scientific expert working through state authority to ameliorate and control the evolutionary progress of the race."[86] The widespread use of these tests, Karier argued, created a sense of fatalism in those people who were subjected to them. Since tests "scientifically determined" that one's lower socioeconomic status was the result of his/her own intellectual inferiority, one could not complain about one's lot. "The tragic character of this phenomenon was not only that the lower class learned to believe in the system," Karier perceptively noted, "but worse, through internalizing that set of beliefs, made it work. It worked because the lowered self-image which the school and society reinforced on the lower-class child did result in lower achievement."[87] Though other historians did not want to admit it, Karier demonstrated how thoroughly the American system of testing and eugenics had predated the German Nazi's involvement in this area, and how this work revealed the seeds of an American fascism hidden thinly beneath the veil of meritocracy and social science technique.[88]

Conclusion and Additional Questions

Criticism of standardized testing in the twentieth century has been rigorous and incisive, and has reflected the perceptions of people undergoing radical social change in the twentieth century. Ideologically diverse, this criticism commented in a variety of ways on the issues pertaining to the validity of standardized testing, and its social and pedagogical implications. There hardly seems to be a significant criticism of standardized testing today that wasn't first voiced during the first half of this century. The bits and pieces of this criticism can be found scattered throughout the historical record of this period. We would do well to examine this record in the interest of reconstructing a more far-reaching criticism of standardized testing than we are generally able to mount today.

Despite the wide-ranging and perceptive criticism of standardized testing in recent decades—criticism that has increasingly made clear the discriminatory nature of these tests against minorities, women, and people from low socioeconomic status (SES) backgrounds—the testing industry and the use of tests continues to grow at a significant rate. A recent report from ETS "concludes that the volume of testing in U.S. schools has increased markedly over the past 20 years."[89] By itself ETS, a "private, non-profit, corporation," had revenue in excess of $345 million for 1993, an increase of more than 30 percent from fiscal year 1989.[90] By 1999, total ETS revenues had soared to more than $490 million.[91] Although roughly half of all teachers do not use portfolios or other forms of authentic assessment, those who do find that they are still required to administer standardized tests and that these tests are considered to be much more important in terms of policy decisions and program evaluations.[92] In the area of professional licensing and certification, the growth of these tests shows no sign of abating, and are in fact made to appear more novel through the introduction of various computer programs that superficially replace the paper/pencil format but leave the essential structure of the tests intact. With respect to teacher certification testing (to take but one example), it is widely recognized that these tests ultimately degrade the complexity of teaching, diminish the responsibility of teacher education institutions, are biased against marginalized groups, and condition beginning teachers to accept the pedagogical, curricular, and ideological dictates of state educational bureaucracies. Despite this recognition, beginning teachers are forced to sit for a variety of costly "minimal competency examinations" whether in the guise of the National Teacher Examination, "Praxis Series" exams, or the newly created New York State Teacher Certification Examination.

Why does standardized testing continue to develop at an unprecedented rate in the U.S. despite the recognition of its obvious shortcomings? There are no easy answers to this question, although a review of the early-twentieth-century criticism of standardized testing may provide us with a few clues. Like the criticism of the rise of propaganda and the "science" of opinion management which closely paralleled the rise of the testing movement, the resistance to standardized testing actually compelled the testers to a more deliberately deceptive practice of their work—drove them undercover and into greater secrecy, fostered a nearly impenetrable jargon which further mystified their work, and enabled them to appear to be attending to the criticism but in actuality sustaining their original practice. Thus, the Educational Testing Service can appear to be addressing the issue of racial and cultural bias in its booklet "An Approach For Identifying and Minimizing Bias In Standardized Tests," when it advises the need for minority participation in the test development process[93]; but such participation cannot alter the central force of these standardized instruments, which is against individual and group differences and uniqueness. Likewise, in response to charges that they are acting arbitrarily when they use a norm-referenced approach to pass or fail a certain number of test takers, the testing industry can utilize a criterion-referenced approach, the scientifically sounding "Angoff Method," to assign the passing point; yet most people do not know what this "Angoff Method" entails or where it comes from, and most people are thus unaware of the fraudulent nature of this practice.[94] The testing industry continues to operate in secrecy, and the testers continue to be sensitive to criticisms of their practices. But, from a public relations standpoint, they have also become increasingly skillful at dealing with and disarming this criticism. One necessary component of any adequate understanding of why standardized testing continues to expand in the U.S., therefore, is a deep recognition of the essentially deceptive character of this work. That much of this deception over time takes the form of self-deception, as Harry Miles Johnson noted in 1929, does not alter this fundamental observation.

Connected to this understanding, of course, would have to be a thorough analysis of the way standardized testing serves power in the United States, and here we would do well to return to the kind of critical historical analysis that Clarence Karier has engaged for the past forty years. More than anything else, standardized testing is an ongoing and comprehensive means of social control. Understanding the ideological assumptions which legitimate this practice, and the economic and political interest that profit from it, would be central to any meaningful critique of standardized testing today.

13

Contradictions of Domestic Containment: Forestalling Human Development During the Cold War

Stephen Preskill

The simple purpose of this essay is to take the concept and practice of "containment"—usually applied to American foreign policy during the cold war—and to explore how it was used domestically during the twenty years after World War II to restrict and limit human development, especially in families and in schools. Also considered are some of the inherent contradictions of domestic containment, contradictions which eventually contributed to containment's demise. The emphasis, nevertheless, is on the harmful impact of containment and on the suffocating legacy of basing educational policy and practice on national interests, instead of the timeless aim of unleashing every child's genius. In *The Individual, Society, and Education*, Clarence Karier delivers a penetrating analysis of the Cold War's chilling impact on human development and human freedom. His analysis provides the backdrop for this essay and two long quotes from his book—one placed near the beginning of this chapter and one inserted at the end—frame and buttress the discussion below.

In the years immediately following World War II most of Europe teetered on the brink of economic and social collapse while the specter of Soviet expansion haunted the architects of American foreign policy. By 1947, State Department strategists had formulated the Truman Doctrine and the Marshall Plan to restore stability to Europe and reassert American hegemony around the globe. In that same year American diplomat George F. Kennan coined the word "containment" to describe the policy he advocated vis à vis the Soviets. "Containment" quickly became the official policy of the United States (though in Kennan's original conceptualization it was less a military counter to Russian might and more, in his view, the restrained, rational response of a country threatened by an alien political ideology). Doubting that the Soviets actually posed a serious military threat to the United States, Kennan cautioned against acting too aggressively and focused more on the political and economic challenge of neutralizing Soviet influence by maintaining a "long-term, patient but firm and vigilant containment."[1] Arguing that hostile measures should be resorted to last, Kennan proposed that economic and political pressure and even psychological manipulation be utilized as the most subtle and most effective strategies for containing Soviet influence.[2] Part of this strategy, then, included projecting an image of American domestic life that was prosperous, secure, and predictable. Americans at home were thus encouraged to contribute to this program by patient but firm containment of all activities that might endanger stability or undermine long term international ambitions.

"Containment" as a concept and a practice soon pervaded almost every aspect of postwar American life. Indeed, one cultural critic has even contended that Kennan's analysis was "much more like a prescription for domestic than foreign policy."[3] "Containment" encouraged intellectuals and scholars to overlook their conflicts and differences and to seek consensus in a variety of disciplinary spheres. This is the era when the literary critic Lionel Trilling claimed that within the United States "liberalism is not only the dominant but even the sole intellectual tradition."[4] While Trilling sought to subject this intellectual tradition to a more searching and critical analysis, his vision was a limited one in that the only competing tradition he cared to explore was conservatism. By the end of the 1950s, Daniel Bell similarly discerned a deeply entrenched individualistic consensus that seemed to discourage lively political debate and to rule out all but the most moderate opinions on capitalism, popular culture, and international relations.[5] Perhaps the height of containment's role in reformulating Americans' view of their own culture was reached when James Gould Cozzen's novel *By Love Possessed* rocketed to the top of the best seller list and stayed there throughout most of 1957. Profiling an ambitious corporate lawyer's growth into a "mature" adult, the book embraces the notion that efforts to improve the world are fruitless and that the truly wise eventually accept their "responsibility to work to sustain the status quo."[6]

"Containment" also slowed the postwar momentum to confront racial injustices and class and cultural inequities. These conflicts were minimized by keeping them out of the popular press and by maintaining the isolation of minority groups. By "containing" these groups a false consensus emerged that gave the appearance of general harmony but disguised the bitter conflict stitched into the social fabric of domestic life. Such a false harmony severely restricted opportunities for these groups to interact, learn from one another, and to identify with one another's problems. Most of all this artificial consensus stalled efforts to address these social problems, all for the sake of preserving a comforting stability.

Ironically, though, "containment" also required that some progress for African Americans occur. The continued subjugation of blacks conflicted blatantly with America's promise to keep the world safe for democracy. As blacks moved North, opportunities for employment in large industries did increase. Protests against Jim Crow laws and other discrimination were on the rise and a series of successful court cases to undermine white supremacy did culminate in the 1954 *Brown* decision. Gunnar Myrdal's *An American Dilemma* reminded many people that the American creed of freedom and opportunity just didn't apply to a very large non-white segment of the population, and Ralph Ellison's best-selling *The Invisible Man*, which depicted the crippling impact of racism on both whites and blacks, left an enduring impression on the seemingly placid waters of the early 1950s.

There were protests and increasing agitation, particularly among African-Americans themselves, for more progress. But government remained surprisingly timid in addressing these problems. Yet, despite this timidity and perhaps even because of it and other efforts to contain change, black people and their allies eventually took it upon themselves to challenge entrenched racial hierarchies and to bring about a significant shift in the politics and social relations of race. Indeed, domestic containment as a policy was first successfully challenged and in time brought down in the early 1960s by the protests and demonstrations that became the Civil Rights Movement. Yet as historian James Patterson has said after recounting the gains of the late forties and early fifties that preceded the Civil Rights Movement, "it is foolish to wax romantic about the rate of ethnic acculturation, or especially about the status of black people [during this period]. Most blacks, northern as well as southern, remained very poor; the vast majority never went to a nightclub or stayed in a hotel; many lacked radios—or even electricity; they encountered discrimination and rejection almost every day of their lives."[7]

In *The Individual, Society, and Education,* Clarence Karier shows that he understood the devastating effects of "containment" as deeply as any social critic of his time. He writes:

> A nation under constant threat, real or perceived, was not prepared to question its fundamental beliefs or carry on a sustained dialog long enough to reconstruct its ideology or its institutions. When the issue is portrayed as military survival, all questions quickly tend to be reduced to the simplicity of military solutions. Thus, the cold war fears in the four postwar decades seem to dominate and stifle any possibility for effective reform. In place of reform, floundering institutions tended to be propped up, and only temporary, superficial remedies seemed possible in an increasingly complicated, uncertain world of threat and violence. The great tragedy remained that, under cold war conditions, the reconstruction of American institutions would not be achieved.[8]

As Karier shows, the Cold War and the expectations of "containment" did not encourage human flourishing. The focus was on limits, boundaries, confinements, and restrictions. Cut-off points beyond which people dare not go were reinforced for behavior, for speech, for politics, and for academic life. This was the period when many people were contemptuous of the "egghead," or the "brain." Intellectuals were dangerous because they unhealthily allowed their obsession with knowledge and inquiry to interfere with the development of what that great American hero, Dwight D. Eisenhower, called the greatest gift of all—"personality." Indeed, one of the most widely used high school psychology texts of the time, T. L. Engle's *Psychology*, counseled students that overstimulating the intellect could adversely affect their physical well-being.[9]

As historian Elaine Tyler May demonstrates, the family was an especially important site where the dangerous forces that supposedly threatened the American way of life could be domesticated and brought under control. Families were urged to help their children adjust to the unpredictability and precariousness of the postwar world, not to challenge the status quo. Families also learned it was their responsibility to engender feelings of well-being and to help everyone feel good about their current situation, no matter how inequitable or threatening the outside world might be. Interestingly, it was an era when families were especially other-directed—intent on keeping up with the Joneses—at the same time that they increasingly withdrew from the harsh realities of the larger society. The family came to be seen once again as a "haven in a heartless land," but primarily for protection, for keeping social forces at bay, not to unleash creativity or promote human development. But most important, the family was a resoundingly conservative institution that "undermined the potential for political activism and reinforced the chilling effects of anti-communism and the cold war consensus."[10]

The analysis that historian Arlene Skolnick advances about family life during the cold war paints an even more devastating picture of how uniquely reactionary the nuclear family was in the twenty years after World War II. It was not the emphasis on domesticity that was surprising during this period, but rather the intense, exaggerated way in which the middle class, nuclear family clung to its domestic norms, which we have come to associate so strongly with the 1950s. These norms—which included large families, the "insistence that marriage and motherhood take up the whole of a woman's identity," and the "increased emphasis on gender difference"—all contributed to the sense that the family could be counted on to uphold the Victorian era's cult of domesticity and devotion to "traditional" values.[11] In Skolnick's view, the cold war family was dominated by "social constraint . . . [by] tightly drawn roles and rules, [and] clearly marked boundaries . . . that one crossed only at great peril." In other words, the bourgeois nuclear family of this period played as large a role as any institution of the time in promoting and sustaining domestic containment.[12]

Despite all of the above, paradox and contradiction clouded this seemingly serene picture. The family appeared to be elevating women to a new status and yet many women had never felt so denigrated. Women claimed to be deeply satisfied with their domestic lot, yet record numbers suffered from anxiety, depression, and nervous tension. And although women were encouraged to remain at home, their participation in the labor force continued to grow. Conflict was roiling beneath the surface of "private traditionalism and public calm." Or, as one pundit put it, "It was as if the whole period was a front . . . the topsoil that protected the seed of rebellion that was germinating below."[13]

A further measure to ensure American stability in the face of Soviet aggression involved the role of schools in containing human development. Containment policies, Edgar Friedenberg insistently argued, discouraged students from feeling and thinking "as deeply as their experience permits."[14] School leaders seemed to sense what was in the postwar air and what, therefore, was expected of them. Their interpretation of the school's mission during this period focused on working hard to maintain tradition, keeping risk taking to a minimum, and avoiding reforms that might threaten the status quo. They saw the world as a particularly treacherous place, where only control and conformity ensured salvation. As historian Robert Hampel has pointed out, the good student was someone who "learn[ed] to control and channel his impulses so that others accord[ed] him approval and respect."[15] The fear of discord, of rupture, of rebellion seemed to be everywhere, making it necessary to introduce stricter disciplinary policies and to foster more structured, less progressive classrooms so that "no matter what happens, (students) do not see too much or get too involved. . . . " Whether educators intended it or not, however, these practices frequently resulted in schools that restricted freedom, inhibited creativity, and discouraged joy in learning.[16]

Interestingly, one of the side effects of this compulsion to control youth, to clamp down on their most boisterous tendencies was a new fear that these externally imposed constraints were inadequate and in the end would only backfire. Historian James Gilbert, drawing on the insights of social critics like Edgar Friedenberg and Paul Goodman, goes so far as to say that young people became the "feared carriers of the failures of modern society."[17] Indeed, Friedenberg even likened teenagers to the so-called Communist threat, for they inspired in the general public the same sense of foreboding and controversy. Despite the attempt to "contain" youth during this period, there were signs of rebellion represented by an alarming increase in juvenile delinquency and the emergence of the "beat generation." But as Friedenberg, Goodman, and others tried to show, this was the reaction of young people who believed that the button-down, status quo–loving, "organizational society" could offer them no meaningful future.[18] The very effort to limit change, to ensure predictability, was creating a breeding ground over the long term for a major cultural shift.

In the meantime, however, the prevailing climate of accepting things as they were and of not questioning basic cultural assumptions had a particularly devastating effect on women. This was especially frustrating given the gains made during World War II in which women were actively encouraged to seek employment outside the home. When millions of soldiers were discharged in 1945 and 1946, however, threatening to produce a dangerous oversupply of labor, women were subjected to an intense propaganda campaign to forgo a career in favor of the flood of male returnees looking for work. They were expected to find a husband, to prepare for a life of domesticity, and to refrain from intellectual pursuits. Although female enrollments in colleges were up in the late forties and early fifties, the proportion of women relative to the total student population was lower than in the past. Furthermore, the drop-out rate for women was increasing, most likely due to the intense pressure to get married and the frustration women repeatedly experienced in securing well-paid and intellectually satisfying work.[19] For many women college became the place "to find a husband and to acquire the polish to carry off the role of the doctor's or lawyer's or organization man's gracious wife."[20]

Perhaps most infuriating of all, however, were the obstacles women and girls encountered in striving to achieve academically. Women reported again and again during this period of the stigma of being "too smart" and of the burdens of being labeled a "brain."[21] And, as Wini Breines has noted, "smart girls could achieve social acceptance only by disguising their book interests."[22] Breines also emphasized how differently boys and girls were treated when it came to academics and intellectual development. Women were actively discouraged from taking advanced courses or from getting too deeply involved in activities that might be defined as intellectual. Men, on the other hand, were frequently given considerable financial and moral support to continue their studies to a more advanced level (though even for men intellectual development could be taken too far).

One well-known and powerful educational reformer, James B. Conant, made his own contribution to the containment of female development during this period. Conant, a chemist and former Harvard president, and key administrator of the Manhattan Project, believed that educating what he called "the academically talented" was an urgent part of America's defense against the Soviet Union. Along with Admiral Hyman Rickover and other cold warriors, he urged the academically talented to elect a course of study that included four years of math, laboratory science, and foreign language, not because of the intrinsic value of these subjects, but because they would give the best and the brightest the preparation they would need for America to compete with the Soviets.[23]

Yet privately, and occasionally in public, Conant tended to use his considerable influence to promote the education of academically talented boys, exclusively. Boys were more likely to become the engineers, scientists, and diplomats that America would need to wage the Cold War. Further, this advanced education only for males (to the near exclusion of females) was, according to Conant, the practical and hardheaded thing to do.

During the process of completing his field work for his study of American high schools, *The American High School Today* (that was published to much acclaim in 1959), Conant realized that many of the talented students who were not going on to college were girls.[24] This struck him as appropriate and fitting, not only because of his desire to prepare males for strategically important careers but also in light of his strong commitment to reducing college enrollments in general. (He was a strong opponent of that segment of the G.I. Bill that indiscriminately financed the higher education of any veteran interested in college.) With smaller enrollments, Conant believed, colleges would be more rigorous, especially in science and math—the fields most urgently needed to prevail over Russia. As for females, Conant said, "A good deal of the talk about the bright people who don't go to college just may be a question of the girls."[25] In other statements, he frequently repeated his assertion that enrolling talented males in math and science courses was the nation's first educational priority.

Significantly, all of this preceded by just a few years the 1963 publication of Betty Friedan's *The Feminine Mystique* and a subsequent movement that actively challenged many of the leading cultural assumptions about women. Although stereotypes about the capacity of females to do well in math and science continued to hang on, thanks in large part to the powerful legacy of the cold war, the end was near for all-male colleges and for professional schools which seemed to cater almost exclusively to men. Sexism would continue to adversely affect the efforts of women to get a good education, but the nadir of the cold war would come to be regarded as a painful memory to which educators must never again descend.

Although females were particularly neglected educationally, most students suffered to one degree or another as a result of an educational vision shaped by containment. The intellectual value of the desirable fields of study was rarely an issue, ensuring that the intellectual and social development of every student was hardly ever an explicit concern. Paul Goodman pointed out in *Compulsory Miseducation* that when Conant insisted that a student's individual development be subordinated to the national interest a new watershed in philosophy of education was established that "puts us back in the ideology of imperial Germany," and was tantamount, ironically, to what the Soviets themselves were championing.[26] When Conant was asked what he would advise a high school boy to do who showed talent in science and math but who preferred to pursue a career as a writer, he unhesitatingly responded that the threat of nuclear annihilation obliged the boy to set aside his personal goals for a career as a scientist or engineer.[27]

In a famous series on education published by *Life* Magazine in 1958, a chart, conceived by Conant, describes a typical comprehensive high school. The least promising students take two years of a combined math and science class, learn to differentiate between the words "clown" and "brown," write a simplified job application letter as their major project for senior English, and are destined, as clearly indicated by *Life*'s crude graphic, for a career in "Joe's Garage."[28] The view of schooling was shockingly simplistic. Good schools, so the cold warriors seemed to be saying, counsel a tiny elite, sometimes against their will, into advanced science and math courses, while most of the rest of the students, including academically able girls, are sorted into various forms of vocational training. In their reform agenda, no consideration was given to the role of teachers in using creative methods to foster enthusiasm for knowledge. No mention was made of promoting a positive attitude toward education or of instilling a sense of joy in learning. No place was found for developing the skills to analyze critically the status quo. Finally, no time was wasted according opportunities for the critics of I.Q. tests and other standardized examinations to explain their analyses or to explore pedagogies and alternative assessments that might greatly augment the ranks of those designated "academically talented." These things were largely irrelevant and elicited in cold warriors like Conant a "distasteful weariness."[29] Their lack of imagination, their unremitting instrumentalism, their complete absence of interest in development for the sake of development were all a legacy of the policy of containment they so vigilantly defended. What cold warriors advocated for American schools in the 1950s still overshadows the enduring hope that society might finally commit itself to the all-around growth of every child.

In the first edition of his 1961 book, *Excellence*, John Gardner, the former head of the Carnegie Foundation and the future Secretary of the Department of Health, Education and Welfare in the Johnson administration, wrote that education has a great role to play in sorting out the talented from the untalented. Although aware of the shortcomings of American institutions in promoting equality of opportunity, Gardner's cold war text with containment as its underlying theme, put much more emphasis on the identification of talent than on its cultivation. Additionally, he forthrightly declared that the school has as much of a responsibility to disclose limitations and deficiencies as it does to discover gifts and abilities. For Gardner, the school of the cold war era was not so much in the business of promoting human development as it was intent on employing mechanisms and techniques to measure incapacity and to use those measures to sort students into vocational tracks. All of which was less urgent than the main business of identifying the 3 to 6 percent of the population destined for education in elite colleges and universities.[30]

In *Growing Up Absurd*, Paul Goodman could not fathom why identifying more creative ways to develop and nurture talent in all children was not in the national interest.[31] But in a sense he answered his own question when he began to speculate that perhaps the conventional school did not serve children very well. To employ more progressive methods, to experiment with bolder designs and more imaginative curricula were simply not options in an era when conservatism reigned and the goal of social stability took precedence over everything else.

Paradoxically, though, there were signs in the postwar era that people wanted to embrace a more inclusive, democratic, and progressive educational agenda. Despite the calls for containment and the tentativeness with which so much educational reform was pursued, there were opposing and contradictory trends. Perhaps the most extraordinary of these was the passage and implementation of the Serviceman's Readjustment Act of 1944—better known as the G.I. Bill. This legislation entitled millions of veterans, who otherwise would not have been able to pay for a university education, to go to the college of their choice. The results were extraordinary and apparently exceeded the expectations of virtually everyone. Not only did many more young men and women elect to go to college than was predicted, their academic performance was superior.[32]

As Clarence Karier has said, these events exposed two myths that propped up so much of the educational policy promoted by Conant, Rickover, and other cold warriors. First, that only a few people were interested in attending college. In fact, of the some 16 million veterans eligible to take advantage of the G.I. Bill, at least half did so, which forced many colleges and universities to erect temporary housing to accommodate the flood of eager learners. The second myth was that only a small percentage of students could profit from going to college. Again the record shows that the veterans who took advantage of the G.I. Bill comprised the most studious and successful cohort of college students in American history.[33]

Nevertheless, when the opportunity to renew the G.I. Bill arose, there was little support for it. Economic conditions had changed, making the need for it far less urgent. Government officials, for the most part, worried primarily about its potential impact on the ranks of those pursuing a military career. And, again as Karier pointed out, "the older elite values of college and university administrators reappeared as they, too, testified against the bill."[34] The old, tired assumptions reemerged that college should be reserved for an elite whose primary interest is in getting an education, not to pursue other extrinsic purposes. Nothing could have been more ironic, however, for the veterans had proved how much an education meant to them intrinsically by their serious and sustained experiences in college, and higher education officials had demonstrated quite clearly that throughout the cold war, anyway, "getting an education" must be subordinated to the more urgent goal of attempting to reunite what Conant called "this divided world."

In the mid-1960s, the journalist Charles Silberman began the investigations that would result in his devastating account of the contemporary American school—*Crisis in the Classroom*. What he found was an institution wallowing in joylessness. He wrote: "It is not possible to spend any prolonged period visiting public school classrooms without being appalled by the mutilation visible everywhere—mutilation of spontaneity, of joy in learning, of pleasure in creating, of sense of self."[35] He attributed much of what he saw to "mindlessness," to the failure of the school as an institution "to think seriously about educational purpose . . . to question established practice."[36] Although educators have never given enough time or thought to investigate the purpose and meaning of schooling, the post-World War II era was particularly impoverished in this respect because of the obsession with containment. What Silberman observed in the 1960s, though he did not acknowledge it himself, was one of the legacies of subordinating the development of every child to what were considered to be the strategic necessities of the day.

As I have attempted to show in this essay, however, domestic containment was not always as simple as it seemed. There were opposing trends and implicit contradictions that often undermined the very intention of containment and in some cases set the stage for new possibilities and substantive reform. It is possible to contend that out of the crucible of "containment" emerged the leading social movements of the 1960s. At the same time, it is almost certainly true that containment badly stalled the momentum generated during World War II to recommit ourselves as a nation to acknowledging, building on, and extending the gifts that all children bring with them to school.

Although it is appropriate for schools to attempt to meet the needs of each new generation, its most important mission has always been timeless—to challenge and motivate young people, to develop their habits of mind and heart, to excite them about learning and doing, to encourage thoughtful critique, and to stimulate their sense of wonder about the world. Whenever we have allowed other objectives to override this central mission, we have not only violated the moral imperative of doing all we can to help each person flourish, we have undermined the role of education in fostering a more meaningful and powerful engagement with our common humanity. Nurturing individual and collective growth and striving to clarify our experience as human beings remain the most compelling reasons to continue to support public education. Ironically, nothing extrinsic to the carrying out of these timeless purposes is as likely to provide as strong a foundation for making and sustaining a good society.

But for a more profound perspective on the devastating impact of the cold war on human development and human freedom, allow Clarence Karier to have the last word:

> In virtually every step along the way in the cold war, Americans learned to fear both the enemy without as well as within. And as they did so, they developed the habit of looking over their shoulders, and managed to survive without freedoms they once regarded as sacrosanct. The price of forty years of cold war cannot be measured in dollars and cents; it has had far greater dimensions. When the time came to reconstruct American political, economic, social and educational institutions, it was clear that the cold war had engendered not only an unnoticed loss of freedoms, but had also cultivated a policy with constricted imagination and limited horizons. Although the need for such reconstruction was clearly evident, the dialog that must necessarily precede any such reconstruction was not readily forthcoming. A society dominated by fear, ever-desirous of security, satiated with image rather than reality, and frantically willing to make any sacrifice to check the enemy without and within, was not a society in any condition to face up to its many problems in order to fulfill the promise of America as the last great hope of humanity. Herein lies the real American tragedy.[37]

14

"What Really Happened": Implications for the Study of African American Educational History

Katrina M. Sanders and Joy Ann Williamson[1]

> Our need today for a broader, more sophisticated educational history, comprehensively conceptualized on sound, structured ideas derived from free minds, playfully interacting with each other and the primary sources perhaps has never been greater, nor given today's social climate, more difficult to produce. Such a history must maintain its crucial cutting edge with the sole purpose of realistically painting the picture of what "really happened" in American education.[2]

In this excerpt from the 1978 Presidential Address for the History of Education Society's annual meeting in Chicago, Clarence J. Karier asks fellow historians to be mindful of how they conduct, interpret, and write American educational history. He warns that producing a truly realistic and responsible historical account is not an easy task. However, a climate of intellectual freedom and free exchange of ideas, a thorough investigation of new and old primary sources, and an interpretation based on sound evidence help one draw a fuller picture of the past. This advice, first articulated over twenty years ago, is still relevant for contemporary historians, perhaps even more so. Current debates regarding "traditional" history and "critical" history reveal a tension between historians and their interpretations of the past. For the purposes of this piece, "traditional" history is defined as a history that supports the status quo, portrays American civilization as a continuous march toward progress, and reflects a particular Eurocentric perspective. "Critical" history is defined as a history in which multiple voices are used to interpret events; it includes an investigation of motivations underlying actions, and reveals a distinctive multicultural perspective. Rather than resolving the tension by advocating some middle ground between the two, Karier advocates critical realistic history.

Though his work was not primarily focused on African American educational history, Karier's advice is applicable to the creation of a more complete picture of the purpose, nature, and direction of African American education from literacy attempts during slavery to the present. The authors of this piece heed his advice and apply it to our investigations of African American history in general, and African American educational history in particular. First, the chapter will begin with a statement of the authors' positions as critical historians, and an assertion of the authors' belief in the value of multiple perspectives in historical interpretation. Second, we will use African American educational history as a point of departure in order to examine two tools that Karier suggests historians can utilize to ensure that personal assumptions do not taint or overwhelm an accurate interpretation of history: ruthless criticism and a thorough investigation of primary sources, including the motivations of historical actors. Neither ensures an accurate historical analysis nor eradicates personal assumptions from historical writing; however, such tools are invaluable in painting a truer picture of "what really happened" and why. In the conclusion we revisit the debate between traditional and critical history and offer a brief discussion of the tenacious nature of traditional history in primary and secondary schools, the authors' ideas on why this is so, and a renewed call for what Karier calls critical realistic history.

Traditional and Critical Histories

The paradigmatic shift from traditional to critical history began in the 1960s and 1970s and continues to spark intense debate among historians. In the historiography since that time, critical history has become respected and popular; however, traditional historians resent the new interpretations and consider them a threat to national character. Though critical history has gained recognition in academic circles, primary and secondary school texts continue to be dominated by traditional history.[3] For instance, scholars attacked the *National Standards for United States History,* published in 1994 and meant as a curriculum and teaching guide to improve the quality of history education in primary and secondary schools. Its use of critical history angered certain scholars who criticized it for its use of multiple perspectives, "politically correct" slant, and omission of "traditional history." Lynne Cheney, former Chairwoman of the National Endowment for the Humanities and perhaps the most vocal critic of the *National Standards,* lamented the change in focus for the history classroom. Whereas "Lessons from History," a previous publication regarding standards in the teaching of history, was "honest about the failings of the U.S., [but] regularly manage[d] a tone of affirmation," the National Standards publication concentrated on "multiple perspectives." Rather than portraying the American Revolution as a part of "the long human struggle for liberty, equality, justice, and dignity,"—as Cheney believes it should be remembered—the National Standards asks students to investigate how the American Revolution did or did not serve the interests of different groups. According to Cheney, investigating such questions revealed a "revisionist agenda" and a "great hatred for traditional history."[4]

Similarly, since history in schools is a vehicle to create civic pride and patriotism, some traditional historians have labeled critical history and those who write it and advocate its use in classrooms as anti-American, anti-Western, and divisive.[5] Critics charge that altering history textbooks to include diverse groups and discussions of oppression, domination, and resistance will alienate White students or make them feel guilty for past wrongs; it will lead to separatism and societal fragmentation; it is an attack on the "common" American identity; it will create a nation full of pessimists and cynics; and including it is more about political correctness and ethnic self-esteem than about historical accuracy. Further, they lament the "disuniting of America" and admonish schools to "teach history for its own sake—as part of the intellectual equipment of civilized persons—and not to degrade history by allowing its contents to be dictated by pressure groups, whether political, economic, religious, or ethnic."[6] Of course, the ideals of equal opportunity, meritocracy, and democracy have been tested, but progress assures us that America's racial problems have either been solved or soon will be. History textbooks should report the common American experience and demonstrate the strength and moral character of our nation rather than focus on the derailed American Dream.

Karier's writings can be used to refute these claims on two fronts. First, Karier contends that historians cannot escape their own value orientations that, in turn, influence their historical research. In *The Individual, Society, and Education: A History of American Educational Ideas*, Karier notes that "History can be and is used to support or discredit every social institution created by men. The student of the past is inevitably involved with the issues of the present."[7] However, Karier warns against those who charge critical historians of presentism and maintain that traditional history is free from advancing particular agendas. Traditional historians, Karier believes, are often themselves guilty of the charges they level against critical historians and can be the least self-reflective of their own research.[8] Traditional history is not without a political agenda—it defends the status quo, promotes patriotism through heroification, and explains contemporary American political, social, and economic structures as the pinnacles of American goodness and progress. Because critical historians choose to investigate history using a different lens and different tools does not mean they are perpetrators of a presentism that distorts historical truth. Instead, they seek a more representative, and therefore more accurate, history.

Second, Karier promotes the issue that most disturbs traditional historians—the use of multiple perspectives in the study of history. Karier maintains that there is no "Historical Truth." Instead, there are "historical truths" that contribute to a fuller understanding of history: "History is not the story of a man's past but rather that which certain men have come to think of as their past. One may read a particular *interpretation* of a historic event but never *the* history of that period."[9] This multiplicity of perspectives on the past exists because people experience events differently. As women and ethnic minority scholars entered the field of history in the late 1960s and early 1970s, traditional interpretations of history began to erode. These scholars, representing groups whose histories had been ignored by the traditional historians, not only reinserted their constituencies back into history, they reinterpreted historical events and eras through a different—but no less valid—lens.

The importance that Karier puts on perception and interpretation in writing history is consistent with the position of other critical historians. They assert that critical histories tell a more comprehensive story with which all students—including women, ethnic minorities, and members of the working class—can identify, and from which all students can learn of the contributions of all people. Traditional historians express concern regarding the alienation White students may encounter in classes that approach the study of history through multiple perspectives. They are afraid to let students learn of the history of oppression in the United States. Critical historians point out that the traditional approach to history does damage of its own, and they ask why traditional historians are unconcerned with alienation of other students. For instance, historian V. P. Franklin reflected on his own educational experience and noted that the events and people meant to "arouse national pride" made him feel "anger, shame or indifference."[10] Similarly, Adrienne Rich discusses the psychic shock many students experience "'when someone with the authority of a teacher' describes your world and 'you are not in it.'"[11] Critical historians must ask if the protection of White esteem (and, as traditional historians would assert, "a united America") is worth the sacrifice of the same esteem in minority groups.

Beyond reducing alienation in the classroom, critical historians demand accuracy in interpretation and an inclusion of all relevant factors when interpreting particular historical events. Ronald Takaki notes the narrow definition of "American" and of American history in historical scholarship. For instance, Oscar Handlin's *The Uprooted*, a study of great migrations that shaped America, excludes a discussion of the migrations of peoples from Africa, Asia, and Latin America. Likewise, Arthur Schlesinger's

The Age of Jackson does not mention two pivotal historical events during Andrew Jackson's tenure as President—Nat Turner's insurrection and the forced Indian removal policies perpetrated by Jackson and the government.[12] The omission of such crucial information allows only a *partial* understanding of the American past and treats historical actors as if they existed in a vacuum. Histories that refuse to recognize and analyze the impact of various groups on the shaping of American politics, economics, and culture cannot offer a complete or balanced picture.

It is important to note that studying the historical record through multiple perspectives does not mean that an accurate representation of history is impossible. Instead, the multiplicity lends itself to a truer understanding of history. When examined from various angles and with various lenses, a more accurate understanding is possible. Historians applaud Russian, German, and Japanese writers for revising their history texts, thereby allowing students to investigate difficult and uncomfortable national histories. "Is the same wisdom not applicable in the world's leading democracy?"[13] Indeed, the promotion of multiple perspectives and historical interpretations fits well with American notions of a democratic tradition that encourages open inquiry and a healthy skepticism.[14]

Employing Ruthless Criticism for Realistic Histories

As previously noted, the paradigmatic shift from traditional to critical history began in the mid-twentieth century. One such study that highlights this shift is Ray Billington's 1966 work, *The Historian's Contribution to Anglo-American Misunderstanding: Report of a Committee on National Bias in Anglo-American History Textbooks*. In this piece, Billington reviews popular textbooks and finds nationalistic bias commonplace.[15] Although Billington notes that the biases generally were unconscious, he found them to be "potentially more dangerous" than the more deliberate distortions of nineteenth-century texts that were meant to build patriotism because the unconscious biases were not as obvious and less easily detected.[16] Noting these biases, Billington points out the critical role the historian plays in constructing history. He writes:

> ... facts never speak for themselves; they must be scrutinized critically no matter how coldly exact they appear. Whenever they have been arrayed on the pages of a history book they have been placed there by some person. He has selected which of the countless facts from mankind's record to include. In doing so he has deliberately or subconsciously chosen items that reflect his own individual interest, national prejudices, or the tensions of his own time and environment; he has arranged those facts in an order that may well convey a different meaning than would be reflected through another sequence and spacing.[17]

In other words, each person knowingly or subconsciously reveals his or her beliefs and prejudices within every line that he or she writes, though one utilizes data which appear to be objective. As one selects, includes, and arranges data, the historian decides what is important and what is not. If one arranged the data in another manner, there could be a different interpretation.

In 1971, Karier also noted the critical role the historian plays in constructing history. He observed that the historian "cultivates the art of history to add meaning to his present existence and that people prefer one history over another because it is that history which most satisfies their quest for meaning."[18] Noting this, it becomes clear why he would seek a "critical realistic history," which he defined as a history that is "critical when it comes to both our inescapable present and past, and realistic with respect to our constant seeking to determine what 'really did happen.'" To obtain this type of history, Karier suggested that historians "take Marx's advice seriously and undertake 'ruthless criticism of everything that exists, ruthless in sense that the criticism will not shrink either from its own conclusion or from conflict with the powers that be.'"[19]

Like Karier, the authors of this piece also seek a critical realistic history. We recognize that by submitting to either the fear of what we will find or to those who favor a more patriotic interpretation, we hinder more comprehensive accounts. Karier's call for a self-reflective examination is not a personal attack on traditional or critical historians but rather a call for historians to examine their own realities and to acknowledge when and how those realities influence how they interpret and write history.

As the twentieth century comes to a close, it is becoming more evident that the call of Karier and those like him is being heeded as historians, increasingly, criticize their own personal motives in their interpretations as well as their data. In Anthony Molho and Gordon S. Wood's *Imagined Histories: American Historians Interpret the Past*, various historians reflect on the numerous ways American historians have traditionally "imagined the pasts" of their own country as well as others. Admitting that this examination is only occurring because "the identity of the United States and the discipline of history are shifting in profound ways," these historians point to a "vast and unsettling transformation" in the writing of history that is forming a "historical revolution" in America and is "affecting the ways Americans have thought about the past."[20] While the traditional historian may view this critical, transformative, historical revolution as undermining traditional American history, the authors find that by acknowledging and analyzing the voices and experiences of diverse historical actors, truer, more comprehensive histories will emerge.

Utilizing ruthless criticism is especially important to the study of African American educational history. Traditional popular accounts often ignore the group's desire for, appreciation of, and efforts to achieve an education.[21] However, when utilizing ruthless criticism we begin to unravel the events surrounding the education of Blacks in America. Increasingly, scholars of African American educational history are revolutionizing the way that history is researched and presented by pushing beyond the top-down interpretations (White ideas on Black education) to identify and analyze bottom-up interpretations (Black ideas on Black education). African American educational historians are not only examining the formal and well-known endeavors in Black education, like those supported by White philanthropists, but also those supported, and in many cases organized, by Blacks themselves.

James D. Anderson, for example, employed a type of ruthless criticism when he went beyond top-down interpretations to examine motivations behind Black education in the south. Anderson found that in the case of the much talked about Hampton Normal and Agricultural Institute, Hampton's theme,

"'Education for Life' meant the training of blacks to adjust to the life that had been carved out for them within an oppressive social order." Anderson's research revealed that philanthropist Samuel Chapman Armstrong had a "lifelong distrust of highly educated black persons" and used Hampton to "de-emphasize" the "black scholar" and to place on a pedestal the "dull plodders."[22] Thus, Anderson's research showed that in many cases White philanthropists and industrialists projected their own views on the purpose, nature, and direction of African American education in order to regulate the labor force and ensure social control.

Karier also applied ruthless criticism to data that related to minority and ethnic group educational experiences. He once noted that "[o]ne must search long and hard to find any evidence in texts on twentieth century American educational history" that key educators were prejudiced against Blacks, southern Europeans, Mexican Americans, Asians, or Jews. However, upon reading the educators' personal letters, Karier found that "one can readily understand why American educational institutions are so profoundly racist." Although he felt that it would be difficult for historians to miss such "blatantly obvious evidence," he noted the possibility due to their perceptual framework. This being the case, he asked historians to question those perceptual frameworks.[23]

Another example of how perceptual frameworks have narrowed interpretations is the omission of bottom-up endeavors like the educational efforts of Myles Horton at the Highlander Folk School and Septima P. Clark's Citizenship schools during the 1930s and 1940s. Although originally organized to educate rural Whites, Highlander also educated Blacks for empowerment. For example, members of the Student Nonviolent Coordinating Committee received teacher training at Highlander along with a wide range of resources including reading classes, protest method classes, and network bases. Just as Highlander educated for empowerment, so did the Citizenship Schools. Utilizing workshop formats and the culture of the oppressed, Citizenship Schools helped people learn to read, write, and fill out money orders and voter registration forms. The goal was to empower the oppressed so that they could help themselves.[24]

Historians are not infallible. Although we often contend that our data are objective, it is important to realize that we are not. Since our realities are different, we are prone to selecting and presenting data that will fit those realities. That being the case, it is important for us to constantly analyze critically what it is that we do and why we do it. As noted in *A Different Mirror: A History of Multicultural America*, "It is very natural that the history written by the victim . . . does not altogether chime with the story of the victor."[25] With this in mind, as we seek accurate and inclusive histories, we will continue to welcome, acknowledge, and criticize ruthlessly those perspectives for the truths that they bring.

Investigating Motivations with Primary Sources

A growing use of primary source data facilitated the shift to critical historiography. Historians combed diaries, newspapers, personal correspondence, and manuscripts and found that traditional interpretations failed to explain phenomena adequately. Also, scholars began to investigate motivations behind historical acts—motivations which previously were excluded from historical writing as irrelevant to the history itself. Accused of rediscovering sin, taking quotes out of context, and writing morality plays backwards, critical historians were attacked for examining the moral tone of the period and of the historical actors. However, the authors agree with Karier's assertion that to divorce the historical actor from his or her intentions and motivations is to pretend that people are not influenced by prevailing ideologies.

If motivations and intentions remain separate from the history of African American education, understanding its development is difficult to impossible. For instance, it is just as important to understand *why* certain educational theorists and philanthropists helped fund African American education during the post-bellum era as it is to know that various historically Black institutions began emerging. Historians must ask, why did African American education develop the way it did? Was it a purely benevolent act to educate the freedmen and freedwomen after being liberated from bondage? Why was the Hampton-Tuskegee Model of education so heavily supported financially? The answers to such questions reveal the motivations and intentions of a particular group attempting to control and dominate another and explain why industrial education for African Americans—rather than liberal education—gained support. It is an uncomfortable history, but it is our history nonetheless.

To ignore motivations and shield students of history from the furious debates of our past is to reduce history to a chronology of insipid facts and innocuous biographies. Historical actors reacted to and shaped the society around them and were driven by motivations, intentions, ideas, and ideologies. Understanding the political climate in which they lived, the debates in which they engaged, and the motivations behind their actions is pivotal if we are to understand the full texture of history. Beyond a contribution to a fuller understanding of history, including a discussion of motivations and of historical debates can illuminate present conditions: "Whether one deems our present society wondrous or awful or both, history reveals how we arrived at this point. Understanding our past is central to our ability to understand ourselves and the world around us."[26] Examining particular intentions and motivations with regard to African American educational history can inform current discussions, from the establishment of historically Black colleges, to affirmative action, to the initiation of Black Studies.

In the field of African American educational history, new primary sources have been unearthed and formerly used sources reinvestigated and examined. Such sources have proven invaluable in reconstructing parts of African American educational history. For instance, Vanessa Siddle Walker investigates the education Black students received in a segregated rural North Carolina school from the mid-1930s to the late-1960s.[27] The common assumption is that Black students languished in such schools. Without denying the unequal distribution of resources, Walker demonstrates that such blanket statements should not pass for overwhelming historical "fact." Through historical ethnography and a pairing of oral and written evidence, she demonstrates that some segregated schools succeeded in providing nurturing environments; hired highly qualified classroom teachers; practiced institutional and interpersonal caring to facilitate student development; cultivated a cadre of parents, teachers, administrators, and staff committed to educational excellence; and produced academically and socially fit graduates. She also disentangles the relationship between lack of resources and educational environment by demonstrating that Black schools—though handicapped by lack of funds and materials—managed to provide their students with valuable and positive schooling experiences. Such historical investigation and use of primary sources not only illuminates a part of African American educational history that has been ignored but can contribute to an understanding of what questions we ought to be asking regarding the education of contemporary African American youth.

Historians, of course, must apply the same degree of critical analysis to primary sources as they bring to bear on other aspects of their work. Karier's critique of David Garrow's Pulitzer Prize winning book, *Bearing the Cross: Martin Luther King, Jr., and The Southern Christian Leadership Conference,* draws attention to the author's misuse and manipulation of primary sources. As Karier says of Garrow,

> Under the guise of being sympathetic but objectively realistic, Garrow created a psychologically damning portrait of America's most important black leader, all done with the heavy use of material furnished by America's secret police agencies. What seems most unfair is that this character assassination is presented as an objective running account of what happened.[28]

Explicit in Karier's discussion is the historian's use of primary sources manipulated to tell a particular story for a particular purpose. Perhaps the most disturbing element of the misuse of primary sources is that misinterpretation often is disguised as "Truth." Beyond the misuse of historical sources, historians can further damage history if they do not practice ruthless criticism of their sources and do not expand their perceptual framework to allow for various possibilities and outcomes. Karier asks, if we assume that the material Garrow uses was carefully censored by the Federal Bureau of Investigation, how would the omitted material reshape what was left in the file? Under what circumstances were the files written? What does this do to the credibility of the evidence? Garrow's failure to investigate such questions and critically examine his evidence leads to a gross misrepresentation of both King and the Civil Rights Movement. Also, Karier demonstrates that Garrow's perceptual framework leads him away from evidence necessary to understand King's psychological state. For instance, only in passing does Garrow mention the well-documented FBI attempts to "break King down," including wiretaps, false correspondence, organization infiltration, and suggestions to commit suicide. Instead, Garrow describes King in a psychological vacuum and as spiritually depressed, emotionally fatigued, and preoccupied with death—as if this were all of King's own making. Ignoring the outside influences on King's mental and emotional state leads Garrow, according to Karier, to false conclusions.

Again, complicating history by investigating the motivations of historical actors is not meant to shame or devalue history or the historical actor. Its purpose is to make the historical figure human, to complicate our understanding of the past, and to provide a context for understanding the actions of the actor. Critical historians argue that exposing students to the horrors of the American past and the jaded motivations of our heroes is not unpatriotic. Instead, investigating "the frailty of national leaders or contradictions between lofty political principles and shabby practices" allows students to think critically and become truly informed citizens.[29]

Conclusion

Why is the traditional interpretation of history so tenacious in our society and in our schools? How can misrepresentations such as Columbus discovering America and the myth of the first Thanksgiving remain "historical fact?" Several explanations exist, including the status assumed by traditional historians for their work and the role of traditional history in schools. First, traditional historians position themselves as the norm and their traditional histories as "True history." Similarly, they have defined their research as "objective," declared their interpretation of history "correct," and described themselves as defenders of the American past and a common identity against the onslaught of "the cult of ethnicity."[30] They label other historical interpretations as revisionist history with an overtly political agenda, as an attack on sacred American ideals, and as highly subjective. Such definitions are a powerful tool used to discredit or at least diminish critical historical scholarship. In spite of these challenges, critical historians continue to advance the field, producing important new work, even if little of it finds its way into schools.

Second, the authors believe that shaping the past in the traditional mold serves the purpose of sanitizing history for public consumption, especially in primary and secondary school settings. Where the historian's choice of sources and perceptual framework can lead to a narrow version of history in works meant for professional consumption, the construction of comfortable histories for youth is more manipulative. "Even when professional historians and instructors are willing to consider a more balanced and comprehensive history among themselves, there remains the tendency to teach children a history that celebrates consensus, progress, assimilation, intergroup harmony and democracy."[31] As the critics cited earlier in this chapter state, why not stress these themes? As James Loewen banters, "we want our children to be optimists, don't we?"[32]

The authors believe it is a disservice to students and to history itself to paint such a bland and flat landscape. History is filled with interesting debates, twists and turns, contradictions, and intrigue. Complicating history—including African American educational history—with a multiplicity of perspectives, a ruthless investigation of sources, and an understanding of the motivations of historical actors will broaden and texturize the field. Further, if we believe that understanding history leads to understanding the present, as the authors of this piece do, students can take the lessons learned and apply the same scrutiny to present conditions. As Karier states,

> The question really is not whether our history is going to be optimistic or pessimistic, nor is it a question of whether it is going to be conflict-oriented or consensus-oriented but rather whether or not it is going to be critical or uncritical and whether or not that historical reality of what

"really did happen" is taken as our guiding goal, a touchstone, constantly sought after....[33]

In short, we do not need optimistic history or pessimistic history; we do not need sanitized history; we do not need a history to offend the least number of people. We need critical realistic history informed by a rigorous examination of historical sources and a multiplicity of perspectives if we are to produce an intelligent and informed citizenry.

15

The Ideology of Progressive Education and Its Implications for American Imperialism

Gilsang Lee

The thought and practice of American education have been formulated in the process of consistent responses to various challenges to the capitalist social order established by, and in favor of, a racially, economically, and politically selected minority, while a number of different rhetorics for the rationalization of this order were used according to the changing circumstances. Schooling has played a constant role as an instrument to overcome these challenges and maintain the social order, while many educational theoreticians have rationalized this role under the disguise of democracy, science, and national interest. In this process American education has constituted the ideological context of American imperialism as well as provided the capitalist-dominated American society with docile consumers.

Fear of the Ignorant Masses

The United States began the twentieth century with the fear of ignorant masses and the hope of a meritocratic society based on a solid educational system. In his first annual message to the Senate and House of Representatives, President Theodore Roosevelt pointed out the danger of increasing antagonism of the wage-worker, the farmer, the small trader, which was aroused in the process of rapid urbanization, industrialization, and the converging wealth of large corporations. He attributed this "antagonism without warrant" to the ignorance of masses who believed, due to ignorance, that "as the rich have grown richer the poor have grown poorer." It was "a well-known sociological law," Roosevelt asserted, that "the ignorant or reckless agitator has been the really effective friend of the evils."[1]

National leaders such as Roosevelt thought it urgent to teach the ignorant masses that the captains of industry have on the whole done great good for the people and to make them accept the social order as a natural result of an emerging "merit" system in society. Roosevelt emphasized that the merit system was in its essence as democratic and American as the common school system itself. Written competitive examinations were offered as a central means for creating a merit-based society.[2]

The expansion of compulsory school attendance was directed at these ignorant masses, "whose regeneration was seen as particularly vital for the security of the state."[3] Compulsory schooling can be understood, in spite of its paternalistic rhetoric, as a preventive measure against the possible ignorant violence that could threaten the sound cooperation among the different classes in this capitalist society. Just as United States intervention into world affairs was usually the externalization of domestic economic decay, so compulsory school attendance was an example of personalization of social decay. The responsibility for social evils was frequently shifted onto the victims of the evils.

The United States Bureau of Education emphasized the social efficiency aspect of schooling clearly in its 1914 bulletin:

> The public schools exist primarily for the benefit of the state rather than for the benefit of the individual. The State seeks to make every citizen intelligent and serviceable.[4]

Public schools were to produce the new serviceable men and women who would be dependent on the industrial society. With this intention, all states had adopted compulsory school attendance laws by 1918. These compulsory education laws, together with the child labor legislation, increased school enrollments to a great extent.

"Cardinal Principles of Secondary Education," the final report of the National Education Association's Commission on the Reorganization of Secondary Education, reflected this trend, which was formulated during the preceding two decades. The individual society relationship embodied in this report was also held by the progressive liberals who established the Progressive Education Association (PEA) the same year.

In 1918 the United States declared its holy crusade to "make the world safe for democracy" abroad and American educators attempted to institutionalize their reform will. The publication of the "Cardinal Principles" and the founding of the PEA meant that educational progressivism formed almost the mainstream of American education. "Cardinal Principles of Secondary Education," reported in 1918, was in sharp contrast to the recommendations of academically oriented "Committee of Ten" led by Charles Eliot twenty-five years previously. The social efficiency element of the Cardinal Principles, which emphasized the school as an institution to adjust the individual to society, became "the cornerstone of the new progressivism" in education.[5]

This social-efficiency oriented view of the world reflected in the Cardinal Principles stemmed from early progressive ideology, and it contained intellectual justification for repressive measures against individual freedom. Progressive theorists derived their notion of freedom, democracy, and the school's role from their organic conception of society and their recognition of individual differences. Charles Cooley, Edward Ross, and Jane Addams, for example, all were concerned with the establishment of a more efficient social mechanism in order to prevent conflict and to establish a harmonious organic community.[6] Harmony between the individual and the society was considered vital for a modern society and essential for the individual's ability to contribute to the larger social order. The major concern of the progressives was about how to differentiate individuals and decide their special function in society. Society's soundness depended on efficient specialization. Human beings were not perceived as equal when Cooley said "The theory of a free order is that everyone is born to serve mankind in a certain way, that he finds out through a wise system of education and experiment what that way is, and is trained to enter upon it."[7] Men were equal only in that they ought to serve the society regardless of their race, class-status, and education.

Like Theodore Roosevelt, progressive theorists worried about the irrationality of the ignorant masses. They saw the masses as unable to think rationally because they were governed by emotion. Progressives attempted to confine rationality to a small, elite group. This concept of the elite and the average person became the basis of the twentieth-century progressive leaders' view of democracy and freedom. Democratic society is one in which everybody is selected reasonably, assigned to a special function, and ultimately satisfied with their role without any resistance. Therefore, the task of sorting individuals for specialized roles was most important. Individuals may enjoy freedom to find their natural place and serve the society. This selection was to be carried out "according to the needs of society" and by elites who allegedly had the ability to grasp those needs and evaluate the talent of individuals.[8]

Few disagreed with the idea that the school could play its role efficiently as a sorting agency. Schools were perceived as a scientific mechanism, able to identify each individual's talent, assign him a proper goal, and train him to achieve it. As long as it was consonant with society's needs, each individual's capacity was to be developed to its fullest.[9] Progressives' notion of individual difference supported their argument of the inherent inferiority of certain races, their support for immigration restriction, their espousal of eugenics for social improvement, and their rationalization of occupying the lands of other people for democracy and civilization.

The increasing menace of inferior races made the society more complex and called for some efficient means of discipline in order to maintain the social order. School education, sports, arts, playgrounds, and various group activities were designed by the elite group as excellent means of discipline by which everybody could find and enjoy their role voluntarily. "Cardinal Principles of Secondary Education," based on the social efficiency spirit of the progressive theorists, gave the schools the task of fitting the children to the needs of the social structure. Most of the educational reforms of the first half of the twentieth century actually reflected or followed the "Cardinal Principles": "the emphasis on experience and projects as the best method of learning, the emergence of the new field of curriculum development, the discovery and celebration of the child-centered school, the appeal to educational science. . . ."[10] For example, the first important purpose of vocational education was without doubt "to match native and acquired talents with the society's manpower demands."[11]

The slogan "equality of educational opportunity" was formulated to overcome "the explicit class nature of the earlier rationale."[12] The equality of educational opportunity ideal was based on the assumption that many children were inherently incapable of intellectual education, and this notion became the conventional wisdom in education by the 1910s. Public schools were to be efficient agencies to sort children into their appropriate positions in the stratified industrial society fairly after giving equal educational opportunity to all. The only questions were how to justify the differentiation, and with what kind of acceptable criteria.

The testing movement, sponsored by corporate foundations, attempted to form an objective set of criteria to differentiate individuals in the name of science. This movement, together with the slogan "equality of educational opportunity," transformed American society into a twentieth-century "meritocracy."[13] The twentieth-century testing movement began with the "Race Betterment" activities, which were based on an American belief in progress, racial superiority of Anglo-Saxon whites, and faith in science.

Fear of ignorant masses and hope in rule by the intelligent elite were explicitly expressed in most progressives' writings. The dream of a "meritocratic society" in which the intelligent minority directs the inferior majority occupied the minds of these intellectuals and, more importantly, began to be disseminated to the public as the twentieth-century brand of democracy. Educators, school administrators, and educational scientists appear to have rationalized the development of a tracking system in secondary schools by the 1920s.

Most schools changed their curriculum to fit a differentiated tracking system, believing that scientific tracking coincided with the ideal of equal educational opportunity. The tracking system in schools was, without doubt, based on the stratified capitalist social structure, which was unilaterally favorable to the capitalist class. It was hopeless to expect that true merit acted as the basis for the selection process because it was not possible to realize equal opportunity in any sense without changing the current racist, capitalist, and elitist society in which the schools operated. Through the class-biased tests and the tracking system in schools, in fact, social classes were to be recapitulated and the hierarchical social order maintained. Test experts insisted that the tests were culture-free and that ordinary people accepted the alleged objectivity of the tests. Even though evidence proved the class nature of the tests and tracking system, the people obsessed by the illusion of objectivity seem to have been intoxicated by exceptional cases of upward social mobility achieved occasionally by lower class children and reported by the mass-media.

Most American high schools since the 1920s, following the Cardinal Principles, used two means to create a sense of unity among students. The first was to teach a well-organized social studies curriculum. The second was to encourage participation in the so-called extracurricular activities. According to Joel Spring, during the 1920s, "extra-curricular activities developed into an educational cult."[14] The basic goal of extracurricular activities was to produce a unified, cooperative "industrial intelligence" with common ideals and goals. Students were, through these activities, to practice democracy that allowed everyone the opportunity to exhibit his or her best talents for the good of unequal society. Schools tended to reinforce the existing unequal social structure in spite of the slogans that schools could break down the walls between classes.

The rhetoric of progressive reformers for "meeting individual needs" and for "learning by doing" resulted in the schools casting people into their social positions and perpetuating social stratification. Extracurricular programs were devised to prevent possible conflict between the classes, but it could not lower the wall that existed between classes. Certainly most people in control of the schools liked to maintain the social structure that allowed them to wield the power in schools. John Dewey was representative of those reformers who wanted change but only without much conflict. His view of the individual and society would represent the framework in which most twentieth-century educational reformers were confined.

Dewey's belief in collective institutional progress transformed the individual into "a means rather than an end to social order."[15] He rationalized the need for state power to control human beings through manipulating their thoughts and actions. He felt the necessity for elites to foster social change and to control the irrationality of the masses. His commitment to systematic social change through collective efforts, belief in elite experts, and the fear of irrational masses led him to look favorably upon educational reforms in collective Russia during the 1920s. In his *Democracy and Education*, Dewey asserted that all men were to be educated in order to realize their different talents in social relationships without causing any disorder.[16] In education, twentieth-century new liberals, including Dewey, supported maintaining a mass system of schooling "dedicated to filling the need of society for a citizen capable of adjusting to the necessities of an industrial system."[17] Their social efficiency-oriented view, reflected in most pragmatic and experimental reforms, ignored education for the sake of individual development.

For the most part, as Michael B. Katz says, progressive education represented "a conservative movement" in that it tried to make changes within the given social order.[18] Considering this nature of progressive and liberal educational reforms, the schools could not but be conservative. Most radical challenges to the role of American public schools, appearing between the two world wars, tended to attempt to change the social settings themselves, which were regarded as the source of evils. They had a strong belief in the power of the school as the liberal reformers did. The conservative nature deeply rooted in American intellectual tradition, however, could not tolerate the radical challenges of some undisciplined intellectuals.

Fear of the Undisciplined Intellectuals

As we observed above, American schools were established by accepting and internalizing a social efficiency principle around the 1920s as an instrument for the conservation of values and the creation of unity out of diversity. These values were those of the dominant group or class in the capitalist society. In the early 1930s Americans were trying in many ways to save the nation from the deep trouble of the Depression. Even though the economic distress deepened, showing no end, few Americans questioned the very principles underlying the capitalistic social system itself or lost their faith in the system completely.[19]

In education, reflecting this faith in the American way, "the illness of society became diagnosed as simply a lack of education," and better education was understood by many as the solution to this problem.[20] A number of New Deal educational reforms were created and operated with the principle of governmental control and planning, which was not a departure from, but a translating into action of, the progressive and the liberal ideologies. New Deal policy on the whole was a conservative approach to social distress in order to save the order from possible ignorant violence. New Deal leaders found the way in education by which they could preserve the main structure of society while expanding political support by assisting the discontents.[21] Some emergency educational agencies such as the Civil Conservation Corps (CCC) and the National Youth Administration (NYA) were created with these explicit and implicit purposes.

Another group appeared by 1932, challenging all conservative efforts at dealing with the national crisis. The economic catastrophe convinced a group of progressive educators that the existing social order and capitalism were not worth saving. George S. Counts, the leader of this movement, argued that the building of a new social order was inevitable and it would be based on a form of socialism. Counts, in his sensational 1932 address *Dare the School Build a New Social Order?*, insisted that the social and moral condition of human beings could not be improved until their social environment had been radically changed. The primary concern of the social reconstructionist educators was different from that of the child-centered progressives, even though both groups were common in their strong belief in collective social improvement and the power of education. The reconstructionists' concern was to rebuild the society through complete planning by the intelligent elite group.

Social reconstructionist educators, in this framework used their view of a new society in determining the kind of individual that education should create. The development of the individual became dependent upon the planner's interpretation of the society to come. As the experts in this social planning, social reconstructionists themselves were filled with a sense of mission, at first to save American society from an undemocratic situation, and later to save the world from undemocratic forces. They attempted to realize a social revolution by inspiring teachers with this sense of mission and disseminating their idea of reform into the society through the schools. They assigned to teachers the role of "an advance guard point" in social reform. Counts, for example, considered teachers as the only group who could stop social evils and restore social justice.[22] This sense of mission, disseminated through the PEA journal *Frontiers of Democracy* and other publications, was based on a strong sense of elitism and cultural superiority.

Social reconstructionists had been deeply influenced by nineteenth-century educational reformers' views as well as the social, economic, and political conditions of the 1930s. Their desire to reform society and their idealistic approach to education were the legacy of nineteenth-century reformers such as Horace Mann. They, as their predecessors had done, had a naïve sense of duty that they could and should contribute to the improvement of society. They had an idealistic view of the power of education to eradicate social evils. They viewed themselves as a force capable of directing social change.

Even though both groups, the nineteenth-century reformers and the twentieth-century reconstructionists, were similar in the impractical view of reform, there was a fundamental difference between the two. While the nineteenth-century reformers wanted to change certain elements in society within a framework of an established system of values, the twentieth-century reconstructionists wished to reform the social system itself. The former believed that dominant social values were beyond criticism. Consequently, they turned their attention to correcting those individuals whose behavior deviated from the dominant social order. On the other hand, individual behavior was not the major concern of social reconstructionists, because they were primarily interested in the problems of the social structure itself.

Because of this difference in the target of reform, the reconstructionists met severe difficulty in finding any realistic way to achieve their purpose. First of all, American teachers did not have sufficient power to lead social change, especially when the society faced an economic crisis. Teachers in America were, as C. A. Bowers pointed out, in those days treated only as public employees who were hired and fired at the discretion of the people who controlled the schools.[23] Their major concern, at that time, was about fluctuating prices and salaries; additionally, the Roosevelt administration's low estimation of educators was felt as a real threat to the teacher's position.[24]

The social reconstructionist believed that experts could perceive where the society should be moving and should inspire teachers with a proper sense of duty. They claimed that educators had a legitimate right to direct the course of social change in a transitional age. Their view on the relation between the education and the role of the elite seems to be similar to that of early progressives and may not be compatible with democratic ideals. The editors of *Frontiers of Democracy* showed their strong belief in intelligence when they wrote that "we have faith in human effort when guided by intelligence."[25] Charles Beard criticized frontier educators' fabulous elitism and interest in power by saying:

> The schools have no access to super-wisdom. If they do, then, educators might well take over the government of the country.[26]

Some criticized the social reconstructionists for being filled with the idea of their own superiority and for having the professional conceit to believe that real improvement could be brought about only by intelligence. For example, the American League Against War and Fascism again blamed the frontier intellectuals for their desire to substitute a planned society for the present chaos and to set up the rule of the "best people" over the masses.[27]

The reconstructionists' belief that the development of a new social order should depend on certain social outlooks predetermined by the planners gave rise to the so-called "indoctrination debate" in the 1930s. Counts argued that some imposition was inevitable in education. This support for the imposition arose partly from the paternalism adopted by many earlier political and educational progressives. Few reforms were based on the assumption that the ordinary people would be capable of rational thinking. The elite group might assume the responsibility of the decision-making. The social reconstructionists' elitism led to the conclusion that the student should accept predetermined social ideals.[28]

In spite of the heated debate about freedom, teachers were, Mary Anne Raywid concluded, imposing only the dominant values of the existing society on the students.[29] The successful influence of conservative pressure groups and the demand of conservative community leaders restricted efficiently both the freedom to criticize and to teach anything inconsistent with the existing social order.[30] Howard K. Beale, in his book *Are American Teachers Free?*, reached a similar conclusion with persuasive evidence that few liberal or radical teachers could be found in the schools during the 1930s.[31]

Because of ideological weakness and their lack of practical means to reform society, the social reconstructionists of the 1930s did not make any radical improvement in the real world of the school. On the contrary, their radical rhetoric, entangled with communist movements in the mid-1930s, contributed to invoke a conservative reactionary suppression in the schools. Consequently the progressives were divided and finally conquered in the midst of dealing with the radical teachers in schools.

It seems that the social reconstructionists and communists had a similar purpose: a radical change in the social structure itself. This similarity in orientation between these two groups made some of the 1930's radical educators wander on the marginal line between socialism and communism. There were surely crucial differences between the two groups in their perceptions of the driving force of social change. While reconstructionists believed that social improvement was possible through the school power, the communists thought that social reform could not but be reserved until education was rescued from the influence of the ruling class. Karl Marx indeed had no objection to the schools being an instrument of society. But he was not content with letting this agency remain in the hands of the ruling class. Earl Browder had the same view that the school was a "captive of the bourgeoisie" and that the communist education was possible only in communist schools.[32] Because schooling was conceived by the communist as "a weapon the effect of which is determined by the hands which wield it, and by who is to be struck down," educational reform without social revolution was helpless and unimaginable.[33] The class struggle by which the commander of education would be determined, therefore, was thought of as an inevitable and historically predetermined way to a classless society.

On the contrary, the social reconstructionists assumed a social revolution which should be initiated and led by the elite. That is, they emphasized the role of the "best minority" rather than mass power. The reconstructionists pinned their hopes on the power of intelligence, while the communists primarily relied on the power of class consciousness among the working class people.

By 1920, American communists were scarcely concerned about activities in schools. However, the onset of the Depression heightened and expanded the activity of the communists in schools. This change provided the occasion for the first large-scale Congressional investigation of the communist activity in American schools in 1930. The final report of this committee, with Hamilton Fish as its leader, concluded that the communist activity in American universities was negligible. American communists, in the mid-1930s, succeeded in stirring up a number of teachers who were depressed as a result of being asked to do more work for less money. And they could associate with some radical progressives irritated by the conservative repression of the teachers' union movement. Even though they took the controlling power of the American Federation of Teachers Local No. 5 (New York) for a while, their success instead provided a timely excuse or legitimized ongoing planned suppression.

By 1935, more than twenty states enacted laws which required loyalty pledges for teachers. It aimed at eradicating or preventing the employment of radical teachers who were accused of "imposing un-American and subversive doctrines on the nation's school children."[34] In the midst of widespread constraints on teachers' freedom, bitter critics were heard against the loyalty oath and other suppressive measures such as censoring library books.[35] People like William Randolph Hearst devoted himself and his business to stirring up reactionary public opinion. And a number of patriotic groups led attacks on radicalism in schools. More important, local businessmen also joined or supported the patriotic associations in order to instill pro-American doctrines in students. The furor over the textbooks of Harold Rugg illustrates the business connection to the conservative suppression. "His hostility to the profit motive, his awareness of chronic inequalities, and his faith in social planning were anathema to conservatives."[36]

It is interesting that the arguments both for and against loyalty oaths were based on the social efficiency principle. The conservatives wanted to socialize the students into an existing value order, while the liberals expected to impose new social ideals on the students by increasing the teacher's freedom to criticize social evils. Individual freedom was not the major issue at that time.

Fear of Undemocratic Forces

Some radical movements in the 1930s were struck down by leading progressives such as John Dewey and George S. Counts, who in a united front with the communists, fought against the conservative forces who wanted to maintain an "undemocratic" social order. The presumed national crisis before America's entrance into World War II made most liberals move in the conservative direction. And they, now along with the conservatives, led the movement to eliminate teachers who prevented the students from accepting the superiority of the American way of life and institutions.

William S. Taylor, the chairman of the NEA's Academic Freedom Committee, cautioned that, "there is . . . always a danger that certain persons may hide under the cloak of academic freedom and disseminate propaganda in our public schools."[37] In 1941, the NEA adopted a resolution which included this item: "The NEA is opposed to the employment, in any school, college, or university, of any person who advocates or who is a member of any organization that advocates changing the form of government of the United States by any means not provided for under the Federal Constitution."[38] The American Federation of Teachers, under Counts, revoked three communist-dominated local unions in 1941 and amended its constitutions to reject any applications of teachers "whose political actions are subject to totalitarian control such as Fascist, Nazi, or Communist."[39] Proof of wrong action was not necessary to expel a teacher from the school. Guilt by association was approved and applied to many cases in the name of protecting democracy.

Political purges in Soviet Russia, Hitler's occupation of some European countries, and the German-Russia Pact inspired a sense of national crisis and promoted the liberal progressives' return to the mainstream of American liberal thought which, to be sure, was conservative. The conservatism of American progressive education in this national crisis can be explained by seeing some leading progressives' positions in a heated argument that occurred just before the United States entered the War. The heated debate on the PEA journal *Frontiers of Democracy*'s statement *This War and America* shows the progressive educators' deeply rooted elitism, cultural superiority, and faith in the expert society.

A handful of liberals and progressive educators objected to America's entrance into the War, remembering the disastrous consequences that had resulted from their failure to face the crisis of World War I. They regarded the war as a clash between rival imperialists. Before Pearl Harbor, Charles Beard, as an isolationist, maintained that "we should concentrate our attention on tilling our own garden. It is a big garden and a good garden though horribly managed and trampled by our greedy folly."[40] By the time of Pearl Harbor, however, the majority of liberals in education were strongly in support of going to war.

Both the NEA and the PEA, in 1940, had abandoned their isolationist position and reversed themselves by calling for "a comprehensive educational program" of national defense. The NEA insisted that the old liberal practice of criticism and protest which the educators adopted so enthusiastically during the Depression years was incompatible with the present national interest.[41] The PEA, in September 1940, prepared a report entitled "National Defense and Education." The report began with a statement which rationalized the use of force as follows:

> While everyone wishes to avoid conflict in which human lives are sacrificed, it has become increasingly apparent that democracy will not survive if democratic countries are unprepared, weak, internally confused or rotten with defeatism.[42]

The report further urged American education to create a bold comprehensive plan adequate for our national needs and for national defense.[43] The October issue of the *Frontiers of Democracy* included the Teachers College faculty's policy statement on "Democracy and Education in the Current Crisis," which recommended that the nation "must be ready to meet force with superior force."[44] Just one year after this statement, in October 1941, twelve of the fourteen members of the Board of Editors of the *Frontiers of Democracy* signed the statement entitled "This War and America," advocating "full responsible participation on the part of the United States in the democratic struggle against the Axis to the extent, if necessary, of actual participation in the war."[45] The frontier educators sanctioned the use of collective force and justified it as the best and the last way to defend the American way of life, the last bulwark of democracy. The meaning of World War II was changed, in their minds, from a conflict between rival imperialistic powers into a democratic struggle against the totalitarian ways of life. They were urging the educators of the United States to expand the cloud of hatred.

After this statement, a number of articles appeared in the *Frontiers of Democracy* explaining why it was urgent for the United States to join the war. The PEA reports, *Frontiers of Democracy* editorials, and the articles following them contained, however, almost no critical analysis of the economic, political, and moral issues that were at the center of the conflict.[46] Instead, the progressive educators appealed to the reader's sense of nationalism, sense of mission, and sense of cultural superiority.

While they attributed the World War to rising nationalism, the frontier thinkers urged the American educators to strengthen the emotion of nationalism among students for national solidarity and unity. Harold Benjamin and Harold C. Hand, two editorial members who did not sign the statement, warned against the rising American nationalism inspired by the elite group:

> Such an attack, if successful, would certainly strengthen the spirit of nationalism among our people and would probably extend the territory over which we could exercise direct political control by imposing our kind of civilization thereon.[47]

Most progressive and liberal educators, apparently and conveniently, forgot that they had criticized the United States just a few years earlier for its lack of democracy. Nationwide, expenditures for rural schools in the 1930s were about half those in urban systems; one-half of black children in the South were not even in school; the average yearly per-pupil cost for blacks was less than $15, compared with a national average of more than $80. The national education honorary society, Phi Delta Kappa, which counted among its members a large number of educational leaders, retained until 1939 a clause in its constitution specifying that "only white males of good character shall be eligible to membership in this fraternity."[48] These were only a segment of the so-called last bulwark of democratic life in the world. These undemocratic practices, frontier reformers insisted from the beginning, should have been removed and reconstructed according to democratic principles. Social reconstructionists had started their movement with their common recognition that capitalistic America had a lot of undemocratic characteristics to be eliminated in order to survive and with their sense of mission that education was the only way to lead to a more democratic society.

Ignoring the real evils at home and forgetting their early arguments, social reconstructionists suddenly transformed undemocratic society to be corrected into the last bulwark of democracy to be defended even by force. They revealed, as Noam

Chomsky pointed out in his "The Manufacture of Consent," America's mysterious collective "historical amnesia" in the name of defending democracy.[49]

The PEA report of 1940 states that "only as the American people are aware of the values of democracy will they be able to resist and curb those who would destroy it."[50] Grayson N. Kefauver insisted, in his "Education in a Democracy at War," that America's entry into the worldwide conflict should be sufficient evidence to justify a very considerable cost and risk in an effort to maintain peace among nations and to contribute to the improvement of the life of all the people of the world.[51] Ernesto Galarza showed this kind of sense of cultural superiority possessed by most American intellectuals in his "The Problem of the Americas" when he said that "there is no doubt that this continent is the last portion of the world where democracy has a chance to survive and grow."[52] Kilpatrick went on to the extent of branding some persons, who objected to the United States' entrance into the war and demanded more democratization at home, as anarchists.[53]

This pro-war statement and the rationalization of using force reveal the kind of ideology which dominated most liberal as well as conservative educators' educational ideals and the educational practices of the first half of this century. However plausible rhetoric may sound about defending democracy or national interest, there can be no doubt that war is the worst preparation for peace and human dignity rather than the best. Nor is war a good or adequate means for defending any way of life. The essentials of humanity have always been impaired by war.

"In any period of emergency," as Howard R. Anderson said, "there are selfish persons who put personal or group interest ahead of the common good. There are still others whose zeal for the common good clouds their judgment. Both groups are likely to be highly vocal in their efforts to reach and influence the people."[54] The *Frontiers of Democracy* statement to support America's entrance into the war shows that most progressive educators, in a time of national crisis in the first half of this century, fell into one or both of these two categories.

Implication for the Coming American Imperialism

As John L. Childs recognized, the manner in which this country both at home and on the war fronts carried on the struggle profoundly conditioned the kind of peace created after the totalitarian powers were defeated.[55] By 1943, the social reconstructionist group turned its attention to the future problem of a postwar world order. The hopeful prospect of playing a crucial role in this new reconstruction task revitalized the social reconstructionist educator's sense of mission. As the guiding leaders in searching for the answer to the question of what kind of world order the United States should build after the war, educational leaders assumed a world in which the American way of life dominated, rather than a world in which different peoples could live according to their own values and traditions. They could not overcome their tendency to ignore or deny the value and significance of other cultures. As Lawrence K. Frank pointed out, "[T]oward other peoples, especially those of a different color, [westerners] have usually acted as the 'master race' which had all the wisdom and enlightenment and therefore was entitled to impose its ideas and religions, its institutions and social practices, and its political and economic control upon their lands and their peoples."[56] Frank argued that:

> The tradition of colonization and of empire, of missionary zeal and trade promotion and economic exploitation are predicated upon this assumption. Like the classical Greeks we will regard those who speak with a different tongue and attempt to order their lives to a different design as barbarians, to be pitied for their benighted condition and to be exploited or degraded whenever they find themselves in the path of the one wise, truly civilized, and really superior people, who bear the "white man's burden!"[57]

Kilpatrick showed this sense of superiority clearly in his "The War in Orient and American Education," when he said about the Chinese people that "They know we have no selfish designs upon them. . . . The people of China have long felt friendly toward us. . . . When the victory is won, that day will offer to this country the greatest opportunity of possible results ever granted in history for one country to help another."[58] Less than one decade after that, however, the people of China turned their back to, and fought against, the United States in the Korean War, calling the United States an imperialist power to be defeated.

American planners of the postwar world order should have recognized, if they really dreamed of a world of peace as they said, that the world order was not to be gained by a regimentation of all peoples to the same pattern of thinking, acting, and believing through a blend of all in a rigid uniformity, and that no single culture could be accepted as the final and the best for all.

Democracy, it is this writer's belief, is a social order in which men who are different from each other can live together in peace and freedom. The prime essence of democracy is the right to be different.[59] Liberalism is the belief in and commitment to a set of methods and policies that have as their common aim greater freedom for individual men and women.[60] Its prime enemy is the use of force. Twentieth-century American education, regardless of prevailed rhetoric about democracy and freedom, contributed to build an efficient society composed of educated people who would recognize that everyone could come to his full being by serving the existing social order.

When the United States came to occupy some other peoples after winning the war, they applied this ideology to foreign people and attempted to build an efficient world society composed of Americanized people who would recognize that every country could become democratic by serving the "master race."

16

Arthur Bestor and Anti-Intellectualism in American Education

Marlene Wentworth

The historian Arthur Bestor died in Seattle, Washington, in December 1994. His obituary in the *New York Times* recognized him as a leading scholar on the constitution, an area in which he had worked extensively following 1956, a year he'd spent at Oxford as Harold Vyvyan Harmsworth professor. Three years earlier, Bestor, then a full professor in the Department of History at the University of Illinois at Urbana-Champaign, published with that institution's university press a book he entitled *Educational Wastelands*, to indicate the erosion of educational ideals which he saw occurring in American schools. The book brought together and expanded upon several articles he had published earlier in various journals, all of which decried the condition of American educational policies. Thus it is Bestor's work in the 1950s which marks his significance for historians of American education.

Fifteen years after the appearance of *Educational Wastelands*, Clarence J. Karier recognized Arthur Bestor as one of the most important commentators on American education in the twentieth century. Karier believed Bestor's criticisms cut more to the heart of the troubles in American education than any of those offered by others who were then describing crises they saw occurring in American schools.

Bestor argued that the function of the school was not to help people adjust to life but to help people learn to think. This was done through the disciplines of science, mathematics, history, literature, English, and foreign languages. The great tragedy of American education, Bestor insisted, resulted from the separation of these disciplines from what went on in the public schools. He believed that what went on was an increasingly insignificant vocational curriculum which was getting more and more anti-intellectual. The public schools, he argued, had lost their natural moorings, the disciplines of knowledge.[1]

The education establishment (or what Bestor called "an interlocking directorate" and David Tyack called "the educational trust") was embedded within the country's school systems by 1953 when *Educational Wastelands* was published. The word "educationists," Bestor explained, corresponded to words like "chemist," "economist," and "physicist," used to indicate those involved in a specific profession. Educators, who like himself were classroom teachers, should be considered distinct from the educationists who formulated and implemented school policies, trained schoolteachers, and set certification requirements for them, and/or prepared graduate students to enter this relatively new profession.

In 1900, at the turn of the century, graduate education as such was practically nonexistent. Studies in the field of pedagogy had a long history, but that field focused on methods of instruction. The new field of education, which began to develop in the early decades of the twentieth century, concentrated instead on administration of schools and school systems, as well as on curriculum development. Driven by efforts of men such as Ellwood Cubberley at Stanford and James Earl Russell at Columbia, the new field grew quickly.

One driving force behind the proliferation of these professionals was the rapid expansion of the high schools during the first two decades of the century. Secondary schools were woefully ill prepared, both in terms of personnel and physical plants, to manage the sudden influx of students brought about by increased immigration and other social factors. Not only was there an urgent need to build more schools quickly, but professionals trained to manage them were also needed. Graduate schools at Columbia, Stanford, Ohio, and other institutions seemingly could not produce fast enough a sufficient number of men and women prepared to fill the multitude of administrative positions in school districts and government agencies, such as state boards of education, which directed the development and management of schools. Consequently, what earlier had been the field of pedagogy was rapidly transformed into one primarily concerned with administration.

Given the critical situation in public high schools, the newly graduated educationists tended to see themselves as coming to society's rescue, and from that perspective it wasn't a huge leap, especially considering the changing demographics of students attending high school, for them to begin to consider themselves the "vicars of society."[2] Unfortunately, this self-perception was accompanied by doubts which had begun to appear early in the century about the adequacy of the traditional curriculum. As it became increasingly necessary to deal with large numbers of students coming from diverse backgrounds, these doubts intensified.

Also at this time, educational psychologists were developing new theories from their investigations into the individual differences found in schoolchildren, theories which would contribute extensively to the philosophy of education being developed by the educationists. Traditionally the focus of educators had been upon the commonalities found among children. With the advent of research on individual differences in the late 1800s this focus shifted to one which could support arguments for the differentiated curriculum. The innovation of providing different subjects for different children, appearing in tandem with beliefs about the need to revamp the classical curriculum, was of great appeal to the educationists. However, despite its pragmatic advantages, the differentiated curriculum had serious faults. Once introduced, it resulted not only in children being sorted, supposedly according to their abilities, but in limiting children to the type of schoolwork they were presumed capable of mastering. At this point the schools departed dramatically from their original mandate to teach the traditional disciplines to all students.

A common belief among school administrators was that for schools to be truly democratic, they should ensure that students were taught the skills necessary to succeed in their likely stations in life as indicated by their individual abilities. Bestor saw this assumption as a travesty of what education was supposed to be. He insisted that the school "becomes an agency of true democratization only if it sends [students] forth with knowledge, cultural appreciation, and disciplined intellectual power," that is to say, the kind of education once accessible only to a privileged few.[3] In rebuttal the educationists charged Bestor with ignoring individual differences in students, and consequently he was judged to be elitist and antidemocratic.

Once the differentiated curriculum became widespread in American schools, the educationists' concern over children who continued to do poorly resulted in the introduction of what came to be known as "life adjustment education." The most vociferous proponents of this type of schooling came from backgrounds in vocational education. Training students for specific skills in particular jobs did not suffice, they argued, to ensure a well-rounded and productive life. These students also needed schooling in social skills. The end result of these arguments was the notorious Prosser resolution, which relegated 60 percent of American children to the study of nonacademic subjects. Bestor specifically attacked this resolution in a presentation made to the American Historical Association (AHA) meeting in 1952.

In conjunction with preparing a paper for presenting to his professional association, Bestor collected signatures from professors in the various disciplines across the country to support a resolution he was drafting to propose reform of teacher education. The resolution urged the creation of a "Permanent Scientific and Scholarly Commission on Secondary Education," to be made up exclusively of scholars and scientists in the various disciplines of learning and to be affiliated with the scholarly and scientific societies of the country, as distinguished from professional education associations and nonprofessional general organizations. It was an attempt to organize historians and other scholars to combat what he saw as dangerously undemocratic trends in American educational policy. He suggested that the best way to begin to correct the situation would be a thorough reorganization of existing teacher training programs across the country. He planned to submit his resolution concurrently with his paper, and accordingly sought scholars to cosponsor it with him.

Bestor secured the support of 695 academicians, including 62 historians. The paper he presented was entitled "Anti-Intellectualism in the Schools—a Challenge to Scholars." It was published by the *New Republic* almost immediately, appearing in its January 19, 1953, issue. *School and Society*, a professional journal for teachers and educationists, printed the resolution in its entirety and without comment in its January 31, 1953, issue.

The AHA Council considered the resolution at its December 1952 meeting, copies of it having been reproduced and distributed in advance to Council members. Its report indicated that "after careful consideration, it was the consensus in the Council that the problem presented by these resolutions is a serious one, meriting close and thoughtful study before any action by the Association."[4] However, the Council felt immediate adoption of the resolution would be "premature" and recommended further study on three grounds: (1) the Association's need to determine its own policy; (2) the need for collaboration with "other learned societies"; and (3) the need to take into consideration "the mature thought of professional educators who are conscious of this problem and would wish to collaborate in the formulation of any comprehensive statement on national educational policy." Incoming president Louis Gottschalk was authorized to appoint a committee to study the resolution.

In Bestor's view the life adjustment program exemplified an unjustifiable response to the issue of individual differences. The fact that its policies denied access to intellectual subjects to large segments of the American school population was, he warned, only one way in which it endangered education in this country. It also posed a threat to that smaller percentage of students who would be going on to college. In an article written for the *New Republic* in March 1957, Bestor pointed out that gifted American children needed an education equal to that afforded to young people in other countries. In their eagerness to address the needs of those they perceived as less intellectually capable, the educationists had established policies which resulted, he feared, in depriving our best and brightest students of intellectual training as demanding as that being received by students of comparable ability in other countries. "American education is dedicated to equality of opportunity," Bestor wrote, but that term must be used carefully and with the full understanding that "equality can be achieved by diminishing as well as by increasing the value of what is given. Unfortunately there is such a thing as equal *denial* of opportunity."[5] The launching of Sputnik in October 1957 lent weight to his words.

Bestor recognized that not all schoolchildren will perform equally well in all subjects. His book, *Restoration of Learning*, addressed ways in which such differences might be addressed in schools. However, when the educationists talked about limits of capacity, as they frequently did, they differed substantially from Bestor's meaning. Bestor assumed that all children were potentially capable of doing high-level academic work, and the limits set on their achievement should be determined only through their efforts in such schoolwork. Consequently he believed it was the responsibility of teacher training institutions to produce teachers skilled in making the most of each child's potential.

The assumption under which the educationists formulated their school policies was the converse of this. Presupposing that a large percentage of schoolchildren lacked sufficient intellectual capacity to succeed in rigorous academic studies, educationists set limits on the school achievement of this group beforehand, thereby precluding any opportunity to demonstrate ability.

Bestor and his colleagues in liberal arts and sciences at the University of Illinois, as well as elsewhere nationwide, had become increasingly concerned about the lack of preparedness of freshmen entering college. What, they asked, was happening in high schools to bring this about? Obviously, Bestor explained, high school teachers were not receiving the education necessary to prepare their students properly, and thus colleges of education became his target, including the college of education at the

University of Illinois, one of the leading teacher training institutions in the country.

"What fanned long-standing differences of opinion about the nature and purposes of education into a raging flame at Illinois," Bestor explained in a letter written to the author in 1988, "was an attempt by the College of Education to undercut the University's graduate requirements by unilaterally exempting its students, who were to become the state's future schoolteachers, from subject-matter requirements generally, including an acquaintance with even one foreign language—this in a world just torn by a global war and becoming increasingly interdependent."[6] Understandably such a proposal would infuriate members of the liberal arts and sciences faculty, especially those who already concurred in Bestor's view that the educationists were overstepping their professional boundaries.

As was the case for many educationists throughout the United States, several of the faculty at the College of Education at Illinois were graduates of Teachers College, Columbia. While working on his doctorate at Yale in the 1930s Bestor had taught history at Columbia for several years. He was, therefore, well acquainted with that institution. In the letter quoted above he went on to say,

> At Teachers College the theories of education in which I believed were not necessarily identical with those of colleagues in other departments, but were by no means heretical. Opinions expressed in my writings in the 1950s were freely canvassed at Teachers College in the 1930s and early 1940s. They were voiced not only by members of "subject-matter" departments but also by many distinguished professors concerned with school administration and with the philosophy of education.
>
> What struck me when I came to the University of Illinois in 1947 was the enormous difference between the attitude and functioning of Teachers College as a part of Columbia University and the attitude and functioning of the College of Education as part of the University of Illinois. Members of the Education faculty at Illinois with degrees from Teachers College seem not to have brought with them the attitude I had known at their alma mater, where education was regarded as a joint enterprise involving scholars from every field of knowledge, not as a fief belonging to specialists in what used to be denominated pedagogy.[7]

What did Bestor mean by the kind of education once afforded to the privileged few? His own education exemplified what he considered the best. In defending his criticisms against them, educationists retorted that he had attended only "blue stocking schools." While it may have been true that Bestor attended some of the best schools then available, the retort overlooked his argument that this was the type of schooling which should be made available to every American child.

Bestor's earliest education was in Chautauqua, New York, where he was born in 1908 and where he spent every summer of his youth. Growing up in the culture of Chautauqua Institution helped shaped his ideas about education. His father was for forty years president of the Institution and his leadership retained the insistence upon the importance of popular education (in the sense of education for the populace) that had been the impetus behind its founding in 1874.

The two Methodist ministers who founded the Institution in 1874 believed that to best know God one must learn as much as possible about God's world. Consequently, religion and education were closely united at Chautauqua. Over time its summer educational programs, created at first for schoolteachers, were expanded to appeal to adult learners in general. Eventually the Institution became more secularized and a greater emphasis was placed on the arts, but whatever the focus of any particular summer program, what did not change was the excitement about learning and its importance in adulthood. The term "lifelong learning" was one used consistently by the founders of Chautauqua Institution to describe its purpose. The term is again in vogue, used frequently within the context of vocationalism.

While Chautauqua was peripheral to Bestor's formal education, his father's philosophy in shaping the Institution had an impact. As Bestor wrote in responding to a paper submitted to him by the author, "I do want to say that it [your paper] brought into consciousness something about myself that I had not really thought about, namely the congruence of my fathers' educational philosophy and my own. . . . Your perceptive account has made me aware of how much I subconsciously absorbed from him in my earlier years, two decades or more before I set down my ideas in 1953 in *Educational Wastelands*."[8]

Bestor attended early elementary grades at the lab school at the University of Chicago, founded by John Dewey, and in Washington, D.C. during World War I when his father was serving as Director of the Speaking Division of the Committee on Public Information. His fifth-grade year was spent traveling abroad with his family, after which the family relocated to New York City. Bestor and his sister were placed in Horace Mann School and later attended Lincoln School. Both Horace Mann and Lincoln were developed and conducted by Teachers College as experimental schools; Lincoln School being the epitome of progressive education as it was understood in the 1920s. Bestor went to Yale in 1926, graduated in 1930, and then after doing some teaching, returned to Yale to work on his Ph.D., which he received in 1938.

Arthur Bestor appreciated his excellent education. His writings reveal that he understood the curriculum he'd studied had value at intellectual, emotional, and moral levels. He believed firmly that such an education was not only the birthright of every American child, but was also the country's best vehicle for achieving and maintaining the sort of democracy envisioned by its founders. Like Jefferson, whose works he studied and wrote about, he urged the critical importance of a well-educated citizenry.

Recalling his schools, Bestor said in his letter to the author, they were "distributed more or less evenly between traditional and progressive schools. I was challenged in both. I learned in both. The courses and their intellectual content were substantially the same in both, and I sensed no real differences in their basic educational objectives. Whatever differences I was conscious of lay in matters peripheral to the curriculums."[9] Given the list of schools he attended, it is understandable why Bestor's critics accused him of having been given an elitist education. Far from denying this, however, Bestor argued that the education he'd received was of the quality which should be afforded to every American child as his or her birthright. He debated educational policy on many campuses and before many parents' and teachers' organizations in the 1950s, defending the importance of rigorous intellectual training and urging for all children a thorough grounding in the liberal arts and sciences.

In recognizing the criticisms made by Bestor as more fundamental than others voiced in the 1950s, Karier traced Bestor's arguments to American educational history in the 1920s, when the former classical curriculum, which had been the cornerstone of schooling for hundreds of years, met its demise. The seeds of life adjustment education were sown then, and with each generation there was an increasing tendency toward vocationalism, to the extent that a whole new meaning of "education" had evolved by mid-century. Karier pointed out that as college professors who had been trained under the old classical regime retired and passed away, they were replaced by those trained more in the modern tradition. The development of new knowledge became more highly specialized within each profession, and correspondingly a new body of knowledge had been developed by those who ran the country's schools. When Bestor was in school, he learned from instructors steeped in the earlier classical tradition, but gradually these men and women were replaced by others who had been taught differently.[10] The educationists operated within a very different philosophy of education from that in which Bestor was reared.

In *Educational Wastelands* Bestor discussed the deterioration of cooperation between scholars and scientists in departments of liberal arts and sciences and people in education, tracing the beginning of this decline to the early part of the twentieth century, when this "promising form of cooperation petered out." As the focus on specialization increased, and scholars took on increased responsibility in their own fields for graduate teaching, research, and the production of new knowledge, it was not surprising that they had less time for concerns about public education, much less for exercising vigilance over developments in American high schools. As the new cadre of professionals in education increased, Bestor saw this particular specialization as preempting too much for itself. Instead of concentrating on pedagogy, he contended, educationists have inflated their discipline to encompass all of education. This attitude had the result of dismissing educators like himself. For many of these professionals, the assumption was that only those trained in their specialization had any business concerning themselves about what went on in American schools.

"A new attitude (alien to that which had made Teachers College a beacon-light in American education) had, by the 1950s, come to prevail in many colleges of education besides that at Illinois," Bestor wrote to the author. "It amounts to a diminution and trivialization of purpose—a redefinition of education, focussing on the processes of teaching instead of keeping steadily in mind the ultimate purpose of education, namely, developing the intellectual power of the nation's citizenry. By the 1950s this attitude seems to me to have turned many colleges of education (not least that at Illinois) into bastions of self-satisfied intellectual isolationism, openly hostile to the intellectual disciplines which are fundamental to modern civilization and which, because of this, had heretofore been recognized as fundamental in education."[11]

Bestor believed teacher education to be the responsibility not of a single college or department but of a university as a whole, and urged that this function must be reclaimed. When scholars and scientists in the established disciplines began to concentrate on their own areas of specialization, he said, they abandoned serious concern for the preparation of schoolteachers and relegated that function to the educationists. The result was that schools were becoming increasingly anti-intellectual.

Bestor urged that more attention be given to schools by people in the liberal arts and sciences, but Karier, in his "Retrospective One" to the 1985 edition of *Educational Wastelands,* explains why this was expecting too much. By mid-century the trend toward vocationalism in American education had already begun to extend beyond the high schools. Bestor recognized that many of his colleagues in the liberal arts and sciences had contributed to the malaise by concentrating too exclusively on their own fields. However, he failed to acknowledge his own uniqueness in being willing to expend large amounts of time working with teachers of history in public schools. Many professors had little concern for how their disciplines were being taught in the public schools. The rewards of the tenure system drove them to produce and publish new knowledge, not to worry about its dissemination to precollege students. In many places undergraduate education was becoming of less concern than graduate education, particularly in larger research institutions like the University of Illinois.

In his interview with the author in 1988, Bestor spoke further on this issue. "Groups get interested," he said, "in something that defines what they are interested in in a particular way and they do not regard the things that are similar to it or even that use the same language as being part of their movement. In a way you know, I would apply that to the whole of people who call themselves educationists. In other words, I'm no longer, although I taught for fifty years, I'm no longer an educator. I'm a historian, and they don't include that. That may be a kind of exclusiveness of a group that wanted to define itself as those people who were doing certain kinds of things."[12] Certainly, the educationists who wrote in opposition to Bestor in the 1950s saw him as an outsider, someone who knew little about public schools, making charges they saw as unfounded because of his lack of expertise in their area of specialization. Despite his long involvement with the teaching of history—both his own teaching in college classes and his work with high school classroom teachers—and despite the fact that he had written extensively on issues of education,[13] he simply was not one of them. A consequence of this was that little credence was given to what he had to say.

Despite changes in school policies, some of which Bestor was instrumental in effecting, cries for school reform have continued to echo across the country. Huge amounts of revenue have been funneled into education, but a solution continues to elude us. In many schools teachers have increasingly been expected to work with children who are in dire straits in terms of health, poverty, and broken or unsupportive families. The recent "culture wars" and the attack on the body of knowledge created by "dead white men" has added new dimensions to curriculum development. The advent of the Internet and the computer as a teaching tool has transformed the way in which teachers cover material in many classrooms. The question of access to knowledge is now frequently interpreted as meaning the acquisition of a sufficient number of computers for each classroom, an issue very different from Arthur Bestor's concern.

On the face of it, use of a computer to access knowledge should not make the acquiring of it more problematic. Yet "information glut" is far removed from the "organized bodies of knowledge" about which Bestor wrote. Certainly the tendency toward fragmentation is encouraged by the use of computers. Neil Postman argues that just as the transition from an oral tradition of teaching to a tradition that was text-based changed not only the method but the nature of what was learned, a shift from textbooks to computer screens may well have similar results.

As Clarence Karier has pointed out, much of our culture is created by those with whom we study, and the scholars from the early 1900s with whom Bestor studied were long ago replaced by those of his own generation. Instructors of Karier's generation are now retiring, and those who studied with them will likely find their grandchildren gleaning as much information from the Internet as from live teachers in their classrooms. Future generations of educators will, as Bestor said in his dedication to *Educational Wastelands*, "need to know more and think harder than ours." The challenge will be to transform huge amounts of information into the kind of knowledge Bestor and Karier gave to their students. Those of us who were privileged to know and work with these men are grateful for all we learned from them.

17

The Emancipatory Power of Language: Critical Language Awareness and the Legacy of Clarence J. Karier

Timothy Reagan

Prolegomenon

Unlike most of the others who have contributed to this *Festschrift* for Clarence Karier, I do not consider myself to be a historian, nor has the bulk of my own scholarship been historical in nature. My career, rather, has focused primarily on issues of language in education—educational linguistics, foreign language education, language planning and policy studies, the education of linguistic minorities, bilingual education, and so on. Nevertheless, I was a student of Clarence's in the late 1970s and early 1980s, and my experiences with him, both in and out of the classroom, played a major role in my development as a scholar. It was from Clarence, more than anyone else, that I learned the power of scholarly tenacity and the value of careful and reasoned argument, and it was as a role model of intellectual rigor, honesty, humility, and humanity that he had the greatest impact on me.[1]

The focus of this chapter, then, is concerned not so much with Karier's historical scholarship *per se* as with the implications of the *kind* of scholarship that he has embodied for the critical study of language in education and society. I will attempt to provide examples that demonstrate how the role of language in general, and of critical linguistic awareness in particular, can provide a potentially powerful tool in helping us to recognize and challenge elements of ideological hegemony, racism, sexism, and classism in society, and hence work toward promoting social justice in American society.

A good starting point for this chapter is the centrality of language itself in the educational endeavor. All too often, educators and policymakers view language and language issues in education (and, indeed, in society in general) as somewhat tangential to our "real" concerns. Discussions of students whose first language is one other than English are largely limited to debates about the relative merits of bilingual education, English as a Second Language, and immersion programs, while foreign language education remains something of a *terra incognita* for most nonforeign language educators, arguably far more marginalized than any other subject matter in the curriculum. As Leo van Lier recently argued,

> There was a time, from the ancient Greeks to the late Middle Ages, when language was central in educational practices, in the form of the three branches of the *trivium*: grammar, logic, and rhetoric. Then, increasingly, language study became separated from other subjects . . . and became merely one other subject. . . . As a result, language lost its centrality and relevance as an educational focal point, and it became difficult to see how it connected to other parts of the curriculum. . . .[2]

Whether recognized or not, though, language has in fact continued to be the central element that not only makes education possible, but which plays a key role in the construction of knowledge on both the part of the student and the part of the teacher. Assumptions and beliefs about language, as well as attitudes toward language, function in important ways to color and set the parameters of the educational experience, and can, in the classroom context, serve either positive or negative ends.

In this chapter, I will outline and briefly discuss two broad areas related to the interface of language issues and educational concerns: the challenge of "ideological monolingualism" and conceptions of "language legitimacy." Each of these areas provides an important example of both the need for, and application of, what a growing number of scholars have termed "critical language awareness" in education.[3] Such "critical language awareness," I would suggest, is very much in keeping with the kind of scholarship that Clarence Karier has always represented.

The Challenge of "Ideological Monolingualism"

One of the most interesting and challenging aspects of dealing with matters of language and language diversity in the U.S. context is that of "ideological monolingualism." In essence, this refers to a set of commonly held beliefs about language among many (perhaps most) English-speakers in society. Dell Hymes has identified what he takes to be six core, albeit generally tacit, assumptions about language in the United States: 1) everyone in the United States speaks only English, or should; 2) bilingualism is inherently unstable, probably injurious, and possibly unnatural; 3) foreign literary languages can be respectively studied, but not foreign languages in their domestic varieties (it is one thing to study the French spoken in Paris, another to study the French spoken in Louisiana); 4) most everyone else in the world is learning English anyway, and that, together with American military and economic power, makes it unnecessary to worry about knowing the language of a country in which one has business, bases, or hostages; 5) differences in language are essentially of two kinds, right and wrong; 6) verbal fluency and noticeable style are suspicious, except as entertainment.[4] Each of these assumptions is fundamentally flawed, and the list as a whole is grounded in a lack of understanding of the nature of language, a confusion of historical mythology with historical fact, and is replete with both factual and normative errors. Nevertheless, the belief system that undergirds and supports "ideological monolingualism" is very powerful, and has direct implications for such educational issues as the role and purpose of foreign language education in the schools, the place of language and language study in multicultural and global education programs, how the schools deal with the presence of nonmainstream varieties of English, and how they seek to meet the needs of children whose native language is other than English.

Since space limitations do not allow us to explore all of these areas, we will focus only on the first here: the implications and manifestations of "ideological monolingualism" with respect to the teaching of foreign languages in the public schools.[5]

Justifications for the study of foreign languages by foreign language educators and policymakers who are supportive of foreign language study are fairly common, and include a variety of arguments. Basically, the arguments normally employed to justify the study of foreign languages fall into three groups: cognitive arguments, cultural arguments, and pragmatic arguments. The cognitive arguments tend to focus on the role of language study in promoting critical thinking, providing mental discipline, increasing mental flexibility and creativity, and improving cognitive functioning.[6] Although the evidence for such benefits is, I think, quite compelling, it is not at all clear that these arguments have any more than rhetorical force in the arena of educational policymaking. The cultural arguments used to support foreign language study are less strong both empirically and anecdotally (all too often, bilingualism accompanies bicultural chauvinism rather than broad cultural tolerance). In addition, such arguments in practice actually seem to further marginalize foreign language study, leading to a view of such study as a nice but unnecessary "extra" in the curriculum. Pragmatic arguments are those grounded in concerns about national security, the economic needs of American society, and the consequences of foreign language study for employment.[7] Typical of such arguments is the following passage from a newspaper column by Sylvia Porter:

> With a language skill added to your other skills, you might double the chances of getting the job you want. There are openings for an auto mechanic who also speaks Arabic, an electronic radio expert who knows Japanese, a chef (even a woman chef) who understands French. It even could be a foreign language would be more useful to you during the next ten years than a college diploma. . . . You should weigh the judgment of one executive: "A person who speaks two languages is worth two people." Language is, in fact, your hidden job insurance.[8]

The fundamental problem with this argument, and its like, is that it is really not credible for most Americans. The United States, as noted earlier, is a profoundly monolingual society, ideologically if not empirically, and relatively few students (or parents, teachers, or policymakers, for that matter) honestly believe that second language skills are really necessary for the marketplace. Claims about language skills being "job insurance" are viewed with considerable suspicion in a society in which monolingualism in English is seen as the norm. Finally, of course, is the issue of competence: the level of language competence required in those jobs that do require language skills are far beyond what students can be expected to learn in a typical foreign language program at the secondary level. Even if a student had been fortunate enough to study Arabic for two or three years at the high school level, for instance, and had also had the benefit of appropriate automotive training, it is hardly likely that that person would be able to function as an Arabic-speaking auto mechanic.

If these justifications for taking a foreign language in secondary school are not compelling, then why do students do so? The answer is really quite simple: taking (and passing) foreign language classes often functions as a necessary condition for admission to college. In other words, "getting through" a couple of years of foreign language classes is simply one of the hurdles that one must endure to get into higher education (which, in turn, is a hurdle that is, for the most part, required for social class maintenance and upward mobility). It is this function, rarely articulated publicly but commonly recognized by both students and others, that is in actual fact served by secondary level foreign language classes.

Finally, foreign language education finds itself working against a widespread and general "social expectation of failure." This "social expectation of failure" is in fact the thread that holds together the other structural and institutional constraints that face foreign language education in the United States. Foreign language education in the United States is clearly not successful for most students, nor could it be given the way that it has been, and continues to be, implemented in the schools. Further, it is clear that most students, parents, teachers, and policymakers do not seriously expect it to succeed. Rather, it serves an important tracking and sorting function in American education—a function quite different from the arguments that foreign language educators sincerely offer for it. It is important to note that, for the most part, the same is true in higher education. At the undergraduate level, completion of a certain number of foreign language classes often serves as a requirement for graduation, while graduate level programs commonly require the demonstration of reading proficiency in a foreign language, but will give no credit for coursework to satisfy this requirement. In fact, in recent years many institutions have attempted to circumvent the foreign language requirement by the establishment of a cognate field, or even the declaration of computer language or statistics as satisfying the foreign language/research tool mandate. Even among the best educated of American society, in short, competence in a second language is increasingly seen as irrelevant, except in its limited role of serving to control and restrict access.

Conceptions of "Language Legitimacy"

Language serves as the primary medium through which much learning takes place, and the acquisition of socially and academically appropriate language forms (both oral and written) is generally seen as one of the principal goals for the educational experience.[9] Underlying all of the educational discourse dealing with issues of language are a number of common assumptions about the nature of language, language structure, language difference, and so on, that are shared by both classroom teachers and the general public. Perhaps the most powerful of these assumptions is that concerning what counts as a "real" language, and, even more important, what does *not* count as a "real" language. In short, what is at issue here is what can be called "linguistic legitimacy": which language varieties are deemed legitimate and which are denied that status.[10]

The concept of "linguistic legitimacy" is a significant one for educators, touching as it does on issues of class, ethnicity, and culture, as well as being embedded in relations of dominance and power. "Linguistic legitimacy" as a construct is also important insofar as it has implications for the development and implementation of educational policy, as the recent national debate about the Oakland, California, school district's decision to recognize Black English as the dominant language of many of that district's students makes clear.[11] Typical of much of the rhetoric surrounding that decision was the columnist Roger Hernandez's assertion that, "The notion that black English is a language and that black kids are actually bilingual is ludicrous and patronizing. Ebonics is ungrammatical English. What students who speak Ebonics need to learn is that they are speaking substandard English and that substandard English brands them as uneducated."[12]

Essentially the same underlying argument, although perhaps more carefully and moderately articulated, is commonly found in educational settings and among educators. For instance, as is true at many tertiary institutions, the California State University (CSU) system has a foreign language requirement. The CSU catalog describes the kinds of languages that can be used to meet this foreign language requirement in the following manner: "Any natural language other than English used by speakers sharing a common culture is acceptable. Excluded by this definition are artificially created languages such as Esperanto, computer languages, and derivative languages such as American Sign Language (ASL) or dialects of English."[13] This is an intriguing passage, since it explicitly distinguishes between those systems of communication which count as "languages" and those which, in some sense, do not. Especially interesting in this passage is the exclusion of Esperanto, ASL, and "dialects of English" (which, presumably, would include Black English). Each of these language varieties is used on a daily basis by significant numbers of people to communicate and yet none counts as a "real" language. Underlying this exclusion, of course, is an implicit assumption of the validity of the concept of "linguistic legitimacy"—that is, that some communications systems are legitimate languages and that others are, in some important sense, not.[14]

There are a variety of arguments used, both implicitly and explicitly, to question (and to reject) the legitimacy of various language varieties. The objections are often language-specific, which is to say that the objections to one language variety will be different from those applied to another. There are also, however, underlying commonalities in different challenges to linguistic legitimacy. At this point, I want to present and respond to the language-specific objections to the legitimacy of Black English and ASL,[15] and will then discuss, in somewhat broader terms, the general themes that hold these objections—and other language-specific objections to linguistic legitimacy—together conceptually.

Black English

There are few debates about language that are capable of producing the kind of heat and passion produced by discussions of Black English,[16] especially with respect to educational issues. In 1979, the *Martin Luther King Junior Elementary School Children vs. Ann Arbor School District* decision (473 F. Supp. 1371, E.D. Mich. 1979) led to a vociferous debate about the nature and status of Black English not unlike that which took place with respect to the Oakland policy.[17] In both instances, strong emotions on both sides of the debate all too often effectively drowned out more moderate, defensible voices. Many well-meaning individuals, educators, and noneducators alike, have raised grave reservations and concerns about both *King* and the Oakland policy with respect to Black English. The concerns that have been articulated most commonly include doubts about the nature of Black English, its recognition in educational settings, and, perhaps most important, its effects on student learning and student achievement. Also raised have been fears about the implications of identifying speakers of Black English as non-English speakers, as well as concerns about the social and economic language needs of speakers of Black English. A fairly typical critical response to the Oakland decision is that of Bill Maxwell, an African American columnist, who wrote that, "Oakland, like many other districts nationwide, is failing in part because grown-ups there lack the courage to call Ebonics what it is: a bastardization that has few redeeming elements. . . . Ebonics is acceptable in rap, poetry, and fiction. But it has precious few redeeming qualities in the real world and, therefore, must be avoided in public."[18] While this response, like that offered above by Roger Hernandez, is clearly polemical in nature, the underlying concerns it reflects are very real and legitimate ones, and are certainly shared by many people. At this point, while a complete treatment of the social phenomenon of Black English is obviously not possible here, it may be useful to present a basic overview of what is actually known about the nature of Black English, as well as a brief discussion of possible educationally sound responses to the presence of large numbers of speakers of Black English in the schools.

The contemporary social and educational debates about Black English rest on two fundamental and distinct arguments.[19] The first of these two arguments focuses on the nature of Black English in general terms, and especially with respect to prescriptivist judgments about what constitutes "proper English," and how such judgments are related to the use of Black English.[20] The second argument concerns the relationship between Black English and other varieties of American English, and is often presented in the terms of whether Black English is really a distinctive language in its own right or whether it is simply a variety of American English. Each of these arguments is important both from a linguistic and an educational standpoint, and each merits our attention here.

That the nature of Black English as a language should be at issue in contemporary discussions is, although perhaps somewhat understandable socially and educationally, nevertheless profoundly puzzling from a linguistic perspective. As Edgar Schneider has noted, "For more than twenty years, the dialect spoken by black Americans has been among the most salient topics of linguistic research in the United States,"[21] and there is a huge body of very competent linguistic research dealing with various aspects of Black English.[22] Indeed, it could be quite credibly argued that in sociolinguistics the study of Black English has provided a central framework for much contemporary research. In other words, from the perspective of linguistics, the status of Black English has long since been answered: Black English is a series of related language varieties, spoken primarily by African Americans, which are rule-governed and which differ in significant ways from other varieties of American English.[23] If the issue is not really the nature of Black English, then what is it? As Tom Trabasso and Deborah Harrison note with respect to the definition of "what is Black English," "It is a political question since language has served as an instrument of political and cultural control whenever two cultures meet. It is a social question since certain forms of speech are admired, prestigeful, codified, and promulgated while others are accorded low esteem, stigmatized, ridiculed, and avoided. It is an economic question since many feel that 'speaking proper' or some variety of Standard English is required for success in middle-class America."[24]

And what of the classroom context of Black English? The debate about Black English is fundamentally an educational one, concerned with the most appropriate manner of meeting the needs of a particular group of students. Arguably the most significant lesson to be learned with respect to the needs of Black English speakers is that language difference does not in any way constitute language deficit. Although this has become something of a politically correct cliché in recent times, it is nonetheless worth emphasizing because while teachers and others may rhetorically accept the distinction between differences and deficits, all too often the distinction is not reflected in actual belief and practice. Speakers of Black English continue to be disproportionately misdiagnosed and mislabeled with respect to both cognitive and speech/language problems, and this alone would constitute a compelling justification for additional teacher preparation with respect to language differences, and specifically those differences commonly found in the language of Black English speakers.[25] In addition, the failure to recognize language differences often leads teachers to misunderstand their students, sometimes in significant ways. For instance, Shirley Brice Heath has reported the following conversation between a teacher and a Black English speaking student:

> A teacher asked one day: "Where is Susan? Isn't she here today?" Lem answered "She ain't ride de bus." The teacher responded: "She *doesn't* ride the bus, Lem." Lem answered: "She *do* be ridin' de bus." The teacher frowned at Lem and turned away.[26]

This is a wonderful example of how a teacher's ignorance of a student's language variety can impede effective communication and lead to misunderstandings in the classroom. Lem did, in fact, respond appropriately to the teacher's question: he indicated that Susan had not ridden the bus on the day in question. The teacher, focusing on what she took to be an error in mainstream English, attempted to correct Lem by rephrasing his answer. Lem not only understood the teacher's correction, but he recognized that she had not understood his point, and replied by using a form of the habitual aspect to emphasize that indeed Susan did *normally* ride the bus, but that she hadn't done so on this particular day. The teacher at this point merely abandons the conversation, no doubt convinced that Lem has communication problems. She is, of course, partially correct: someone in the conversation has missed the point, though it wasn't Lem.

Embedded in much contemporary educational discourse about Black English are strongly held views of linguistic inferiority. A powerful example of this tendency is found in a recent book by Eleanor Wilson Orr, entitled *Twice as less: Black English and the performance of Black students in mathematics and science*.[27] The thesis offered by Orr, an experienced classroom teacher, is that "For students whose first language is BEV [Black English Vernacular] . . . language can be a barrier to success in mathematics and science."[28] Orr's argument is that certain linguistic features of Black English (such as prepositions in the expression of selected quantitative relationships, as/than modes of expressing comparisons, etc.) can result in erroneous understanding of certain key mathematical relationships. The fundamental problem with Orr's book, in essence, is that she is simply wrong. Not only is the linguistic base with regard to what we actually know about the structure of Black English dated and inaccurate, but, as John Baugh has pointed out, "despite claims to the contrary, Orr's book merely serves to perpetuate racist myths about the relationship between language and thought."[29]

Basically, then, what the case of Black English would seem to emphasize is that there is a fundamental distinction between what might be called "language-as-system" (that is, language as a linguistic phenomenon) and "language-as-social marker" (the sociological role of language). Further, in every society there is a hierarchy of linguistic variations, generally reflective of social class. It is this distinction which helps us to understand why, in contemporary American society, Black English and mainstream English can have the same *linguistic* status, while having markedly different *sociolinguistic* status.

American Sign Language

Challenges to the legitimacy of ASL have increased in recent years as efforts have been made to include it as a foreign language option in many secondary schools and colleges and universities.[30] Many objections to the teaching of ASL as a foreign language, as well as to its use in the education of deaf children, are based on the idea that ASL is in some manner linguistically inferior to spoken language. Characteristic of this view is Myklebust's assertion that, "Sign language cannot be considered comparable to a verbal symbol system,"[31] and, more recently, van Uden's claim that, "The informative power of the natural sign language of the deaf is extremely weak."[32] However common and popular such views may be, though, they are nonetheless clearly and demonstrably false in both spirit and detail. Since the 1960 publication of William Stokoe's landmark study, *Sign Language Structures*,[33] there has been a veritable explosion of linguistic, psycholinguistic, and sociolinguistic research dealing with ASL,[34] as well as with other natural sign languages.[35] The result is that we now know far more about the nature and workings of natural sign languages than we did thirty years ago, and the now well-established research base has been summarized by Robert Hoffmeister as follows:

> ASL is a language that has been misunderstood, misused, and misrepresented over the past 100 years. It is structured very differently from English. The structure of ASL is based on visual/manual properties, in contrast to the auditory/spoken properties of English. ASL is able to convey the same meanings, information, and complexities as English. The mode of expression is different, but only at the delivery level. The underlying principles of ASL . . . are based on the same basic principles found in all languages. ASL is able to identify and codify agents, actions, objects, locations, subjects, verbs, aspects, tense,

and modality, just as English does. ASL is therefore capable of stating all the information expressed in English and of doing this within the same conceptual frame. ASL is able to communicate the meaning of a concept, through a single sign or through a combination of signs, that may be conveyed by a word or phrase (combination of words) in English.[36]

In fact, as a result of this growing body of research concerned with the linguistics of natural sign languages, a 1985 UNESCO report went so far as to assert as an operating principle that, "We must recognize the legitimacy of the sign language as a linguistic system and it should be accorded the same status as other languages."[37]

Perhaps among the more intriguing objections to viewing ASL as a foreign language in American educational settings that have been raised in recent years is that offered by Howard Mancing, head of the foreign language department at Purdue University. Mancing has argued that, "In no way do I impugn the integrity of ASL as a legitimate academic subject or as a well-developed, intellectual, emotional, subtle, sophisticated language.... It is all of that, but since it is *American* Sign Language it is not foreign by definition."[38] The issue raised by Mancing is essentially one of definition. The obvious, ordinary language sense of "foreign" in the term "foreign language" is that the language is foreign *to the learner*. To employ Mancing's definition would require that we also exclude native American languages, such as Navajo, and even, perhaps, Spanish, which is at least as "indigenous" to North America as English, and is certainly widely spoken as a native language in the United States. In short, although the argument that ASL is not "foreign" may initially appear to be compelling, this is in fact far from the case. The danger in the argument presented by Mancing is that by granting the legitimacy of ASL as a language, but denying its "foreignness," one is presented with what falsely appears to be a balanced position—yet another way in which a particular language or linguistic system can be effectively delegitimized.[39]

Traditional defenses for the study of foreign languages as a part of a liberal education often rely on the close connection between language and culture. It is commonly argued that only through the study of a people's language can their culture be properly understood, and that such study can provide an essential international or global component in an individual's education. Critics of the acceptance of ASL as a foreign language have suggested that it does not meet this aspect of foreign language education on two counts: first, because the terms "language" and "culture," when applied to ASL and the culture of the Deaf community,[40] are used metaphorically rather than literally, and second, because it is an indigenous rather than international language. As Thomas Kerth, chairman of the German and Slavic Languages Department at SUNY, Stony Brook, explained, "I think these people who talk about deaf culture and foreignness are using it in a metaphorical way, not literally, and when you get into the realm of metaphor the meaning gets obscured. Most would read a foreign language as one not spoken by Americans."[41] With regard to this claim that discussions of the Deaf culture are metaphorical rather than literal, all one can say is that this is a serious distortion of what writers on (and members of) that culture have actually said, written, and meant. There are a number of works devoted to the history, sociology, and anthropology of the American Deaf community, written by both deaf and hearing scholars.[42] Nowhere in this extensive body of writings is there the suggestion, or even so much as a hint, that cultural deafness is to be understood metaphorically; indeed, the overwhelming sense of these works is that the term is used in an absolutely literal sense. The preponderance of the evidence clearly supports the view that the deaf community constitutes a cultural community in precisely the same way as would any other cultural community.

Kerth's second claim is closely related to the idea that ASL is not "foreign." However, here the suggestion is that since ASL is used almost exclusively in North America, it cannot provide students with an international or global perspective. This is true in the case of ASL, of course, to the same extent that it is a valid criticism of the study of the indigenous languages and cultures of North America, as noted earlier. The study of the Hopi, for instance, is also not international in the narrow sense that is being applied to ASL and the Deaf community. However, one could certainly argue that the point of such an international requirement in a student's education is to expose the student to cultures and languages different from his or her own, and that there is no logical reason for this exposure necessarily to entail study of a culture and language of a different country.

A third argument, at least at the tertiary level, against accepting ASL as a foreign language has been that it is not a written language, and hence does not have a literature to which students can be exposed. This objection actually has two separate components; first, the claim that ASL is not a written language, and second, that it does not possess a literature. Although it is technically not quite true that ASL is not a written language—there actually are several notational systems that can be used for reducing it to written form—it is true that it is not a commonly written language. Indeed, the written language of the American Deaf community is, in fact, English. Having granted, then, this first objection, what of the second—that is, the claim that there is, therefore, a lack of a literature in ASL?

Since ASL is not normally written down, it obviously does not have a written literature in the way that French, German, Russian, and English, amongst others, do. Of course, the same might be said of the vast majority of the languages currently spoken around the world. What ASL *does* have is a literary tradition comparable to the oral traditions found in spoken languages.[43] Nancy Frishberg has identified three major indigenous literary genres in ASL: oratory, folklore, and performance art. She compellingly argues that:

> ASL has been excluded from fulfilling foreign or second language requirements in some institutions because of claims that it has no . . . tradition of literature . . . [However,] a literary aesthetic can be defined prior to a written literary tradition, as in the case of Greek and Balkan epic poetry. We know that other languages which are socially stigmatized nonetheless adapt literature through translation and develop their own literary institutions. Non-Western cultures without writing traditions convey their traditions of history and philosophy within community-defined forms of expression. And, finally, the presence or absence of writing (systematized orthography) has little relationship to the existence of a traditional verbal art form.[44]

Further, it can be argued that the advent of the movie camera, and, more recently, the VCR, have made possible the compilation and transmission of the literary traditions and even the canon of ASL in a way simply not possible before this century. Nor is it the case that such a literature is merely possible in theory; the extensive body of ASL literature exists as a fact.[45] In short, ASL does have a well-developed literature, albeit one not easily reducible to a written form, that is now both accessible and worthy of serious study.

Toward a Critique of "Linguistic Legitimacy"

The challenges to the legitimacy of Black English and ASL would appear to be quite different, and this is hardly surprising, since they are in many significant ways very different linguistic systems with very different histories, user communities, and so on. And yet, there are some remarkably similar common themes. In both instances, concerns about the legitimacy of the language inevitably involves related concerns about culture, and, specifically, about the perceived lack of a cultural community tied to the language. The language communities that choose to use each of the languages under consideration are, in essence, themselves delegitimated as well—the African American cultural community is simply not discussed at all in the context of Black English, while in the case of ASL, the Deaf community is seen by outsiders as unsophisticated and parochial. Daniel Ling, for instance, has gone so far in attempting to delegitimize the feelings and concerns of the Deaf community as to argue that, "Members of the adult deaf community are not, by virtue of their deafness, experts on the education of hearing-impaired children and to argue otherwise is comparable to claiming expertise in pulmonary medicine simply because one breathes."[46] Indeed, as this quote suggests, in both of the cases discussed here, the very *existence* of a concomitant cultural community is often denied by those challenging the legitimacy of the language. Further, questions are raised about the linguistic structures of both languages—Black English is dismissed as simply "broken English," ASL is rejected as a derivative of English or as syntax-free or syntactically limited.

Finally, it is interesting to note that challenges to the linguistic legitimacy of Black English and ASL are very commonly offered by those who are not themselves competent in the respective language.

We see, then, that the challenges to the legitimacy of both of these language varieties have been based on a variety of assumptions that, upon careful examination, prove to be both empirically and conceptually problematic. In both cases, it can be argued that the resistance to the language under consideration is misguided, misleading, and inappropriate. However, the debate is not simply a matter of misunderstanding. Rather, it reflects more general issues of language and cultural rights in society, and the way in which such rights are often overlooked or ignored. What is actually at issue in this debate is the question of how the "Other" in society is perceived and treated, and the extent to which the dominant group in society is willing seriously to countenance pluralism. By challenging the legitimacy of particular languages (whether Black English, ASL, or whatever), we in essence denigrate and even reject the speaker communities of these languages, their cultures, and their worlds. The rejection of the "linguistic legitimacy" of a language—*any* language used by *any* linguistic community—in short, amounts to little more than an example of the "tyranny of the majority." Such a rejection merely reinforces the long tradition and history of linguistic imperialism in our society. The harm, though, is done not only to those whose languages we reject, but in fact to all of us, as we are made poorer by an unnecessary narrowing of our cultural and linguistic universe. So long as we reject the legitimacy of others' languages, we inevitably set overly parochial limits on our own culture, language, and world.

Toward "Critical Language Awareness" in American Education

The thread that holds all of the issues raised in this chapter together is that of the need for a critical perspective on language and language issues in education. Language, as we have seen, is at the core of the educational experience, and at the nexus of language and education are a host of issues that reflect issues of dominance and domination, hegemony, racism, sexism, and classism. In addition to the cases discussed in this chapter, one could easily add others: linguicism in its many forms in educational discourse and practice,[47] the challenge (and denial) of language rights in educational settings and by educational institutions,[48] the social and ideological aspects of opposition to bilingual education in the United States,[49] and, by no means least, the growing support for English-only legislation of various types in the United States.[50] In each of these instances, we see the use of linguistic issues in social and educational settings being manipulated to accomplish what are clearly ideological ends. It is also in such matters, I would suggest, that the critical legacy of scholars like Clarence Karier has so much to teach us.

Appendix

Bibliography of Published Works by Clarence J. Karier

1956
"Political Apathy and the Citizenship Teacher," *Wiscouncilor*.

1960
"The Humanist Protest in American Education 1890–1930," unpublished dissertation, University of Wisconsin.

1963
"The Rebel and the Revolutionary: Sigmund Freud and John Dewey," *Teachers College Record* 64 (7) (April): 605–613.

1964
"Totalitarianism of the Right," *Educational Theory* 14 (1) (January): 40–49.

1965
"American Educational Theory: An Essay Review of Charles Brauner's *American Educational Theory*," *Studies in Philosophy and Education* 4 (1): 27–34.

1967
"Elite Views on American Education," *The Journal of Contemporary History* 2 (3). Reprinted in *Education and Social Structure in the Twentieth Century*, edited by Walter Laqueur and George L. Mosse, vol. VI (New York: Harper and Row), 149–163.

Man, Society, and Education: A History of American Educational Ideas, Glenview, IL: Scott, Foresman. (Translated in Korean).

1969
"A Review of Henry Steele Commanger's *The Commonwealth of Learning*," *Choice*.

"A Response to Professor Messerli's *Booker T. Washington: A Pilgrim's Progress and the Perils of Piecemeal Reform*," delivered AERA meeting.

"'Humanitas' and the Triumph of the Machine," *Journal of Aesthetic Education* 3 (2) (April): 11–28.

1970
"A Review of Howard V. David, *Frank Parson: Prophet, Innovator, Counselor*," *Choice* 7 (1).

"A Review of Donald N. Michael, *The Unprepared Society: Planning for a Precarious Future*," *Journal of Aesthetic Education* 4 (1) (January): 141–144.

"Review of Patricia Albjerg Graham's *Progressive Education: From Arcady to Academe*," *Educational Theory* 20 (2) (Spring): 197–201.

1972
"Testing for Order and Control in the Corporate Liberal State," *Educational Theory* 22 (2) (Spring): 154–180. Reprinted in Roger Dale, Geoff Esland, and Madeline MacDonald, *Schooling and Capitalism: A Sociological Reader* (London: Routledge & Kegan Paul/The Open University Press, 1976), pp. 128–141, and in *The IQ Controversy: Critical Readings*, edited by N. J. Block and Gerald Dworkin (New York: Pantheon Books, 1976), pp. 339–369.

"Liberalism and the Quest for Orderly Change," *History of Education Quarterly* 12 (1) (Spring): 57–77. Reprinted in *Education in American History: Readings on the Social Issues*, edited by Michael B. Katz (New York: Praeger Publishers, 1973), pp. 303–318, and in Roger Dale, Geoff Esland, and Madeline MacDonald, *Schooling and Capitalism: A Sociological Reader* (London: Routledge & Kegan Paul/The Open University Press, 1976), pp. 90–97.

1973
With Paul C. Violas and Joel Spring, *Roots of Crisis: American Education in the Twentieth Century*. Chicago: Rand McNally College Publishing Company.

"American Educational History: A Perspective," *The Educational Forum* 37 (3) (March): 293–302.

"A Revisionist Response to Maxine Greene's 'Identities and Contours: An Approach to Educational History'," *Educational Researcher*.

1975
"John Dewey and the New Liberalism: Some Reflections and Responses," *History of Education Quarterly* 15 (4) (Winter): 417–443.

Shaping the American Educational State: 1900 to the Present. New York: The Free Press/Collier Macmillan Publishers.

1976
"The Ethics of a Therapeutic Man: C.G. Jung," *Psychoanalytic Review* 63 (1) (Spring): 115–146.

"The Odd Couple: Radical Economics and Liberal History," an essay review of Samuel Bowles and Herbert Gintis, *Schooling in Capitalist America*, *Educational Studies* 7 (185–193).

"Business Values and the Educational State," reprinted in Roger Dale, Geoff Esland, and Madeline MacDonald, *Schooling and Capitalism: A Sociological Reader* (London: Routledge & Kegan Paul/The Open University Press, 1976), pp. 21–31.

1977
"Making the World Safe for Democracy: An Historical Critique of John Dewey's Pragmatic Liberal Philosophy in the Warfare State," *Educational Theory* 27 (1) (Winter): 12–47.

"Recensiones: Lawrence A. Cremin's *Traditions of American Education*," *Pedagogica Historica*, 456–461.

"Science, Racism and the Oppression of the Poor," An essay review of Allan Chase's *The Legacy of Mathus: The Social Costs of the New Scientific Racism*, *The Review of Education* (September/October): 330–342.

1978

"Education of the American Citizen: An Historical Critique," Research for Better Schools.

With David Hogan, "Professionalizing the Role of 'Truth Seekers'," *Interchange* 9 (2): 45–71.

1979

"A Review of Julie Roy Jeffrey's *Education for Children of the Poor*," for *The American Historical Review* 84 (April): 592–593.

With David Hogan, "Schooling, Education and the Structure of Social Reality," *Educational Studies*, 10 (3) (Fall): 245–266.

"The Quest for Orderly Change: Some Reflections," *History of Education Quarterly* 19 (2) (Summer): 159–177.

"Art in a Therapeutic Age: Part I," *The Journal of Aesthetic Education* 13 (3) (July): 51–66.

"Art in a Therapeutic Age: Part II," *The Journal of Aesthetic Education* 13 (4) (October): 65–79.

1980

"Therapeutic Uses of Illusions: A Critique of the Psycho-Social Ideology of Otto Rank," *The Meritocratic Intellect*. Aberdeen University Press.

"In Praise of Great Men," an essay review of L. S. Hearnshaw, *Cyril Burt, Psychologist, History of Education Quarterly*.

1982

"Supervision in a Historic Perspective," *Association for Supervision and Curriculum Development Yearbook*, pp. 2–15.

"Foreword," for Robert B. Everhart, ed., *The Public School Monopoly: A Critical Analysis of Education and the State in American Society*, pp. xv–xxi. San Francisco: Pacific Institute for Public Policy Research.

1983
"G. Stanley Hall: A Priestly Prophet of a New Dispensation," *The Journal of Libertarian Studies*.

1984
A Review of Ellen Lagemann's *Private Power for the Public Good: A History of the Carnegie Foundation for the Advancement of Teaching*, in *The Journal of American History* 70 (March): 913–914.

"In Search of Self in a Moral Universe: Notes on George Herbert Mead's Functionalist Theory of Morality," *Journal of the History of Ideas* (January): 153–162.

1985
"Retrospective One," pp. 233–259, in Arthur Bestor, *Educational Wastelands: The Retreat from Learning in Our Public Schools*, 2d ed. Urbana: University of Illinois Press.

"The Image and the Reality," a review of Ernest L. Boyer's *High School*, for *Curriculum and Inquiry* 15 (Winter): 435–449.

1986
Scientists of the Mind: Intellectual Founders of Modern Psychology. Urbana: University of Illinois Press. (Translated in Spanish and Portuguese).

The Individual, Society, and Education: A History of American Educational Ideas, 2d ed. Urbana: University of Illinois Press. (Translated in Korean).

1987
"Some Reflections on the Coming of an American Fascism," *Educational Theory* 37 (3) (Summer): 251–263.

"Review Article—The Reassassination of Martin Luther King, Jr.," (an essay review of David J. Garrow's *Bearing the Cross: Martin Luther King, Jr., and the Southern Christian Leadership Conference*), *Educational Theory* 37 (4) (Fall): 463–475.

1989

A Review of Bernard J. Baars, *The Cognitive Revolution in Psychology*, for *The Journal of the History of the Behavioral Sciences* 25 (1) (January): 77–81.

1990

"Humanizing the Humanities: Some Reflections on George Steiner's Brutal Paradox," *Journal of Aesthetic Education* 24 (2) (Summer): 49–63.

"Nineteenth Century Romantic and Neo-Romantic Thought and Some Disturbing Twentieth-Century Applications," pp. 93–113 in *The Educational Legacy of Romanticism*, edited by John Willinsky. Waterloo, Ontario: Wilfrid Laurier University Press for the Calgary Institute for the Humanities.

"Review Article—John Dewey and the Polish Study Reconsidered: Mary V. Dearborn's *Love in the Promised Land*," in *Educational Theory* 40 (2) (Spring): 255–265.

"A Review of Henry L. Minton's *Lewis M. Terman: Pioneer in Psychological Testing*," for *The Journal of American History*, 76 (4) (March): 1294.

"A Review of David Holmes, *Stalking the Academic Communist: Intellectual Freedom and the Firing of Alex Novikoff*," in the *Journal of Higher Education*, 61 (2) (March/April): 229–232.

1995

The Rise of the National Security State and the Demise of Democracy. Urbana, IL: Unpublished book manuscript.

Notes

Preface

1. Clarence J. Karier, "Recensiones: Lawrence A. Cremin's *Traditions of American Education*," *Pedagogica Historica* (1977): 457–458.

Chapter 1

1. D. H. Lawrence, "Things Men Have Made," *Complete Poems* (New York: Penguin Books, 1971), cited in Thomas More, *The Education of the Heart* (New York: HarperCollins, 1996), 234.

2. Chungliang Al Huang and Jerry Lynch, *Mentoring: The Tao of Giving and Receiving Wisdom* (San Francisco: HarperCollins, 1995), xi.

3. D. M. Dooling, *A Way of Working: The Spiritual Dimension of Craft* (New York: Parabola Books, 1979), 37.

4. Huang and Lynch, *Mentoring*, 3.

5. Henri Nouwen, *Reaching Out: The Three Movements of the Spiritual Life* (New York: Doubleday/Image Books, 1966), 71.

6. Joseph Campbell, *An Open Life* (New York: Harper & Row, 1989), 24.

7. Correspondence from author to Ms. Emma Kenning, July 14, 1973.

8. Alfred North Whitehead, *The Aims of Education and Other Essays* (New York: Macmillan, 1929).

9. Henry David Thoreau, *Walden* (Boston: Houghton Mifflin, 1854), 98.

10. G. Stanley Hall, *Adolescence and Its Relations to Physiology, Anthropology, Sociology, Sex, Crime, Religion, and Education* (New York: D. Appleton and Co., 1904). Also see: G. Stanley Hall, *Life and Confessions of a Psychologist* (New York: D. Appleton and Co., 1923); G. Stanley Hall, *Jesus the Christ in the Light of Psychology* (Chicago: University of Chicago Press, 1972); G. Stanley Hall, *Educational Problems* (New York: D. Appleton and Co., 1911).

11. Mihaly Csikszentmihalyi, *Flow: The Psychology of Optimal Experience* (New York: HarperPerennial, 1991); Mihaly Csikszentmihalyi, *Finding Flow: The*

Psychology of Engagement with Everyday Life (New York: Basic Books, 1977); Barry Sears, *The Zone: A Dietary Road Map* (New York: HarperCollins, 1995).

12. Nouwen, *Reaching Out*, 52.

13. Greta Nagel, *The Tao of Teaching: The Special Meaning of the Tao Te Ching as Related to the Art and Pleasures of Teaching* (New York: Primus/Donald I. Fine, Inc., 1994), 83.

14. Thoreau, *Walden*, cited in Bill Devall, *Simple in Means, Rich in Ends: Practicing Deep Ecology* (Salt Lake City: Peregrine Smith Books, 1988), 81.

15. Thomas Del Prete, *Thomas Merton and the Education of the Whole Person* (Birmingham, AL: Religious Education Press, 1990), 10.

16. Thomas Merton, *Conjectures of a Guilty Bystander* (New York: Doubleday Dell Publishing Group, 1966), cited in Thomas Moore, *The Education of the Heart* (New York: HarperCollins Publishers, 1996), 278.

17. Clarence J. Karier, Paul C. Violas, and Joel Spring, *Roots of Crisis: American Education in the Twentieth Century* (Chicago: Rand McNally College Publishing Co., 1973); Clarence J. Karier, *The Individual, Society, and Education: A History of American Educational Ideas*, 2d ed. (Urbana: University of Illinois Press, 1986); Clarence J. Karier, *Shaping the American Educational State: 1900 to the Present* (New York: The Free Press, 1975); Clarence J. Karier, *Scientists of the Mind: Intellectual Founders of Modern Psychology* (Urbana: University of Illinois Press, 1986); Clarence J. Karier, "Making the World Safe for Democracy: An Historical Critique of John Dewey's Pragmatic Liberal Philosophy in the Warfare State," *Educational Theory* 27 (1977): 12–47; Clarence J. Karier and David Hogan, "Professionalizing the Role of Truth Seekers," *Interchange* 9 (1978): 45–71; Clarence J. Karier and David Hogan, "Schooling, Education, and the Structure of Social Reality," *Educational Studies* 10 (Fall 1979): 245–266.

18. Karier, *Shaping the American Educational State*, xvii.

19. Ibid.

20. Ibid.

21. Ibid.

22. Clarence J. Karier, *The Rise of the National Security State and the Demise of Democracy* (Unpublished book manuscript, Urbana, IL). Some of the themes developed in much greater detail in this manuscript may be read in the following chapter: "War by Peaceful Means," in Karier, *The Individual, Society, and Education*, 286–362.

23. Manning Marable, *Speaking Truth to Power: Essays on Race, Resistance, and Radicalism* (Boulder, CO: Westview Press/HarperCollins Publishers, 1996), 122.

24. Open Memo to Dean J. Myron Atkin from Clarence J. Karier, Chairman, "New Positions for 1974–1975 and 1975–1976," August 19, 1974, 1.

25. Ibid., 1–2.

26. Ibid., 2.

27. Hermann Hesse, *Narcissus and Goldmund* (New York: Farrar, Straus and Giroux, 1968), 272.

28. Huang and Lynch, *Mentoring*, 103.

Chapter 2

1. Arthur J. May, *A History of the University of Rochester, 1850–1962* (Princeton: Princeton University Press, 1977), 323.

2. Ibid., 253, 325.

3. Parker J. Palmer, *The Courage To Teach* (San Francisco: Jossey-Bass Publishers, 1998), 11.

4. Ibid., 104. Italics in original.

5. Clarence J. Karier, *Man, Society, and Education: A History of American Educational Ideas* (Glenview, IL: Scott, Foresman, and Company, 1967), xcii. Italics in original.

6. R. Freeman Butts and Lawrence A. Cremin, *A History of Education in American Culture* (New York: Holt, Rinehart, and Winston, 1953).

7. Adelia Peters, telephone conversation with author, 5 September 1999. Adelia began the History of Education doctoral program in 1965 and completed her dissertation in 1969. Her teaching career was spent at Bowling Green University.

8. Jerry Gaff, "Making a Difference: The Impacts of Faculty," *Journal of Higher Education* 44 (1973): 609; Ohmar Milton, "The Changing Nature of Instruction," *The Journal of Research and Development in Education* (1973): 117.

9. Carl Rogers, *Freedom To Learn* (Columbus, OH: Charles E. Merrill Publishing Co., 1969), chapter 4.

10. Neil Postman and Charles Weingartner, *Teaching as a Subversive Activity* (New York: Delacorte Press, 1969), 49.

11. Ibid., chapters III and V.

12. Kenneth Eble, *Professors as Teachers* (San Francisco: Jossey-Bass, 1972), 5–6.

13. Palmer, *Courage*, 11, 27.

14. Richard Ognibene, "The Art of Teaching: A Critical Reexamination," *Improving College and University Teaching* 23 (1975): 190–192.

15. Palmer, *Courage*, 11.

16. Richard Ognibene, "Social Foundations and School Reform Networks: The Case Against E.D. Hirsch," *Educational Foundations* 12 (4) (1998): 5–27. This article emerged from a graduate philosophy of education class I taught. Hirsch's recent book, *The Schools We Need*, had been assigned as an example of contemporary educational conservatism. The book was so filled with flawed assertions, illogical deductions, and misuse of evidence that I was unable to sustain a neutral pose as a means of provoking discussion. Searching for truth made pedagogical role playing impossible in this instance.

Chapter 3

1. Clarence J. Karier, Paul Violas, and Joel Spring, *Roots of Crisis: American Education in the Twentieth Century* (Chicago: Rand McNally College Publishing Company, 1973).

2. Clarence J. Karier, "Business Values and the Educational State," in ibid., 6.

3. Ibid., 7.

Chapter 4

1. See Merle Curti, *The Social Ideas of American Educators* (New York: C. Scribner's Sons, 1935), and Lawrence Arthur Cremin, *The Transformation of the School: Progressivism in American Education, 1876–1957* (New York: Knopf, 1961).

2. Clarence J. Karier, *The Individual, Society, and Education: A History of American Educational Ideas*, 2d ed. (Urbana: University of Illinois Press, 1986), ix–x.

3. See, for example, ibid., x; Clarence J. Karier, "The Quest for Orderly Change: Some Reflections," *History of Education Quarterly* 19 (Summer 1979): 159–160;

Clarence J. Karier, "John Dewey and the New Liberalism: Some Reflections and Responses," *History of Education Quarterly* 15 (Winter 1975): 437.

4. Plato, *Republic*, trans. G.M.A. Grube, revised by C.D.C. Reeve (Indianapolis: Hackett Publishing Co., 1992), 186–192.

Chapter 5

1. Clarence J. Karier, *Shaping the American Educational State: 1900 to the Present* (New York: The Free Press, 1975), xviii–xix. During my initial conversation with Clarence in 1990, he called attention to the gender-specific language in his earlier work, and told me how he came to understand the problems inherent in such usage. Clarence reinforced this example, of not holding oneself above honest criticism, again and again. It was a priceless lesson.

2. Audre Lorde, "Learning from the 60s," in *Sister Outsider: Essays and Speeches by Audre Lorde* (Freedom, CA: The Crossing Press, 1984), 141.

3. Clarence J. Karier's *The Individual, Society, and Education* was first published as *Man, Society, and Education: A History of American Educational Ideas* (Glenview, IL: Scott, Foresman and Co., 1967). References in this paper are to Karier, *The Individual, Society, and Education: A History of American Educational Ideas*, 2d ed. (Urbana: University of Illinois Press, 1986).

4. B. Edward McClellan, "Progressivism Reconsidered: Review of Clarence J. Karier, Paul Violas, Joel Spring, *Roots of Crisis: American Education in the Twentieth Century*," *Educational Theory* 24 (Summer 1974): 312.

5. Michael B. Katz, "Book review—*Roots of Crisis: American Education in the Twentieth Century*," *Harvard Educational Review* 43 (August 1973): 435, 442.

6. "Liberalism vs. Fascism," *The New Republic* 50 (March 2, 1927): 35.

7. Ibid.

8. See Clarence J. Karier, Paul Violas, and Joel Spring, *Roots of Crisis: American Education in the Twentieth Century* (Chicago: Rand McNally, 1973), 3–4 and Steven E. Tozer, Paul C. Violas, and Guy Senese, *School and Society: Historical and Contemporary Perspectives*, 3d ed. (Boston: McGraw-Hill, 1998), 99–104 for a full description of New Liberal ideology. Violas's essay, "Progressive Social Philosophy: Charles Horton Cooley and Edward Alsworth Ross," in *Roots of Crisis*, pp. 40–65, especially, is useful in understanding the major tenets of New Liberalism.

9. Clarence J. Karier, "American Educational History: A Perspective," *The Educational Forum* 37 (March 1973): 294–295, 301. Parts of this article appear in the introduction to Karier, Violas, and Spring, *Roots of Crisis*, 1–5.

10. Karier, "American Educational History," 302; Clarence J. Karier, "Liberal Ideology and the Quest for Orderly Change," in *Roots of Crisis*, 85–86, 107.

11. See Cornel West, "Black Strivings in a Twilight Civilization," in Henry Louis Gates, Jr. and Cornel West, *The Future of the Race* (New York: Alfred A. Knopf, 1996), 107–112.

12. Karier, *Shaping the American Educational State*, xviii–xix; Lorde, "Learning from the 60s," 141.

13. Hayden V. White, quoted in Karier, *The Individual, Society, and Education*, xi.

14. Lorde, "Learning from the 60s," 141.

15. Clarence J. Karier, "John Dewey and the New Liberalism: Some Reflections and Responses," *History of Education Quarterly* 15 (Winter 1975): 439. See the discussion on the significance of different assumptions held by liberal and radical historians in Karier, Violas, and Spring, *Roots of Crisis*, 3–5.

16. Karier, "Liberal Ideology and the Quest for Orderly Change," 85, 106.

17. Ibid., 88, 91. This theme is addressed in other essays in *Roots of Crisis*, and is a theme that I extend in chapter 6 of Karen Graves, *Girls' Schooling during the Progressive Era: From Female Scholar to Domesticated Citizen* (New York: Garland Publishing, 1998), 228–244.

18. Karier, "Liberal Ideology and the Quest for Orderly Change," 93, 105; see also, Karier, "John Dewey and the New Liberalism," 441–442; Clarence J. Karier, "The Quest for Orderly Change: Some Reflections," *History of Education Quarterly* 19 (Summer 1979): 170–171.

19. See Clarence Karier, "Making the World Safe for Democracy: An Historical Critique of John Dewey's Pragmatic Liberal Philosophy in the Warfare State," *Educational Theory* 27 (Winter 1977): 12–47; Karier, "Liberal Ideology and the Quest for Orderly Change," 105; Karier, "John Dewey and the New Liberalism," 417–443; Karier, "The Quest for Orderly Change," 170–171.

20. Karier, "Liberal Ideology and the Quest for Orderly Change," 84–85.

21. See Dewey's definitions of these terms in ibid., 90–91.

22. Charles W. Eliot, "The Function of Education in Democratic Society," *The Outlook* 57 (1897): 573–574.

23. Dewey, quoted in Karier, "Liberal Ideology and the Quest for Orderly Change," 101.

24. Karier, "Liberal Ideology and the Quest for Orderly Change," 87–91.

25. Edward L. Thorndike, "Intelligence and Its Uses," in Karier, *Shaping the American Educational State*, 232.

26. Karier, "Liberal Ideology and the Quest for Orderly Change," 94–95; 102–104; "An Apology for Fascism," *New Republic* 49 (January 12, 1927): 207–209; "Liberalism vs. Fascism," 33–35; Charles A. Beard, "Making the Fascist State," *New Republic* 57 (January 23, 1929): 277–278. Karier clearly notes that Beard, Croly, Kallen, and Steffens reversed their opinions on fascism in the 1930s.

27. Beard, "Making the Fascist State," 278.

28. Karier, "Making the World Safe for Democracy," 22.

29. "Liberalism vs. Fascism," 35.

30. Karier, "Making the World Safe for Democracy," 26–30.

31. Larry Everest and Jose Palafox, "Urban Warrior In Oakland," *Z Magazine* 12 (July/August 1999): 50, 52, 54–55.

32. Jerry Brown, quoted in ibid., 55.

33. Jerry Brown, quoted in ibid.

34. Karier, *The Individual, Society, and Education*, ix; Karier, *Shaping the American Educational State*, xvi; Karier, "John Dewey and the New Liberalism," 437.

35. Karier, "American Educational History: A Perspective," 293; Karier, *Shaping the American Educational State*, xvii; Karier, Violas, Spring, *Roots of Crisis*, 2; Karier, "The Quest for Orderly Change," 160, 165–166.

36. Karier, *Shaping the American Educational State*, xvii.

37. Karier, "John Dewey and the New Liberalism," 418; Karier, "Making the World Safe for Democracy," 47.

38. See Karier, "Making the World Safe for Democracy," 47.

39. Paul Violas, quoted in Karier, "The Quest for Orderly Change," 160.

40. Karier, "The Quest for Orderly Change," 160.

41. Ibid., 164–165.

42. W.E.B. DuBois, "Of Mr. Booker T. Washington and Others," in *The Souls of Black Folk, with an introduction by John Edgar Wideman* (New York: Vintage Books, 1990), 39.

43. Karier, Violas, and Spring, *Roots of Crisis*, 5; Karier, "Liberal Ideology and the Quest for Orderly Change," 85; Karier, *Shaping the American Educational State*, xvii.

44. John Higham, quoted in Karier, "The Quest for Orderly Change," 161–162.

45. Karier, "The Quest for Orderly Change," 164–165.

46. Ibid., 169–170.

47. Ibid., 170.

48. Ibid., 167. See the discussion beginning on page 166.

49. Ibid., 167; Karier, "Liberal Ideology and the Quest for Orderly Change," 96.

50. Karier, "Making the World Safe for Democracy," 26–31.

51. Karier's *Individual, Society, and Education* is recognized by many as the preeminent intellectual history of education in the United States, and his later research has been instrumental in transforming historical inquiry into American education. Unfortunately, Karier has not received the kind of scholarly recognition that his work obviously demands, and this book is an effort to redress these "inexcusable omissions." It is important to note, however, that liberal scholars now accept key aspects of Karier and other critical historians' work as points of departure in their own scholarship. Arguments advanced by radical historians, derided by liberal scholars in the 1970s, have now become settled into mainstream academic thought, but often with, at best, parsimonious acknowledgment of the earlier scholarship.

52. Jennifer Reingold and Ronald Grover, "Executive Pay," *Business Week* (April 19, 1999): 72, 78.

53. Holly Sklar, Chuck Collins, and Betsy Leondar-Wright, "The Growing Wealth Gap," *Z Magazine* 12 (May 1999): 47–51.

54. Dan Balz, "Bush's Fund-Raising Opens Huge Disparity," *The Washington Post* (1 July 1999): A1.

55. Marlin Fitzwater, quoted in Howard Zinn, *A People's History of the United States: 1492–Present* (New York: HarperPerennial, 1995), 634.

56. Christian Parenti, "Swat Nation," *The Nation* 268 (31 May 1999): 16, 18.

57. William J. Broad and Judith Miller, "Pentagon Seeks Command for Emergencies in the U.S.," *The New York Times* (28 January 1999): A21; see also, Ron Martz, "Marching Across the Thin Blue Line; Waco Revelations Have Fueled the Debate Over the U.S. Military's Role in Civilian Law Enforcement," *The Atlanta Journal and Constitution* (10 October 1999): 1B; Tozer, Violas, and Senese, *School and Society*, 485.

58. Rudy Acuña, quoted in Elizabeth Martínez, "Brown David v. White Goliath: Racism at the University of California," in *De Colores Means All of Us: Latina Views for a Multi-Colored Century* (Cambridge, MA: South End Press, 1998), 151.

Chapter 6

1. Clarence J. Karier, *Man, Society, and Education* (Glenview, IL: Scott, Foresman and Co., 1967).

2. Clarence J. Karier, "Liberal Ideology and the Quest for Orderly Change," *History of Education Quarterly* 12 (Spring 1972): 57–80; Clarence J. Karier, "Testing for Order and Control in the Corporate Liberal State," *Educational Theory* 22 (Spring 1972): 154–176.

3. Clarence J. Karier, Paul Violas, and Joel Spring, *Roots of Crisis: American Education in the Twentieth Century* (Chicago: Rand McNally, 1973).

4. Clarence J. Karier, *Shaping the American Educational State: 1900 to the Present* (New York: The Free Press, 1975).

5. Karier, *Shaping the American Educational State*, xvii.

6. See, for instance, Michelle Fine, *Framing Dropouts: Notes on the Politics of an Urban Public High School* (Albany: State University of New York, 1991); Amy Stuart Wells and Robert L. Crain, *Stepping over the Color Line: African-American Students in White Suburban Schools* (New Haven: Yale University Press, 1997); Jean Anyon, *Ghetto Schooling: A Political Economy of Urban Educational Reform* (New York: Teachers College Press, 1997).

7. See, for instance, Michael W. Sedlak, Christoper W. Wheeler, Diana C. Pullin, and Philip A. Cusick, *Selling Students Short: Classroom Bargains and Academic Reform in the American High School* (New York: Teachers College Press, 1986); Reba Neukom Page, *Lower-Track Classrooms: A Curricular and Cultural Perspective* (New York: Teachers College Press, 1991); Seymour B. Sarason, *Revisiting "The Culture of The School and The Problem of Change"* (New York: Teachers College Press, 1996); David L. Angus and Jeffrey E. Mirel, *The Failed Promise of the American High School, 1890–1995* (New York: Teachers College Press, 1999).

8. Clarence J. Karier, "Liberal Ideology and the Quest for Orderly Change," in Karier, Violas, and Spring, *Roots of Crisis*, 93.

Chapter 7

1. Kingsley Davis, "Mental Hygiene and the Class Structure," *Psychiatry* 1 (1938): 55.

2. Clarence J. Karier (ed.), *Shaping the American Educational State: 1900 to the Present* (New York: Free Press, 1975), xvi.

3. Clarence J. Karier, "The Ethics of a Therapeutic Man: C. G. Jung," *Psychoanalytic Review* 63 (1976): 125.

4. Herbert Marcuse, *Reason and Revolution: Hegel and the Rise of Social Theory* (New York: Oxford University Press, 1941).

5. Karier, "The Ethics of a Therapeutic Man," 116.

6. Marcuse, "Remarks on a Redefinition of Culture, " *Daedalus* (Winter, 1965): 201. Cf. Karier, "The Rebel and the Revolutionary: Sigmund Freud and John Dewey," *Teachers College Record* 64 (1963).

7. Karier, "Art in a Therapeutic Age, Part I," *Journal of Aesthetic Education* 13 (1979): 60.

8. Ibid.

9. Waldo Frank, *The Bridegroom Cometh* (New York: Doubleday, 1938–39), 548–549, as quoted in Karier, "Art in a Therapeutic Age, Part II," *Journal of Aesthetic Education* 13 (1979): 75.

10. Jerome D. Frank, *Persuasion and Healing: A Comparative Study of Psychotherapy*, revised ed. (Baltimore: Johns Hopkins University Press, 1973), 2–3.

11. Thomas S. Szasz, *The Manufacture of Madness: A Comparative Study of the Inquisition and the Mental Health Movement* (New York: Dell, 1970).

12. Sigmund Freud, *The Question of Lay Analysis* (New York: W. W. Norton, 1950), Ch. 5.

13. William Ryan, *Blaming the Victim* (New York: Pantheon, 1976).

14. Kenneth D. Benne, "The Process of Re-Education: An Assessment of Kurt Lewin's Views," *Groups and Organizational Studies* 1 (1976): 33.

15. David Moberg, *The Church as a Social Institution: The Sociology of American Religion* (Englewood Cliffs, NJ: Prentice-Hall, 1962), 180.

16. Ibid., 179–181.

17. Karier, "The Ethics of a Therapeutic Man," 121.

18. James K. Feibleman, *The Institutions of Society* (London: Allen & Unwin, 1956), 222, 224.

19. Clarence J. Karier, *The Individual, Society, and Education: A History of American Educational Ideas*, 2d ed. (Urbana: University of Illinois Press, 1986), 159.

20. Clarence J. Karier, *Scientists of the Mind: Intellectual Founders of Modern Psychology* (Urbana: University of Illinois Press, 1986), 8.

21. Ibid., 20–21.

22. Christopher Lasch, "Review Article—*Scientists of the Mind*," *Educational Theory* 37 (1987): 202. This account is a somewhat curious, if natural, interpretation by Lasch in that he has been accused of objectifying the subjects of some of his own studies and thus rendering them as rather passive objects of social control. See Henry Abelove, Betsy Blackmar, Pete Dimock, and Jonathan Schneer (eds.), *Visions of History* (New York: Pantheon, 1983), 82.

23. Karier, *Scientists of the Mind*, 21.

24. Karier, *The Individual, Society, and Education*, 289.

25. Karier, "The Ethics of a Therapeutic Man," 143.

26. C. Wright Mills, as quoted in Richard Gillam, "Richard Hofstadter, C. Wright Mills, and 'the Cultural Ideal,'" *The American Scholar* 47 (1977/78): 76.

27. Harold D. Lasswell, "Psychopathology and Politics," in his *The Political Writings of Harold Lasswell* (Glencoe, IL: Free Press, 1951), 194, 202.

28. Lasswell, "What Psychiatrists and Political Scientists Can Learn From One Another," *Psychiatry* 1 (1938): 33.

29. Peter Sedgwick, as cited in Anthony Clare, *Psychiatry in Dissent: Controversial Issues in Thought and Practice* (Philadelphia: Institute for the Study of Human Issues, 1976), 24–26.

30. Thomas J. Schaff, *Being Mentally Ill: A Sociological Theory* (Chicago: Aldine, 1966); and his "Schizophrenia as Ideology," *Schizophrenia Bulletin* 2 (1970): 15–19.

31. Szasz, "The Myth of Mental Illness," *American Psychologist* 15 (1960): 115.

32. Karier, *The Individual, Society, and Education*, 259. This distinction is drawn from Karier's interpretation of Herbert J. Muller in his *Issues of Freedom* (New York: Harper and Brothers, 1960).

33. Marcuse, *Eros and Civilization: A Philosophical Inquiry into Freud* (New York: Vintage, 1962), 32–34.

34. Karier, "Art in a Therapeutic Age, Part II," *Journal of Aesthetic Education* 13 (1979): 76.

35. Karier, *The Individual, Society, and Education*, 159; and *Scientists of the Mind*, 216.

36. William James, quoted in Gordon Allport (ed.), *William James' Psychology: The Briefer Course* (New York: Harper Torchbooks, 1961), 334–335, as cited in Karier, *The Individual, Society, and Education*, 150.

Chapter 8

1. Consider the first two sentences of the preface to Clarence Karier, *Man, Society, and Education* (Glenview, IL: Scott, Foresman and Company, 1967): "Although men like Emerson and Dewey often spoke of education as being as 'broad as man,' seldom has the history of education been pursued from that point of view. Most often it has been pursued as if education were as 'broad as the school.'"

2. See Karier's "Making the World Safe for Democracy: An Historical Critique of John Dewey's Pragmatic Liberal Philosophy in the Warfare State," *Educational Theory* 27 (1) (Winter 1977): 47.

3. See his chapter, "The Eighteenth-Century Age of Enlightenment" in Karier, *Man, Society, and Education*, 20–42.

4. When Karier published *Man, Society, and Education*, few historians were willing to see certain unshakable Jeffersonian commitments, such as his belief in the existence of a human moral sense and his belief in the concept of small ward-republics, as anything other than intellectual eccentricities. The reason, of course, is that these ideas had become seriously out of step with twentieth-century versions of liberalism. Part of Karier's intellectual project, then, was to chronicle how a nation could move from a point at which

Jefferson's ideas resonated with the people to the point at which his ideas could be considered eccentric. For a variety of reasons, Jefferson's radical ideas are currently receiving much greater scholarly attention. See, for example, Richard K. Matthews, *The Radical Philosophy of Thomas Jefferson* (Baltimore: The Johns Hopkins University Press, 1991) by Garrett Ward Sheldon.

5. See "Nineteenth-Century Neo-Enlightenment Views of the Good Society" in Karier, *Man, Society, and Education,* 95–120.

6. This became the title of one of Karier's highly acclaimed books. See Clarence J. Karier, *Scientists of the Mind: Intellectual Founders of Modern Psychology* (Urbana: University of Illinois Press, 1986).

7. Clarence Karier, "Testing for Order and Control in the Corporate State," *Educational Theory* 22 (Spring 1972): 162.

8. Karier, "Making the World Safe," 12.

9. Ibid.

10. Clarence Karier, "Romantic and Neo-Romantic Reflections on Human Nature, Education and the Social Order: A Perspective." A paper prepared for the Calgary Institute for the Humanities Conference on the Educational Legacy of Romanticism, October 13–16, 1988, Calgary, Canada.

11. Ibid., 1.

12. Karier, "Making the World Safe," 12.

13. Ibid., 14.

14. Ibid., 16.

15. Ibid., 20.

16. Clarence Karier, "The Educational Legacy of War." A paper presented at the Seventeenth Annual Alice L. Foley Lecture, Nazareth College, Rochester, NY, July 15, 1992 (p. 6).

17. Ibid., 2.

18. Clarence Karier, "Review Article—The Reassassination of Martin Luther King, Jr.," *Educational Theory* 37 (Fall 1987): 463–475.

Chapter 9

1. Mark Sorenson, "Navajo Parents' Perceptions of Their Tribally Controlled Grant School." Unpublished Ph.D. dissertation, University of Northern Arizona, 1993.

2. Guy Senese, *Self-Determination and the Social Education of Native Americans* (New York: Praeger, 1991).

3. John Collier, *Indians of the Americas: The Long Hope* (New York: The New American Library, 1947).

4. Lawrence C. Kelly, *The Assault on Assimilation: John Collier and the Origins of Indian Policy Reform* (Albuquerque: University of New Mexico Press, 1983); Stephen Kunitz, "The Social Philosophy of John Collier," *Ethnohistory* 18 (Summer 1971).

5. Kenneth R. Philp, "John Collier and the Controversy over the Wheeler-Howard Bill," in *Indian-White Relations—A Persistent Paradox*, edited by Janet Smith and Robert M. Kvasnicka (Washington, DC: Howard University Press, 1976).

6. Institute for Government Research, Brookings Institution, "Problem of Indian Administration."

7. Kelly, *The Assault on Assimilation*, 36.

8. *Report of the Commissioner of Indian Affairs to the Secretary of the Interior* (Washington, DC: U.S. Government Printing Office, 1933, 1935).

9. Paul A.F. Walter, "Santa Fe Taos Art Movement," *Art and Archeology* 2 (6) (December 1916).

10. Oliver LaFarge, ed., *The Changing Indian* (Norman: The University of Oklahoma Press, 1942).

11. R. Lawrence Moore, "Directions of Thought in Progressive America," in *The Progressive Era*, edited by Lewis L. Gould (Syracuse: Syracuse University Press, 1974).

12. Francis P. Prucha, ed., *Documents of U.S. Indian Policy* (Lincoln: University of Nebraska Press, 1975).

Chapter 10

1. Clarence J. Karier, *Man, Society, and Education: A History of American Educational Ideas* (Glenview, IL: Scott, Foresman, and Co., 1967), vii.

2. Clarence J. Karier, Paul Violas, and Joel Spring, *Roots of Crisis: American Education in the Twentieth Century* (Chicago: Rand McNally College Publishing Co., 1973); Clarence J. Karier, *Shaping the American Educational State: 1900 to the Present* (New York: The Free Press, 1975); Clarence J. Karier, *The Individual, Society, and Education*, 2d ed. (Urbana: University of Illinois Press, 1986).

3. See, for example, Steve Tozer and Stuart McAninch, "Social Foundations of Education in Historical Perspective," *Educational Foundations* 1(1) (Fall 1986): 13–33.

4. Ibid., 9. See also R. Freeman Butts, *First Person Singular* (San Francisco: Caddo Gap Press, 1994), and Harold Rugg and William Withers, *Social Foundations of Education* (1955).

5. Levi Seeley, *The Foundations of Education* (Lake Forest, IL: Lake Forest College Press, 1901).

6. George S. Counts, *The Social Foundations of Education* (New York: Charles Scribner's Sons, 1934); Harold Rugg, ed., *Readings in the Foundations of Education* (New York: Columbia University Press, 1941).

7. Steven E. Tozer, B. Armbruster, and T. H. Anderson, "Psychological and Social Foundations in Teacher Education: A Thematic Introduction," *Teachers College Record* 91 (3) (Spring 1990): 293–299.

8. Council of Learned Societies in Education, *Standards for Academic and Professional Instruction in Foundations of Education, Educational Studies, and Educational Policy Studies*, 2d ed. (San Francisco: Caddo Gap Press, 1996). The *Standards* can be obtained at caddogap.aol.com.

9. Ibid., 1.

10. Karier, *Man, Society, and Education*, xi–xii.

11. For a brief analysis of the postwar influences that led to leading social foundations textbooks becoming much less critical and more conservative, see Tozer and McAninch, "Social Foundations of Education in Historical Perspective." For useful treatments of the emergence of Cultural Studies and Cultural Studies in Education, see Kathy Hytten, "Cultural Studies of Education: Mapping the Terrain," *Educational Foundations* (Fall 1997): 39–60, and Kathy Hytten, "The Promise of Cultural Studies of Education," *Educational Theory* 49 (4) (Fall 1999): 527–543.

12. Karier, *Man, Society, and Education*, xvii.

13. Clarence J. Karier, "Liberal Ideology and the Quest for Orderly Change," in Karier, Violas, Spring, *Roots of Crisis*, 84–107; Clarence J. Karier, "Testing for Order and Control in the Corporate Liberal State," in Karier, Violas, Spring, *Roots of Crisis*, 108–137.

14. For several examples, see Henry A. Giroux and Peter McLaren, eds., *Between Borders: Pedagogy and the Politics of Cultural Studies* (New York: Routledge, 1994).

15. Tony Bennett, "Putting Policy into Cultural Studies," in John Storey, ed., *What Is Cultural Studies: A Reader* (London: Arnold, 1996), 307.

16. Clarence J. Karier, "Business Values and the Educational State," in Karier, Violas, Spring, *Roots of Crisis*, 6–29.

17. See Leslie G. Roman, "Spectacle in the Dark: Youth as Transgression, Display, and Repression," *Educational Theory* 46 (1) (Winter 1996): 1–22.

18. I take as a sound account of postmodern ethics and epistemology, Richard J. Bernstein, *The New Constellation: The Ethical-Political Horizons of Modernity/Postmodernity* (Cambridge: MIT Press, 1995).

19. Karier, *Man, Society, and Education*, 9.

20. Karier, "Liberal Ideology and the Quest for Orderly Change," 95.

21. Karier, *Shaping the American Educational State*, xvi–xvii.

22. Ibid., xvii.

23. Karier, "Business Values and the Educational State," 29.

24. Ibid., 8–9.

25. Quoted in *Shaping the American Educational State*, xvi.

26. Clarence J. Karier, *Roots of Crisis*, 5.

27. Patti Lather, "Deconstructing/Deconstructive Inquiry: The Politics of Knowing and Being Known," *Educational Theory* 41 (2) (Spring 1991).

28. Rugg, ed., *Readings in the Foundations of Education*, xi.

29. Ibid., xii.

30. Karier, *Shaping the American Educational State*, 121.

31. Ibid., 7.

32. Carnegie Forum on Education and the Economy, Task Force on Teaching as a Profession, *A Nation Prepared: Teachers for the 21st Century* (New York: Carnegie Forum on Education and the Economy, 1986); Holmes Group, *Tomorrow's Teachers* (Michigan State University, 1986). Interstate New Teacher Assessment and Support Consortium, *Model Standards for Beginning Teacher Licensing and Development: A Resource for State Dialogue* (Washington, DC: Council of Chief State School Officers, 1992); National Board for Professional Teaching Standards, *What Teachers Should Know and Be Able To Do* (Washington, DC: 1994); National Commission on Teaching & America's Future, *What Matters Most: Teaching for America's Future* (New York: Columbia University, Teachers College, 1996); National Council for Accreditation of Teacher Education, *Quality Assurance for the Teaching Profession* (Washington, DC: n.d.).

33. Karier, "Testing for Order and Control," 135–136.

34. Karier, *Shaping the American Educational State*, 9.

35. Karier, "Liberal Ideology and the Quest for Orderly Change," 93.

36. Karier, *Shaping the American Educational State*, 52.

37. L. E. Beyer, "A Critical Appraisal of the 'New Orthodoxy' in Teacher Education," American Educational Research Association, Montreal, Quebec, Canada, April 1999.

38. Karier, *Shaping the American Educational State*, xvii.

39. Ibid., 9.

Chapter 11

1. Clarence J. Karier, *Man, Society, and Education: A History of American Educational Ideas* (Glenview, IL: Scott, Foresman and Co., 1967), xii.

2. Ibid., 156.

3. Clarence J. Karier, "Liberalism and the Quest for Orderly Change," *History of Education Quarterly* 12 (1) (Spring): 57–80; Clarence J. Karier, "Liberal Ideology and the Quest for Orderly Change," pp. 84–107 in Clarence J. Karier, Paul Violas, and Joel Spring, *Roots of Crisis: American Education in the Twentieth Century* (Chicago: Rand McNally, 1973).

4. Robert Paul Wolff, *The Poverty of Liberalism* (Boston: Beacon Press, 1968); Isaiah Berlin, *Four Essays on Liberty* (London: Oxford University Press, 1970);

Gabriel Kolko, *The Triumph of Conservatism: A Re-Interpretation of American History, 1900–1916* (New York: Free Press of Glencoe, 1963); James Weinstein, *The Corporate Ideal in the Liberal State, 1900–1918* (Boston: Beacon Press, 1968); C. Wright Mills, *Sociology and Pragmatism: The Higher Learning in America* (New York: Oxford University Press, 1966).

5. Clarence J. Karier, "Making the World Safe for Democracy: An Historical Critique of John Dewey's Pragmatic Liberal Philosophy in the Warfare State," *Educational Theory* 27 (1) (Winter): 12–47.

6. Karier, *Man, Society, and Education*; Karier, Violas, and Spring, *Roots of Crisis*; Clarence J. Karier, "Business Values and the Educational State," pp. 6–29 in *Roots of Crisis*; Clarence J. Karier, *The Individual, Society, and Education: A History of American Educational Ideas*, 2d ed. (Urbana: University of Illinois Press, 1986); Clarence J. Karier, *Scientists of the Mind: Intellectual Founders of Modern Psychology* (Urbana: University of Illinois Press, 1986).

7. Karier, "Liberal Ideology and the Quest for Orderly Change," 85.

Chapter 12

1. P. H. Pearson, "The I.Q's and other Q's," *Education* 49 (March 1929): 388.

2. As quoted in D. A. Worcester, "Has Standardized Testing Been Over-Emphasized," *School Executive Magazine* 51 (July 1932): 467.

3. This paper does not treat the associated history of schools that banned the use of standardized testing. While the complete record of such activity is unknown at this time, the reader is encouraged to consult: "I.Q. to Coventry," *The Survey* 65 (January 15, 1931): 448–449. Helen W. Gribben, et al., "Why We Eliminated Uniform Examinations at the Forest Hills High School," *High Points* (January 1943): 36–39. Kent P. Schwirian, "Testing At Issue: A Case Study of School and Community Conflict," *Theory Into Practice* 2 (October 1963): 226–234.

4. Educational Testing Service, *ETS Standards for Quality and Fairness*, (Princeton, NJ: Educational Testing Service, 1987), 37.

5. These articles are reprinted in Clarence J. Karier (ed.), *Shaping the American Educational State: 1900 to Present* (New York: The Free Press/Collier Macmillan Publishers, 1975).

6. Ibid., 286–287.

7. Ibid., 283, 296.

8. Ibid., 292.

9. Ibid., 303.

10. Harry Miles Johnson, "Science and Sorcery in Mental Tests," *The Forum* 82 (December 1929): 366.

11. Ibid., 367.

12. Ibid., 369.

13. Ibid., 367.

14. Ibid., 371–372.

15. C. C. Grover, "When Is an Intelligence Test Intelligent?" *The Nation's Schools* 9 (May 1932): 53.

16. Anna Gillingham, "What is Measurable?" *Child Study* (November 1934): 37.

17. Walter S. Monroe, "Hazards in the Measurement of Achievement," *School and Society* 41 (January 12, 1935): 48.

18. Ibid., 52.

19. James Mursell, "Mental Testing: A Protest," *Harper's Magazine* 180 (April 1940): 526.

20. Ibid.

21. John Wahlquist, "Is the IQ Controversy Philosophical?" *School and Society* (November 30, 1940): 540.

22. Ibid., 547.

23. Pitirim A. Sorokin, "Testomania," *Harvard Educational Review* 25 (Fall 1955): 199–200.

24. Ibid., 202, 203–204, 206.

25. Ibid., 204.

26. Ibid., 206.

27. Ibid.

28. Ibid., 210–211.

29. Ibid., 211.

30. Ibid., 212.

31. Ibid., 213.

32. Banesh Hoffmann, "'Best Answers' or Better Minds?" *The American Scholar* 28 (Spring 1959): 195–202; Banesh Hoffmann, "The Tyranny of Multiple-Choice Tests, "*Harper's Magazine* (March 1961): 37–44; Banesh Hoffman, *The Tyranny of Testing* (New York: Collier Books, 1962).

33. Hoffman, "The Tyranny of Multiple-Choice Tests," 37.

34. Ibid., 39.

35. Ibid., 38.

36. Ibid., 41.

37. Ibid., 42.

38. "Letters: The Testers' Dilemma," *Harper's Magazine* (May 1961): 83.

39. Ibid., 84.

40. See, for instance, William H. Whyte, *The Organization Man* (New York: Doubleday & Company, 1957); Martin L. Gross, *The Brain Watchers* (New York: Random House, 1962); Hillel Black, *They Shall Not Pass* (New York: William Morrow and Company, 1963).

41. Harl R. Douglass, "Some Dangers of the Testing Movement," *Journal of the National Education Association* (March 1934): 17–18.

42. Alfred North Whitehead, "The Aims of Education" *The Aims of Education and Other Essays* (New York: The Free Press, 1967), 9. Originally published in 1929.

43. Ibid., 5.

44. Lorne J. Henry, "Dangers in the Use of Objective Tests," *The School* 17 (June 1929), 941.

45. As quoted in Montagu Frank Modder, "Three Enemies of Education," *Peabody Journal of Education* 7 (July 1929), 18.

46. H. H. Rigg, "Are We Making Blank Fillers Out Students," *School Executive Magazine* 51 (March 1932), 329.

47. D. A. Worcester, "Has Standardized Testing Been Over-Emphasized," 469.

48. H. A. Jeep, "Must Objective Tests Be Dogmatic?" *Educational Administration and Supervision* 19 (March 1933), 181.

49. Ibid., 182.

50. Douglass, "Some Dangers of the Testing Movement," 17.

51. Ibid.

52. See Leon Nordau, "Mental Testing: Technique Without Vision," *Educational Method* 22 (January 1943): 160–166; Leon Nordau, "Science and the Mental Test: A Study in Contradiction," *School Science and Mathematics* 44 (November 1944), 743–755; Leon Nordau, "Intelligence: Amulet or Guide?" *Educational Administration and Supervision* 31 (March 1945), 157–167; and Leon Nordau, "A Cure for the Intelligence Test," *Educational Administration and Supervision* 32 (January 1946), 27–36.

53. Nordau, "Science and the Mental Test," 743.

54. Nordau, "Mental Testing," 161.

55. Ibid., 163.

56. Nordau, "Science and the Mental Test," 573–574.

57. Nordau, "A Cure for the Intelligence Test," 29.

58. Frank Freeman, "The Monopoly of Objective Tests," *The Educational Forum* 10 (May 1946), 389.

59. Ibid.

60. Emerson W. Shideler, "What Do Examinations Teach?" *American Association of University Professors Bulletin* 46 (September 1960), 277–280.

61. Ibid., 277.

62. Ibid.

63. Ibid., 278.

64. Ibid.

65. Ibid., 279.

66. Ibid.

67. Roy P. Fairfield, "Letters: The Testers' Dilemma," *Harper's Magazine* (May 1961), 83.

68. Arthur E. Traxler, "Are the Professional Test-Makers Determining What We Teach?," *School Review* 66 (June 1958), 144.

69. Ibid., 151.

70. John Dixon, "Are Mental Tests in the Schools Democratic?" *The American School Board Journal* 79 (December 1929): 33.

71. P. H. Pearson, "An Educational Tight-Box: A Plea for the Consideration of Individuality," *School Executive Magazine* 49 (November 1929): 120.

72. Ibid.

73. Ibid., 122.

74. F. L. Wells, "Multiple Choice Minds," *School and Society* 47 (January 15, 1938): 85.

75. Ibid.

76. Morley Mays, "Testing: Boon or Scandal?" *Journal of Higher Education* 26 (May 1955): 261.

77. Ibid., 262.

78. Harold C. Hand, "Recipe for Control by the Few," *The Educational Forum* 30 (March 1966): 263.

79. Ibid., 270.

80. Mursell, "Mental Testing," 533.

81. "I.Q. Testing Is Out!" *Phi Delta Kappan* 46 (November 1964): 105.

82. David A. Goslin, "The Social Impact of Standardized Testing," *NEA Journal* 52 (October 1963): 20.

83. Clarence J. Karier, "Testing for Order and Control in the Corporate Liberal State," in *The IQ Controversy: Critical Readings*, edited by N. J. Block and Gerald Dworking (New York: Pantheon Books, 1976).

84. Especially important among this work is Joel Spring, *The Sorting Machine Revisited* (New York: Longman, 1989, originally published in 1976); Leon Kamin, *The Science and Politics of I.Q.* (Potomac, MD: Lawrence Erlbaum Associates, Inc., 1974); and later, Stephen Jay Gould, *The Mismeasure of Man* (New York: W.W. Norton & Company, 1981).

85. Karier, "Testing for Order and Control," 342.

86. Ibid., 342.

87. Ibid., 354.

88. See, for instance, Clarence Karier, "Some Reflections on the Coming of an American Fascism," *Educational Theory* 37 (Summer 1987): 251–263.

89. See "Testing Still Exploding in U.S.," *FairTest Examiner* 8 (Fall 1994): 3.

90. Educational Testing Service, *Educational Testing Service Annual Report, 1993* (Princeton, NJ: Educational Testing Service, 1993).

91. Educational Testing Service, Consolidated Financial Statements, June 30, 1998 and 1999. Available for download on ETS website: www.ets.org.

92. "Testing is Still Exploding in U.S.," 3.

93. Office of Minority Education, Educational Testing Service, *An Approach For Identifying and Minimizing Bias In Standardized Tests: A Set of Guidelines* (Princeton, NJ: Educational Testing Service, 1980).

94. The Angoff Method is named after William H. Angoff, who worked as a research scientist for the Educational Testing Service from 1950 until his death in 1993. Although Angoff wisely tried to claim that others were responsible for developing the method that bears his name, he has been credited for the method largely on the basis of a single paragraph and a single footnote in his long chapter, "Scales, Norms, and Equivalent Scores," which appeared in Robert L. Thorndike's 1971 text, *Educational Measurement*. Briefly, the method entails asking a small group of experts to look at each item on a certification or licensure examination and to estimate "What percentage of minimal competent candidates will answer this question correctly?" The results are tallied and then divided by the number of items on the tests. The results of each expert's work is then tallied and divided by the number of experts engaged in the method, resulting in the passing point for that particular version of the examination. The highly subjective nature of this enterprise does not appear to trouble the objective testers, nor does the fact that participants are asked to provide an answer to one question ("What total number of questions must a candidate answer correctly in order to demonstrate minimal competency?") by posing a fundamentally

different question. I have explored this issue elsewhere. See Timothy Glander, "A Critique of Using the Modified Angoff Method in Establishing the Passing Point for the New York State Teacher Certification Examination." Paper presented at the annual conference of the New York State Foundations of Education Association, Oneonta, New York, April 19–20, 1996.

Chapter 13

1. Stephen Ambrose, *Rise to Globalism: American Foreign Policy, 1938–1980*, 2d ed. (New York: Penguin, 1980), 147.

2. John Gaddis, *Strategies of Containment: A Critical Appraisal of Postwar American National Security Policy* (New York: Oxford University Press, 1982).

3. Andrew Ross, *Intellectuals and Popular Culture* (New York: Routledge, 1989), 47.

4. Lionel Trilling, *The Liberal Imagination* (New York: Anchor Books, 1950), 5.

5. Daniel Bell, *The End of Ideology* (Glencoe, IL: The Free Press, 1960).

6. Peter Carroll and David Noble, *The Free and the Unfree: A New History of the United States* (New York: Penguin, 1977), 364. See also, Stephen Whitfield, *The Culture of the Cold War* (Baltimore: Johns Hopkins University Press, 1991).

7. James Patterson, *Grand Expectations: The United States, 1945–1974* (New York: Oxford University Press, 1996), 30.

8. Clarence Karier, *The Individual, Society, and Education: A History of American Educational Ideas*, 2d ed (Urbana: University of Illinois Press, 1986), 291–292.

9. Robert Hampel, *The Last Little Citadel: American High Schools Since 1940* (Boston: Houghton Mifflin, 1986), 49.

10. Elaine Tyler May, *Homeward Bound: American Families in the Cold War* (New York: Basic Books, 1988), 14.

11. Arlene Skolnick, *Embattled Paradise: The American Family in an Age of Uncertainty* (New York: Basic Books, 1991), 52.

12. Ibid., 72.

13. Ibid., 53.

14. Edgar Friedenberg, *The Vanishing Adolescent* (New York: Vintage, 1959), 104–105.

15. Hampel, *The Last Little Citadel*, 44.

16. Friedenberg, *The Vanishing Adolescent*, 79; Charles Silberman, *Crisis in the Classroom* (New York: Vintage, 1970). Also see, Frances Fitzgerald, *America Revised* (New York: Vintage, 1980) for how social studies textbooks in the fifties contribute to this climate of educational containment.

17. James Gilbert, *A Cycle of Outrage: America's Reaction to the Juvenile Delinquent in the 1950s* (New York: Oxford University Press, 1986), 200.

18. Ibid.

19. May, *Homeward Bound*.

20. Skolnick, *Embattled Paradise*, 53.

21. Wini Breines, *Young, White and Miserable: Growing Up Female in the Fifties* (Boston: Beacon Press, 1992), 73–74.

22. Ibid., 74.

23. James B. Conant, *The Child, the Parent, and the State* (New York: McGraw-Hill, 1959).

24. James B. Conant, *The American High School Today* (New York: McGraw-Hill, 1959).

25. Hampel, *The Last Little Citadel*, 69.

26. Paul Goodman, *Compulsory Miseducation and the Community of Scholars* (New York: Vintage, 1964), 18.

27. Stephen Preskill, "Harvard Goes to Roseville: The Conant Report's Impact on One School." Paper presented at the Social Science History Association Meeting (Minneapolis, MN, 1990).

28. "A Famous Educator's Plan for a School that will Advance Students According to Ability," *Life* (April 14, 1958), 120–121.

29. Conant, *The Child, the Parent, and the State*, 1.

30. John Gardner, *Excellence* (New York: Harper and Row, 1961).

31. Paul Goodman, *Growing Up Absurd* (New York: Vintage, 1960).

32. Karier, *The Individual, Society, and Education*, 303–304.

33. Ibid., 306.

34. Ibid., 303–304.

35. Silberman, *Crisis in the Classroom*, 10.

36. Ibid., 11.

37. Karier, *The Individual, Society, and Education*, 359.

Chapter 14

1. The authors' names are in alphabetical order; both contributed equally to this chapter.

2. Clarence J. Karier, "The Quest for Orderly Change: Some Reflections," *History of Education Quarterly* 19, no. 2 (1979): 175.

3. This will be discussed further in a later section of the chapter.

4. Lynne V. Cheney, "The End of History," *The Wall Street Journal*, 20 October 1994, A22.

5. Gary B. Nash, Charlotte Crabtree, and Ross E. Dunn, *History on Trial: Culture Wars and the Teaching of the Past* (New York: Alfred A. Knopf, 1997), 10.

6. Arthur Schlesinger, Jr., *The Disuniting of America* (New York: W. W. Norton & Company, 1992), 137. See also, Diane Ravitch, "Multiculturalism: E Pluribus Plures," *The American Scholar* (Summer 1990): 337–354. Critical historians have addressed the issue of alienation regarding pedagogy and how to approach issues dealing with ethnic and minority populations in ways that will not alienate white students. See Gary R. Howard, *We Can't Teach What We Don't Know: White Teachers, Multiracial Schools* (New York: Teachers College Press, 1999) and Sonia Nieto, *Affirming Diversity: The Sociopolitical Context of Multicultural Education*, 3d ed. (New York: Addison Wesley, Longman, 2000).

7. Clarence J. Karier, *The Individual, Society, and Education: A History of American Educational Ideas* (Urbana: University of Illinois Press, 1986), xviii.

8. Karier, "The Quest for Orderly Change," 160–161.

9. Karier, *The Individual, Society, and Education*, xvii.

10. John Langston Gwaltney, *Drylongso: Black People Speak Freely About Themselves and White America—for the First Time* (New York: Random House, 1980), 4–5, cited in V. P. Franklin, *Black Self-Determination: A Cultural History of African-American Resistance* (Brooklyn: Lawrence Hill Books, 1992), 3.

11. Adrienne Rich, *Blood, Bread, and Poetry: Selected Prose, 1979-1985* (New York: Norton, 1986), 199, cited in Ronald Takaki, *A Different Mirror: A History of Multicultural America* (New York: Little, Brown, and Company, 1993), 16.

12. Takaki, *A Different Mirror*, 3.

13. Nash, Crabtree, and Dunn, *History on Trial*, 17.

14. Ibid., 11.

15. Ray Allen Billington, *The Historian's Contribution to Anglo-American Misunderstanding: Report of a Committee on National Bias in Anglo-American History Textbooks* (New York: Hobbs, Dorman and Company, 1966), 2. Billington analyzed fourteen American textbooks, five at the junior high level, nine at the senior high level. Two examples are Mabel B. Casner and Ralph H. Gabriel, *Story of the American Nation* (New York: Harcourt, Brace, and World, 1962) and Henry W. Bragdon and Samuel P. McCutchen, *History of a Free People* (New York: MacMillan, 1964).

16. Billington, *The Historian's Contributions to Anglo-American Misunderstanding*, 2. For further information on the context of nineteenth-century texts, see Ruth Miller Elson, *Guardians of Tradition: American Schoolbooks of the Nineteenth Century* (Lincoln, NE: University of Nebraska Press, 1964).

17. Billington, *The Historian's Contributions to Anglo-American Misunderstanding*, 2.

18. Karier, "American Educational History: A Perspective," *The Educational Forum* 37, no. 3 (1973), 294.

19. Karier, "Quest for Orderly Change," 165.

20. Anthony Molho and Gordon S. Wood, eds., *Imagined Histories: American Historians Interpret the Past* (Princeton: Princeton University Press, 1998), 3.

21. For instance, see Thomas Sowell, "The Blacks," in *Ethnic America: A History* (New York: Basic Books, 1981) and Bertram Wyatt-Brown, "Black Schooling During Reconstruction," in Walter Fraser, Jr., Frank Saunders, Jr., and Jon Wakelyn, eds., *The Web of Southern Social Relations: Women, Family, and Education* (Athens, GA: The University of Georgia Press, 1985).

22. James D. Anderson, *The Education of Blacks in the South, 1860–1935* (Chapel Hill: University of North Carolina Press, 1988), 57.

23. Karier, "American Educational History," 301.

24. See John M. Glen, *Highlander, No Ordinary School: 1932–1962* (Lexington: University Press of Kentucky: 1988), and Septima P. Clark, *Ready from Within: Septima Clark and the Civil Rights Movement* (Navarro, CA: Wild Trees Press, 1986).

25. Takaki, *A Different Mirror*, 14.

26. James W. Loewen, *Lies My Teacher Told Me: Everything Your American History Textbook Got Wrong* (New York: The New Press, 1995), 2.

27. Vanessa Siddle Walker, *Their Highest Potential: An African American School Community in the Segregated South* (Chapel Hill: University of North Carolina Press, 1996).

28. Clarence J. Karier, "The Reassassination of Martin Luther King, Jr." Review of *Bearing the Cross: Martin Luther King, Jr., and The Southern Christian Leadership Conference*, by David Garrow, *Educational Theory* 37, no. 4 (1987): 475.

29. Nash, *History on Trial*, 15.

30. Schesinger, *The Disuniting of America*, 119.

31. James D. Anderson, "How We Learn About Race Through History," in *Learning History in America: Schools, Cultures, and Politics*, eds. Lloyd Kramer, Donald Reid, and William L. Barney (Minneapolis: University of Minnesota Press, 1994), 89.

32. Loewen, *Lies My Teacher Told Me*, 286.

33. Karier, "The Quest for Orderly Change," 164.

Chapter 15

1. "Message," *Foreign Relations of the United States* 1901, Department of the State, XIV-XVI.

2. Ibid.

3. Paul Violas, *The Training of the Urban Working Class: A History of Twentieth Century American Education* (Chicago: Rand McNally, 1978), 28.

4. Ibid., 23.

5. Diane Ravitch, *The Troubled Crusade: American Education 1945–1980* (New York: Basic Books, 1983), 48.

6. Social philosophy of the progressive theorists is well examined in Violas' two essays: "Progressive Social Philosophy: Charles Horton Cooley and Edward Alsworth Ross," pp. 40–65, and "Jane Addams and the New Liberalism," pp. 66–83. In Clarence J. Karier, Paul Violas, and Joel Spring, *Roots of Crisis: American Education in the Twentieth Century* (Chicago: Rand McNally, 1973).

7. Quoted in Violas, "Progressive Social Philosophy,"47.

8. Ibid., 51.

9. Ibid., 53.

10. Ravitch, *The Troubled Crusade*, 51.

11. Clarence J. Karier, "Business Values and the Educational State," pp. 6–29 in *Roots of Crisis*, 19.

12. Violas, *The Training of The Urban Working Class*, 144.

13. For this part I am drawing most explanations from Clarence J. Karier, "Testing for Order and Control in the Corporate Liberal State," pp. 108–137 in *Roots of Crisis*.

14. Joel Spring, *Education and the Rise of the Corporate State* (Boston: Beacon Press, 1972), 111.

15. Clarence J. Karier, "Liberalism and the Quest for Orderly Change," in *Education in American History: Readings on the Social Issues*, edited by Michael B. Katz (New York: Praeger Publishers, 1973), 304.

16. Ibid., 312.

17. Ibid., 317.

18. Michael B. Katz, *Class, Bureaucracy, and Schools* (New York: Praeger Publisher, 1974), 113.

19. It is a controversial issue whether American people lost their faith in capitalism and wanted the reversal or they wanted a change in the given framework. For the former position see Paul Violas, "Fears and the Constraints on Academic Freedom of Public School Teachers, 1930–1960," *Educational Theory* 21 (Spring 1977): 70–71. For the latter position see David

Tyack, Robert Lowe, and Elisabeth Hansot, *Public Schools in Hard Times* (Cambridge: Harvard University Press, 1984), 14.

20. Katz, *Class, Bureaucracy, and Schools*, 109.

21. This is the main idea of Tyack, Lowe, and Hansot in *Public Schools in Hard Times*.

22. See George S. Counts, *Dare the School Build a New Social Order?* (Carbondale, IL: Southern Illinois University Press, 1982.) Counts gave the address at the annual PEA meeting in 1932.

23. C. A. Bowers, *The Progressive Educators and the Depression: The Radical Years* (New York: Random House, 1968), 57.

24. About Roosevelt's low opinion of teachers, see Tyack, Lowe, and Hansot, *Public Schools in Hard Times*, 108.

25. "This War and America," *Frontiers of Democracy* 8 (October 15, 1941), 11.

26. Quoted in C. A. Bowers, *The Progressive Educators and the Depression*, 33.

27. "What Do You Mean Fascism?," 395–396.

28. Paul Violas, "The Indoctrination Debate and the Great Depression," pp. 148–162 in *Roots of Crisis*, 149–152.

29. See Mary Anne Raywid, *The Ax Grinders* (New York: McMillan, 1962).

30. Violas, "The Indoctrination Debate," 161.

31. See Howard K. Beale, *Are American Teachers Free?* (New York: Scribner's, 1936).

32. Robert W. Iversen, *The Communist and the Schools* (New York: Harcourt, Brace and Co., 1959), 61.

33. Ibid., 63.

34. Violas, "Fears and the Constraints on Academic Freedom of Public School Teachers, 1930–1960," 71.

35. About various cases that were practiced in schools, see Raywid, *The Ax Grinders*.

36. Tyack, Lowe, and Hansot, *Public Schools in Hard Times*, 65.

37. William S. Taylor, "Academic Freedom," *NEA Addresses and Proceedings* 78 (1940): 879.

38. "Secretary's Report," *NEA Addresses and Proceedings* 79 (1941): 906.

39. Violas, "Fears and the Constraints on Academic Freedom," 75–76.

40. Charles Beard, *The Devil Theory of War* (New York: Vanguard, 1936), 120.

41. C. A. Bowers, *The Progressive Educators and the Depression*, 187.

42. "National Defense and Education," A Report of the Executive Secretary to the Board of Directors of the PEA, 1940, 1.

43. Ibid., 2.

44. See *Frontiers of Democracy* 7 (October 15, 1940).

45. *Frontiers of Democracy* 8 (October 15, 1941): 10–11. This statement was signed by the following members of the Board of Editors: Russell Babcock, Ruth Benedict, John L. Childs, James L. Hymes, Jr., William Heard Kilpatrick, Robert D. Leigh, Jesse H. Newlon, W. Carson Byan, Harold Rugg, Mark Starr, V. T. Thayer, and Laura Zirbes.

46. C. A. Bowers, *The Progressive Educators and the Depression*, 190.

47. Harold Benjamin and Harold C. Hand, "Objection . . . ," *Frontiers of Democracy* 8 (October 15, 1941): 19.

48. Tyack, Lowe, and Hansot, *Public Schools in Hard Times*, 29–32.

49. Noam Chomsky, "The Manufacture of Consent," an Address Given at the Community Church of Boston, December 9, 1984, 4.

50. *National Defense and Education*, 5.

51. Grayson N. Kefauver, "Education in a Democracy at War," *Frontiers of Democracy* 8 (January 15, 1941): 116.

52. Ernesto Galarza, "The Problem of the Americas," *Frontiers of Democracy* 8 (October 15, 1941): 87.

53. William H. Kilpatrick, "Reply . . . ," *Frontiers of Democracy* 8 (October 15, 1941): 17.

54. Howard R. Anderson, "The National Emergency—What Shall We Do?" *NEA Proceedings* 79 (1941): 541.

55. John L. Childs, "This War and American Education,"*Frontiers of Democracy* 8 (October 15, 1941): 102.

56. Lawrence K. Frank, "World Order and Cultural Diversity," *Frontiers of Democracy* 9 (October 15, 1942): 12–13.

57. Ibid., 13.

58. William H. Kilpatrick, "The War in the Orient and American Education,"*Frontiers of Democracy* 8 (January 15, 1942): 103.

59. Horace H. Kallen, "The New Education and the Future of Peace," *Progressive Education* 8 (October 15, 1941): 280–281.

60. *International Encyclopedia of Social Science* 9(New York: The McMillan Company & The Free Press, 1968), 276.

Chapter 16

1. Clarence J. Karier, *The Individual, Society, and Education: A History of American Educational Ideas*, 2d ed. (Urbana: University of Illinois Press, 1986), 315.

2. William O. Stanley, Professor of Education at the University of Illinois, expounded upon this in his textbook, *Education and Social Integration* (New York: Teachers College Press, 1953).

3. Arthur Bestor, *Educational Wastelands: The Retreat from Learning in Our Public Schools*, 2d ed. (Urbana: University of Illinois Press, 1985), 28. Originally published in 1953.

4. "This Year's Business, 1952" *American Historical Review* (April 1953): 777.

5. Arthur Bestor, "The Education of the Gifted Child," *The New Republic* (March 4, 1957): 12–16.

6. Arthur Bestor, letter to the author, November 28, 1988.

7. Ibid.

8. Ibid.

9. Ibid.

10. Karier, *The Individual, Society, and Education*, 317.

11. Bestor, letter to the author, November 28, 1988.

Notes 301

12. Arthur Bestor, interview with the author which took place in Bestor's home in Seattle, Washington, January 29–31, 1989.

13. The 1986 edition of *Educational Wastelands* includes "Publications of Arthur Bestor on Educational Questions. A Select List, in Chronological Order," 289–292.

Chapter 17

1. Although given the different subject matter the connection is indirect, among the publications that most clearly reflect the kind of critical scholarship that is intended here, and that I believe have most influenced me, are Clarence J. Karier, "Business Values and the Educational State," in *Roots of Crisis: American Education in the Twentieth Century*, ed. Clarence J. Karier, Paul C. Violas, and Joel Spring (Chicago: Rand McNally, 1973), 6–29; Clarence J. Karier, "Liberal Ideology and the Quest for Orderly Change," in *Roots of Crisis*, ed. Karier, Violas, and Spring, 84–107; Clarence J. Karier, "Elite Views on American Education," in *Education and Social Structure in the Twentieth Century*, ed. Walter Laqueur and George Mosse (New York: Harper and Row, 1967), 149–163; Clarence J. Karier, *Scientists of the Mind: Intellectual Founders of Modern Psychology* (Urbana: University of Illinois Press, 1986).

2. Leo van Lier, *Introducing Language Awareness* (New York: Penguin, 1995), 7–8.

3. See, for example, Norman Fairclugh, ed., *Critical Language Awareness* (London: Longman, 1992); Hilary Janks, "A Critical Approach to the Teaching of Language," *Educational Review* 43 (1991): 191–199; Hilary Janks, "Critical Discourse Analysis as a Research Tool," *Discourse: Studies in the Cultural Politics of Education* 19 (1997): 329–342; Lynda Wilkinson and Hilary Janks, "Teaching Direct and Reported Speech from a Critical Language Awareness (CLA) Perspective," *Educational Review* 50 (1998): 181–190; Hilary Janks, "Critical Language Awareness: Theory and Practice," *Interpretations* 30 (1997): 1–29.

4. Dell Hymes, *Ethnography, Linguistics, Narrative Inequality: Toward an Understanding of Voice* (London: Taylor and Francis, 1996), 84–85.

5. See Timothy Reagan and Terry A. Osborn, "Power, Authority, and Domination in Foreign Language Education: Toward an Analysis of Educational Failure," *Educational Foundations* 12 (1998): 45–62; Terry Osborn and Timothy Reagan, "Why Johnny Can't *Hablar, Parler*, or *Sprechen*: Foreign Language Education and Multicultural Education," *Multicultural Education* 6 (1998): 2–9.

6. See Gilbert Jarvis, "The Value of Second-Language Learning," in *Learning a Second Language: Seventy-Ninth Yearbook of the National Society for the Study of Education, Part II*, ed. Frank Grittner (Chicago, IL: National Society for the Study of Education, distributed by the University of Chicago Press, 1980), 26–43.

7. See Paul Simon, *The Tongue-Tied American: Confronting the Foreign Language Crisis* (New York: Continuum, 1980).

8. Quoted in Jarvis, "The Value of Second-Language Learning," 31–32.

9. See Linda Cleary and Michael Linn, eds., *Linguistics for Teachers* (New York: McGraw-Hill, 1993).

10. For a more detailed treatment of these issues, see Timothy Reagan, "When is a Language Not a Language? Challenges to 'Linguistic Legitimacy' in Educational Discourse," *Educational Foundations* 11 (1997): 5–28.

11. See, for example, J. Bennet, "Administration Rejects Black English as a Second Language," *The New York Times* (25 December 1996), A-22; S. Holmes, "Voice of Inner City Streets is Defended and Criticized," *The New York Times* (30 December 1996), A-9; L. Olszewski, "Oakland Schools OK Black English: Ebonics to be Regarded as Different, not Wrong," *San Francisco Chronicle* (19 December 1996), A-1, A-19; J. Schorr, "Give Oakland's Schools a Break," *The New York Times* (2 January 1997), A-19; B. Staples, "The Trap of Ethnic Identity: How Africa Came to Oakland," *The New York Times* (4 January 1997), A-22.

12. Roger Hernandez, "Never Mind Teaching Ebonics: Teach Proper English," *The Hartford Courant* (26 December 1996), A-21.

13. California State University, *California State University School and College Review* 6 (1987): 3.

14. One could, of course, argue that the CSU definition only indirectly involves judgments about linguistic legitimacy, and that this prescriptive definition is intended solely with respect to specific institutional needs. Even such a generous reading of the policy, though, still clearly demonstrates an underlying view of linguistic legitimacy, and is thus still highly problematic.

15. For the equally compelling case for Esperanto, see Reagan, "When is a Language Not a Language?"; Alvino Fantini and Timothy Reagan, *Esperanto and Education: Toward a Research Agenda* (Washington, DC: Esperantic Studies Foundation, 1992).

16. Even the term "Black English" is controversial; the more populist term "Ebonics" is also widely used, as are the terms "Black English Vernacular"

and "African American Vernacular English." See, for instance, John McWhorter, *The Word on the Street: Fact and Fable About American English* (New York: Plenum, 1998), 127–261; Salifofo Mufwene, John Rickford, Guy Bailey, and John Baugh, eds., *African-American English: Structure, History and Use* (London: Routledge, 1998); Theresa Perry and Lisa Delpit, eds., *The Real Ebonics Debate: Power, Language, and the Education of African-American Children* (Boston: Beacon Press, 1998).

17. See, for instance, J. Chambers, ed., *Black English: Educational Equity and the Law* (Ann Arbor, MI: Karoma, 1983); Geneva Smitherman, "'What Go Round Come Round': *King* in Perspective," *Harvard Educational Review* 51 (1981): 40–56; Geneva Smitherman, *Talkin and Testifyin: The Language of Black America* (Detroit: Wayne State University Press, 1977); Marcia Farr Whiteman, ed., *Reactions to Ann Arbor: Vernacular Black English and Education* (Arlington, VA: Center for Applied Linguistics, 1980).

18. Bill Maxwell, "Miss Bonaparte Wouldn't Approve!" *New Britain Herald* (2 January 1997), B-2.

19. E. Schneider, *American Earlier Black English: Morphological and Syntactic Variables* (Tuscaloosa, AL: The University of Alabama Press, 1989), 2–3.

20. The same point would be true, of course, for other nonmainstream varieties of English. See Walt Wolfram and Donna Christian, *Appalachian Speech* (Arlington, VA: Center for Applied Linguistics, 1976). For an excellent history of linguistic prescriptivism in the U.S. context, see Dennis Baron, *Grammar and Good Taste: Reforming the American Language* (New Haven: Yale University Press, 1982).

21. Schneider, *American Earlier Black English*, 1.

22. Some of the most recent works are listed in note 16. See also, for example, Robbins Burling, *English in Black and White* (New York: Holt, Rinehart and Winston, 1973); Johanna DeStefano, ed., *Language, Society and Education: A Profile of Black English* (Worthington, OH: Charles A. Jones, 1973); J. L. Dillard, *Black English: Its History and Usage in the United States* (New York: Vintage, 1972); J. L. Dillard, ed., *Perspectives on Black English* (The Hague: Mouton, 1975); Thomas Kochman, *Black and White Styles in Conflict* (Chicago: University of Chicago Press, 1981); Thomas Kochman, ed., *Rappin' and Stylin' Out: Communication in Black Urban America* (Urbana, IL: University of Illinois Press, 1972); William Labov, *The Study of Nonstandard English* (Urbana, IL: National Council of Teachers of English, 1978); William Labov, *Language in the Inner City: Studies in the Black English Vernacular* (Philadelphia: University of Pennsylvania Press, 1972); William Labov, *Sociolinguistic Patterns* (Philadelphia: University of Pennsylvania Press, 1972); S. Mufwene, ed., *Africanisms in Afro-American Language Varieties* (Athens, GA: The University of Georgia Press, 1993); Walt Wolfram and

Ralph Fasold, *The Study of Social Dialects in American English* (Englewood Cliffs, NJ: Prentice-Hall, 1974).

23. See John Baugh, *Black Street Speech: Its History, Structure and Survival* (Austin: University of Texas Press, 1983); E. Whatley, "Language Among Black Americans," *Language in the U.S.A.*, ed. Charles Ferguson and Shirley Brice Heath (Cambridge: Cambridge University Press, 1981), 92–107.

24. Tom Trabasso and Deborah Harrison, "Introduction," in *Black English: A Seminar*, ed. Deborah Harrison and Tom Trabasso (Hillsdale, NJ: Lawrence Erlbaum, 1976), 2.

25. See Walt Wolfram, *Speech Pathology and Dialect Differences* (Arlington, VA: Center for Applied Linguistics, 1979). An additional issue worth mentioning here is the effect on African American students' view of Black English; the poet June Jordan reports that, in studying Alice Walker's *The Color Purple*, her students "soon discovered that along with the grammar of standard English, they had also acquired through their schooling a set of negative attitudes toward the very language that they themselves would use in their informal conversations." Quoted in Eleanor Kutz, *Language and Literacy: Studying Discourse in Communities and Classrooms* (Portsmouth, NH: Heinemann, 1997), 124.

26. Shirley Brice Heath, *Ways with Words: Language, Life, and Work in Communities and Classrooms* (Cambridge: Cambridge University Press, 1983), 277.

27. Eleanor Wilson Orr, *Twice as Less: Black English and the Performance of Black Students in Mathematics and Science* (New York: Norton, 1987).

28. Orr, *Twice as Less*, 9.

29. John Baugh, "Review of *Twice as Less*," *Harvard Educational Review* 58 (1988): 403.

30. Rhonda Jacobs, "Just How Hard is it to Learn ASL? The Case for ASL as a Truly Foreign Language," in *Multicultural Aspects of Sociolinguistics in Deaf Communities*, ed. Ceil Lucas (Washington, DC: Gallaudet University Press, 1996), 183–226; Sherman Wilcox and Phyllis Wilcox, *Learning to See: American Sign Language as a Second Language*, 2d ed. (Englewood Cliffs, NJ: Prentice Hall, 1997).

31. Quoted in Harlan Lane, *The Mask of Benevolence: Disabling the Deaf Community* (New York: Alfred A. Knopf, 1992), 45.

32. A. van Uden, *Sign Languages of Deaf People and Psycholinguistics* (Lisse: Swets & Zeitlinger B. V., 1986), 89.

33. William Stokoe, *Sign Language Structures* (Silver Spring, MD: Linstok Press, 1993; original publication 1960).

34. See Susan Fischer and Patricia Siple, eds., *Theoretical Issues in Sign Language Research: Volume 1, Linguistics* (Chicago: University of Chicago Press, 1990); Diane Lillo-Martin, *Universal Grammar and American Sign Language: Setting the Null Argument Parameters* (Dordrecht: Kluwer, 1991); Ceil Lucas, ed., *The Sociolinguistics of the Deaf Community* (San Diego, CA: Academic Press, 1989); Ceil Lucas, ed., *Sign Language Research: Theoretical Issues* (Washington, DC: Gallaudet University Press, 1990); Ceil Lucas, ed., *Sociolinguistics in Deaf Communities* (Washington, DC: Gallaudet University Press, 1995); Ceil Lucas and Clayton Valli, *Language Contact in the American Deaf Community* (San Diego, CA: Academic Press, 1992); Patricia Siple and Susan Fischer, eds., *Theoretical Issues in Sign Language Research: Volume 2, Psychology* (Chicago: University of Chicago Press, 1991); Clayton Valli and Ceil Lucas, *Linguistics of American Sign Language: An Introduction*, 2nd ed. (Washington, DC: Gallaudet University Press, 1995).

35. For discussions of other natural sign languages in general, see W. Edmondson and F. Karlsson, eds., *SLR '87: Papers from the Fourth International Symposium on Sign Language Research* (Hamburg: Signum Press, 1990); Karen Emmorey and Judy Reilly, eds., *Language, Gesture, and Space* (Hillsdale, NJ: Lawrence Erlbaum, 1995); J. G. Kyle and B. Woll, *Sign Language: The Study of Deaf People and Their Language* (Cambridge: Cambridge University Press, 1985); Siegmund Prillwitz and Tomas Vollhaber, eds., *Current Trends in European Sign Language Research* (Hamburg: Signum Press, 1990); Siegmund Prillwitz and Tomas Vollhaber, eds., *Sign Language Research and Application* (Hamburg: Signum Press, 1990); Timothy Reagan, "The Development and Reform of Sign Languages," in *Language Reform: History and Future,* ed. Istvan Fodor and Claude Hagege (Hamburg: Helmut Buske Verlag, 1990), 253–267; Timothy Reagan, "The Comparative Analysis of Sign Languages: Issues and Challenges," in *Language as Barrier and Bridge,* ed. Kurt Kurt Müller (Lanham, MD: University Press of America and the Center for Research and Documentation on World Language Problems, 1992), 103–114. For a detailed case study of the politics of natural sign language in a non-U.S. setting, see Claire Penn and Timothy Reagan, "How Do You Sign 'Apartheid'? The Politics of South African Sign Language," *Language Problems and Language Planning* 14 (1990): 91–103; Timothy Reagan and Claire Penn, "Language Policy, South African Sign Language, and the Deaf: Social and Educational Implications," *Southern African Journal of Applied Language Studies* 5 (1997): 1–13.

36. Robert Hoffmeister, "ASL and its Implications for Education," in *Manual Communication: Implications for Education,* ed. Harry Bornstein (Washington, DC: Gallaudet University Press, 1990), 81.

37. Quoted in Lane, *The Mask of Benevolence*, 46.

38. Quoted in "Sign Language: A Way to Talk, But is it Foreign?" *The New York Times* (7 January 1992), my emphasis.

39. The concept of "foreignness" is itself highly problematic. See *Standards for Foreign Language Learning: Preparing for the 21st Century* (Lawrence, KS: National Standards in Foreign Language Education Project, 1996), 23; Terry Osborn, *The Concept of "Foreignness" in U.S. Secondary Language Curricula: A Critical Philosophical Analysis* (Ph.D. dissertation, University of Connecticut, 1998).

40. There is an additional facet to this argument as well, and that is the role of deaf studies in the broader context of the growing field of disability studies. See, for instance, Lennard J. Davis, *Enforcing Normalcy: Disability, Deafness, and the Body* (London: Verso, 1995); Lennard J. Davis, ed., *The Disability Studies Reader* (New York: Routledge, 1997); Simi Linton, *Claiming Disability: Knowledge and Identity* (New York: New York University Press, 1998); Arthur Shapiro, *Everybody Belongs: Changing Negative Attitudes Toward Classmates with Disabilities* (New York: Garland, 1999).

41. Quoted in "Sign Language."

42. See, for example, Leah Cohen, *Train Go Sorry: Inside a Deaf World* (Boston: Houghton Mifflin, 1994); Renate Fischer and Harlan Lane, eds., *Looking Back: A Reader on the History of Deaf Communities and Their Sign Languages* (Hamburg: Signum Press, 1993); Susan Gregory and Gillian Hartley, eds., *Constructing Deafness* (London: Pinter Publishers, in association with the Open University, 1991); Harlan Lane, Robert Hoffmeister, and Benjamin Bahan, *A Journey into the Deaf-World* (San Diego, CA: DawnSign Press, 1996); Carol Padden and Tom Humphries, *Deaf in America: Voices from a Culture* (Cambridge, MA: Harvard University Press, 1988); Ila Parasnis, ed., *Cultural and Linguistic Diversity and the Deaf Experience* (Cambridge: Cambridge University Press, 1998); Timothy Reagan, "Cultural Considerations in the Education of Deaf Children," in *Research in Educational and Developmental Aspects of Deafness*, ed. Donald Moores and Kay Meadow-Orlans (Washington, DC: Gallaudet University Press, 1990), 74–84; Timothy Reagan, "The Deaf as a Linguistic Minority: Educational Considerations," reprinted in *Special Education at the Century's End: Evolution of Theory and Practice Since 1970*, ed. Thomas Hehir and Thomas Latus (Cambridge, MA: Harvard Educational Review, 1992), 305–320; Timothy Reagan, "A Sociocultural Understanding of Deafness: American Sign Language and the Culture of Deaf People," *International Journal of Intercultural Relations* 19 (1995): 239–251; Sherman Wilcox, ed., *American Deaf Culture: An Anthology* (Burtonsville, MD: Linstok Press, 1989).

43. See the discussion of this matter in a broader context in Timothy Reagan, *Non-Western Educational Traditions: Alternative Approaches to Educational Thought and Practice* (Mahwah, NJ: Lawrence Erlbaum, 1996), 7–9.

44. Nancy Frishberg, "Signers of Tales: The Case for Literary Status of an Unwritten Language," *Sign Language Studies* 59 (1988): 165–166.

45. Benjamin Bahan, "American Sign Language Literature: Inside the Story," in *Deaf Studies: What's Up?— Conference Proceedings* (Washington, DC: College for Continuing Education, Gallaudet University, 1992), 153–164; E. Lynn Jacobowitz, "American Sign Language Literature: Curriculum Considerations," in *Deaf Studies for Educators: Conference Proceedings* (Washington, DC: College for Continuing Education, Gallaudet University, 1992), 76–82; Wendy Low, "Colors of ASL . . . A World Expressed: ASL Poetry in the Curriculum," in *Deaf Studies for Educators: Conference Proceedings* (Washington, DC: College for Continuing Education, Gallaudet University, 1992), 53–59; Susan Rutherford, *A Study of American Deaf Folklore* (Silver Spring, MD: Linstok Press, 1993).

46. Quoted in Arden Neisser, *The Other Side of Silence: Sign Language and the Deaf Community in America* (New York: Alfred A. Knopf, 1983), 113.

47. See Robert Phillipson, "Linguicism: Structures and Ideologies in Linguistic Imperialism," in *Minority Education: From Shame to Struggle*, ed. Tove Skutnabb-Kangas and Jim Cummins (Clevedon: Multilingual Matters, 1988), 339–358; John Attinasi, J. (1997). "Racism, Language Variety, and Urban Minorities: Issues in Bilingualism and Bidialectalism," in *Latinos and Education: A Critical Reader*, ed. Antonia Darder, Rodolfo Torres, and Henry Gutiérrez (New York: Routledge, 1997), 279–301.

48. See Tove Skutnabb-Kangas and Robert Phillipson, eds., *Linguistic Human Rights: Overcoming Linguistic Discrimination* (Berlin: Mouton de Gruyter, 1995).

49. See, for example, Stephen D. Krashen, *Under Attack: The Case Against Bilingual Education* (Culver City, CA: Language Education Associates, 1996); Katharine D. Samway and Denise McKeon, *Myths and Realities: Best Practices for Language Minority Students* (Portsmouth, NH: Heinemann, 1999); Patrick Courts, *Multicultural Literacies: Dialect, Discourse, and Diversity* (New York: Peter Lang, 1997).

50. Relevant here are Dennis Baron, *The English-Only Question: An Official Language for Americans?* (New Haven: Yale University Press, 1990); James Crawford, *Hold Your Tongue: Bilingualism and the Politics of "English Only"* (Reading, MA: Addison-Wesley, 1992); James Crawford, ed., *Language Loyalties: A Source Book on the Official English Controversy* (Chicago: University of Chicago Press, 1992).

Contributors

JAMES D. ANDERSON is Professor of History of Education and Head of the Department of Educational Policy Studies at the University of Illinois at Urbana-Champaign. A past-president of the History of Education Society, Professor Anderson is the author of *The Education of Blacks in the South, 1860–1935*, and editor (with Vincent Franklin) of *New Perspectives on Black Educational History*. His articles and reviews have appeared in *History of Education Quarterly, Peabody Journal of Education, Journal of Ethnic Studies,* and many other journals.

JOSEPH L. DeVITIS is Professor of Education and Human Development at SUNY at Binghamton. He is the author and editor of several books including *Theories of Moral Development, Helping and Intervention, Competition in Education* (with John Martin Rich), *The Success Ethic, Education, and the American Dream* (with John Martin Rich), and *School Reform in the Deep South: A Critical Appraisal* (with David J. Vold).

TIMOTHY GLANDER is Associate Professor of Education and Chair of the Department of Education at Rockhurst University. He is author of *Origins of Mass Communications Research During the American Cold War: Educational Effects and Contemporary Implications*.

KAREN L. GRAVES is Associate Professor of Education at Denison University. She is author of *Girls' Schooling During the Progressive Era: From Female Scholar to Domesticated Citizen*.

GILSANG LEE is Professor of History of Education at the Graduate School, The Academy of Korean Studies, in the Republic of Korea. He completed his dissertation, "Ideological Context of American Educational Policy in Occupied Korea, 1945–1948," at the University of Illinois at Urbana-Champaign in 1989. In 1997 he researched educational policy and history at the University of Wisconsin-Madison.

STUART McANINCH is Associate Professor in the division of Urban Leadership and Policy Studies in Education at the University of Missouri–Kansas City, where he teaches undergraduate and graduate courses on the social and historical foundations of American education. He has authored or coauthored articles published in *Educational Foundations, Educational Studies, Educational Theory, and Theory and Research in Social Education*, as well as chapters which have appeared in several books.

RICHARD OGNIBENE holds an M.A. in History and an Ed.D. in Educational Foundations from the University of Rochester. He has served as a department chair in teacher education at three colleges, as graduate dean at the College of St. Rose (NY), and dean of the College of Education and Human Services at Seton Hall University. He is currently Professor in the Educational Studies Department at Seton Hall University. His most recent articles have appeared in *Educational Foundations*, the *SRATE Journal, Scholar and Educator, Journal of Education and Economic Competitiveness,* and *Planning and Changing.*

STEPHEN PRESKILL is currently Associate Professor of Education and the Director of the Division of Educational Leadership and Organizational Learning at the University of New Mexico. He has written widely on the history of American education, educational leaders, the relationship between democracy and discussion, and the role of teaching narratives in professional development. His books include *Discussion as a Way of Teaching* (with Stephen Bass) and *Narratives of Teaching and the Quest for the Second Self* (with Robin Smith Jacobvitz), forthcoming.

TIMOTHY REAGAN is Professor of Language, Literacy and Society at the University of Connecticut. He is author of *Non-Western Educational Theories: Alternative Approaches to Educational Thought and Practice,* among other works.

Contributors

RONALD ROCHON is Associate Professor and Director of Graduate Education in the School of Education at the University of Wisconsin-LaCrosse.

KATRINA SANDERS is Assistant Professor of History of Education at the University of Iowa. Her articles appear in the *Journal of the Midwest History of Education Society*, the *Journal of Gender, Race, and Justice*, and the *Journal of Intergroup Relations*. Her book, *And the White People Listened: Charles S. Johnson and the Fisk University Race Relations Institute*, is forthcoming with Peter Lang Publishing.

GAETANO "GUY" B. SENESE did his Ph.D. in Educational Policy Studies in the years 1982–1985. He is Associate Professor of Educational Foundations and Leadership at Northern Arizona University. He taught at Northern Illinois University for eleven years, at Blackburn College, and was on staff of the Illinois Board of Education. He is author of *Simulation, Spectacle, and the Ironies of Education Reform*, and is coauthor (with Steve Tozer and Paul Violas) of *School & Society: Educational Practice as Social Expression*.

CHRISTINE SHEA is Associate Professor in the Department of Foundations, Research and Reading at East Carolina University. She has also taught at Hampshire College, West Virginia University, the North Carolina Center for the Advancement of Teaching, and Georgia Southern University. She is coauthor of *Learning to Teach: Critical Approaches to the Field Experience* and coeditor of *The New Servants of Power: A Critique of the 1980s Educational Reform Movement*.

PETER SOLA is a Graduate Professor of Education in the Department of Educational Administration and Policy at Howard University. In his twenty years at the university he has edited and coedited three texts on education, educational ethics, teacher education programs, and a critique of the 1980's educational reform movement. He is currently coediting a book on health ethics.

MARK W. SORENSEN is Director of Little Singer Tribal School and Wellness Center, in Birdsprings, Navajo Nation, Arizona. He has been principal at the Rough Rock Demonstration School, and Superintendent of the Leupp Boarding School. He is also director of the Native American Grant School Association, an organization of community tribal schools across the state of Arizona. He received the doctorate degree in Educational Leadership from Northern Arizona University, and wrote his master's degree thesis under Professor Karier during graduate studies at the University of Illinois. He has been an educator on the Navajo Nation for 23 years.

JOEL SPRING is the author of many books, including *The Sorting Machine Revisited: National Educational Policy Since 1945; Education and the Rise of the Global Economy; Political Agendas for Education: From the Christian Coalition to the Green Party; Images of American Life: A History of Ideological Management in Schools, Movies, Radio, and Television; American Education* (now in its ninth edition); *Wheels in the Head: Educational Philosophies of Authority, Freedom, and Culture from Socrates to Human Rights; The Cultural Transformation of a Native American Family and Its Tribe, 1763–1995.* He is currently on faculty at New School University.

PAUL THEOBALD is Professor and Dean of Education at Wayne State College in Wayne, Nebraska. He is the author of *Call School: Rural Education in the Midwest to 1918* and *Teaching the Commons: Place, Pride, and the Renewal of Community.*

STEVE TOZER is Professor and Chair of the Educational Policy Studies Program at the University of Illinois at Chicago. His articles on the social foundations of education have appeared in *Teachers College Record, Educational Theory, Educational Studies,* and other journals. He is author (with Paul Violas and Guy Senese) of *School & Society: Educational Practice as Social Expression,* and editor (with Kenneth D. Benne) of *Society as Educator in an Age of Transition.*

Contributors

MARLENE WENTWORTH is an administrator for off-campus programming in the Office of Continuing Education at the University of Illinois at Urbana-Champaign. She completed her dissertation, "From Chautauqua to Wastelands: The Bestors and American Education, 1905–1955," in the Department of Educational Policy Studies at the University of Illinois at Urbana-Champaign in 1992.

JOY ANN WILLIAMSON is Assistant Professor of History of Education at Stanford University. Her articles have appeared in the *Journal of the Midwest History of Education Society* and the *Journal of Negro Education*. She is currently working on a manuscript for the University of Illinois Press on the 1960's Black student movement at the University of Illinois and the nature of higher educational reform.

History of Schools and Schooling

THIS SERIES EXPLORES THE HISTORY OF SCHOOLS AND SCHOOLING in the United States and other countries. Books in this series examine the historical development of schools and educational processes, with special emphasis on issues of educational policy, curriculum and pedagogy, as well as issues relating to race, class, gender, and ethnicity. Special emphasis will be placed on the lessons to be learned from the past for contemporary educational reform and policy. Although the series will publish books related to education in the broadest societal and cultural context, it especially seeks books on the history of specific schools and on the lives of educational leaders and school founders.

For additional information about this series or for the submission of manuscripts, please contact the general editors:

Alan R. Sadovnik
Rutgers University-Newark
Education Dept.
155 Conklin Hall
175 University Avenue
Newark, NJ 07102

Susan F. Semel
Curriculum and Teaching Dept.
243 Gallon Wing
Hofstra University
Hempstead, NY 11550

To order other books in this series, please contact our Customer Service Department:

800-770-LANG (within the U.S.)
212-647-7706 (outside the U.S.)
212-647-7707 FAX

Or browse online by series at:

www.peterlangusa.com